CRITICAL ACCLAIM FOR
GIRL IN A DUMPSTER

"*Girl in a Dumpster* marks the return of Holland Taylor and what a welcome return it is! Not to be missed!"

—D.M. Barr, author of
the domestic thriller *Deadly When Disturbed*

"I wished I had written it... a riveting, edge of your seat gumshoe thriller in the tradition of Sam Spade."

—Vincent Zandri, *New York Times* and
USA Today bestselling Thriller and
Shamus Award-winning author of *Moonlight Weeps*

"A gritty but surprisingly heartfelt PI novel; the kind you thought they don't write anymore, but David Housewright does."

— Scott McCrea, author of *Targets West*

"A solid, traditional private eye story filled with plenty of twists and turns and featuring a solid, traditional private eye—the tough guy with a soft center who plays by his own rules. You won't want to put it down before the heart-stopping but satisfying finish."

—Austin Camacho, Coordinator,
Creatures, Crimes & Creativity Con

GIRL IN A DUMPSTER

ALSO BY DAVID HOUSEWRIGHT

Featuring Rushmore McKenzie
A Hard Ticket Home
Tin City
Pretty Girl Gone
Dead Boyfriends
Madman on a Drum
Jelly's Gold
The Taking of Libbie, SD
Highway 61
Curse of the Jade Lily
The Last Kind Word
The Devil May Care
Unidentified Woman #15
Stealing the Countess
What the Dead Leave Behind
Like to Die
Dead Man's Mistress
From the Grave
What Doesn't Kill Us
Something Wicked
In a Hard Wind

Featuring Holland Taylor
Penance
Practice to Deceive
Dearly Departed
Darkness, Sing Me A Song
First Kill the Lawyers
Girl in a Dumpster

Other Novels
The Devil and the Diva (with Renée Valois)
Finders Keepers
Full House (Short Stories)

DAVID HOUSEWRIGHT

GIRL IN A DUMPSTER
A HOLLAND TAYLOR MYSTERY

Cover design by JT Lindroos

ISBN-13: 978-1-970861-24-2

For Renée

CHAPTER ONE

Violent movement and the loud rumble of a truck engine jolted her awake. Her eyes snapped open, yet she couldn't see in the bleak darkness that surrounded her. She could feel the debris she was lying on; the wetness that penetrated her clothes and pasted her auburn hair to her forehead. She could smell it, too, the sickening stench of garbage. And the shocking taste in her mouth that made her gag. Despite what her senses told her, though, she didn't realize that she was inside a dumpster until it was hoisted into the air and tilted forward. The roof flapped open and bright sunlight revealed the stained walls of the metal box.

She screamed.

The contents began sliding toward the sewage bin of the garbage truck, her along with it. She grasped at the flat walls of the dumpster with her hands, used her heels in a futile attempt to brace herself, anything to keep from falling into the bowels of the truck.

She screamed some more.

Even as she screamed, she told herself that this was a terrifying dream, and she would soon wake up. Only she didn't.

"Please." She didn't know whom she was speaking to. Someone. Anyone. "Please, please…"

Somehow, the driver heard the screams over the sound of his engines, heard the woman's plea for mercy. He pounded the red emergency stop button. The hydraulic lift ceased its movement. The dumpster hovered in midair, yet the screaming continued. He hit a couple more buttons and the giant arms slowly lowered the dumpster back to earth; the metal roof clattering shut over the top.

The woman kept screaming until the driver lifted off the roof and peered inside.

"What you doin' in there, lady?" he asked.

Approximately forty-eight hours later she arrived unannounced at the offices that I shared with Sidney Poitier Fredericks. I say offices even though it's actually one long rectangle with six large windows facing downtown Minneapolis and a single door in the middle of the wall across from the windows. Freddie's desk, chairs, and file cabinets were on the right; I was set up on the left. In the middle was a coffeemaker resting on top of our safe, a small refrigerator, a low, round table, and four stuffed chairs arranged around the table.

She sat in a chair with her back to a window. I sat in a chair across from her. Freddie rested on the edge of his desk where he could get a good view of the woman's legs when she crossed them, which she did several times in the space of only a couple of minutes.

"What exactly *were* you doing in the dumpster?" I asked.

"That, Mr. Taylor, is what I need you to find out."

She had stepped across our threshold minutes earlier and asked "Fredericks and Taylor Private Investigations?" as if she didn't trust the sign on the door. She was young and pretty, yet she dressed in a mature black suit jacket, white shirt and black skirt that covered her knees as if she didn't want us to notice.

"I don't have an appointment," she said. "Is that alright?"

"Certainly."

"Which is Mr. Fredericks and which is Mr. Taylor?"

Freddie and I introduced ourselves. She shook our hands and

said "Pleased to meet you" as if she really were. "I'm Henrietta Weller."

Afterward, I directed her to the chair and poured a cup of caramel cream coffee that she drank from a mug, her pinky extended. That's when she told us her story in a particularly calm and relaxed voice. If she hadn't been constantly crossing and re-crossing her legs, I might not have noticed how anxious she was.

"Where is the dumpster?" I asked.

"In an alley behind a bar called Dillman's on the north side of Minneapolis."

"'Kay," Freddie said.

Henrietta sighed as if she knew what Freddie was thinking and didn't like it.

"As far as I remember, I have never set foot inside that bar," she said. "Not once in my life."

"What do you remember?" I asked.

"I remember leaving my apartment at exactly five-thirty-five Thursday evening, to meet a friend in a club in Uptown for Happy Hour. I would have gone there directly after leaving work except I was wearing slacks and I wanted to change into a skirt in case we went somewhere after. There's a small lot behind my building. You need to pay extra if you want to park there. Anyway, I remember walking to my car. Just as I reached it, I felt as if I was falling, yet I don't remember tripping on anything. The next thing I knew—the next thing I knew, I was soaked with garbage and screaming my head off."

"Where is your car now?"

"I found it in the parking lot at my apartment building exactly where I left it."

"Tell us about your friend," Freddie said.

"Lori Hertz. We were roommates at the University of Minnesota before I was tossed out. She was angry with me for standing her up. She said she called and called; only I never answered. Finally, when I did return her call—it was Saturday. I told her I had been sick, too sick to answer the phone. Lori didn't believe me. I told the people I work with the same thing. They didn't believe me, either. They probably think I went on a drunken bender or hooked up with someone."

"Why did you lie?" I asked. "Why not tell them the truth? Why not contact the police and report exactly what happened?"

"I don't know what happened."

"What I mean..."

"I need to learn the truth before I decide if I want anyone else to learn the truth."

"That requires explanation."

"Mr. Taylor, Mr. Fredericks, I make no claims to virtue. There was a time in my life...It doesn't matter."

"Yeah, it does," Freddie said. "At least it might."

"My mother is—my mother is a prominent woman. While I was growing up, she seemed to be more interested in her career than me. I did things to get her attention. Stupid things. When that didn't work, I decided the best way to hurt her was to hurt myself. Sex. Drugs. Rock and roll. That'll teach her, I thought. It's a cliché, I know. I like to think I put that kind of self-destructive behavior behind me. But maybe not. That's what I need to find out. I'm not addicted to alcohol or drugs in the classic sense. I've done both, though, to the point where I lost more than days, sometimes a week. Did that happen again? You tell me."

Over Henrietta's shoulder, I could see Freddie resting two fingers against his cheek. It was something we did whenever we came across an unlikely tidbit of information that might or might not be significant to a case we were working. We'd make a production out of resting our fingers against our cheeks and saying "Hmm" except this time Freddie remained quiet.

"Tell us again about the last thing you remember," I said.

"I left my apartment Thursday..."

"Is this a thing, goin' out after work?" Freddie asked.

"Not a habit, but not unusual, either."

"Do you often go to your apartment to change?" I asked.

"When I go out, yes. What I wear at work isn't particularly flattering."

"Do your friends know that, that you go home to change?"

"My friends wouldn't hurt me."

"How about those pretending to be your friends?" Freddie asked.

"You're exploring possible scenarios," Henrietta said. "Believe me, gentlemen. I've been doing the same thing all weekend."

"Money? Credit cards?"

"I still have them. I found my purse in the dumpster; I had to crawl back inside to fetch it. My cell phone, credit card, bank card, my cash, everything was still there. Everything except my driver's license. I had to bring my passport and social security card down to the DMV this morning to replace it. They insisted I file a Law Enforcement Alert for Victims of Identity Theft with the Minnesota Department of Public Safety, which I did, but I lied on the form. I'm sure it's illegal, saying that my purse was snatched when I was walking down the street."

Freddie made a gimme gesture. "Let's see your cards." Henrietta left the chair and moved to Freddie's desk. She set her bag on top and dug inside for a worn wallet. She opened the wallet and slipped the cards out of their slots. Freddie fired up his computer, found a few websites. "Do you remember your password?" Henrietta did, it was the same password for all of her accounts. Freddie gave her a lecture about the necessity of having a different password for each account while he worked the numbers. "It's like makin' a hundred copies of your house key and leavin' 'em scattered around. Hacker finds one and now he has access to everything." Henrietta nodded like she believed him.

Freddie called up each of Henrietta's three credit card accounts as well as her checking and savings account and found, "There's been no activity since Thursday afternoon."

"That was when I charged lunch at a café near my work," Henrietta said.

Still, Freddie told her that if she was smart, she'd contact the credit card companies and her bank, tell them that her accounts have been compromised, and get new numbers and passwords. Also, contact the major credit bureaus and place a fraud alert. Henrietta said she would.

"Do you carry a lot of cash?" I asked.

"No," Henrietta said. "Why do you ask?"

"You went missing for nearly two days. How did you pay for it?"

"I hadn't thought of that. I did mention the sex part, though, right?"

"Speaking of which..." Freddie said.

"I wasn't raped," Henrietta said. "At least not violently. I was still wearing my clothes when I climbed out of that dumpster. Once I got my head together, I went to Hennepin County Medical Center. I paid for a rape kit exam. It took them hours. The results—the doctor said he didn't think I was sexually assaulted, but they stored all the evidence in case I want to file a police report later. Just to be safe, I've been popping morning-after pills like they were M&Ms ever since. Anyway, I was dehydrated and hungry, only I wasn't hurt. None of the drugs they tested for were in my system."

"Have you heard of Flunitrazepam?" I asked. "Also called Rohypnol? It doesn't stay in the system very long..."

"You think I was roofied? Okay. Tell me who did it."

"How old are you?" Freddie asked.

"Why does that matter?"

"Tell me."

"I turned twenty-seven last month."

"The hard living you describe didn't seem to do much damage. If you had told me you were eighteen, I woulda believed you."

"I've always been lucky that way. I'm still carded at clubs I've been going to since—that wasn't meant as a compliment, was it?"

"Sometimes girls are snatched off the street," I said. "Human traffickers hustle them out of town, sell them for sex slaves. Usually, it's young girls. Easier to control. Cops can be convinced that they're runaways despite what the family might say. Older women, though, are harder to dominate; cops tend to search for them more diligently."

"You're saying that someone might have kidnapped me thinking I was a kid, found out I was an ancient twenty-seven-year-old, and tossed me into a dumpster," Henrietta said. "If that's true, I want to know."

"Talk about your boyfriends," Freddie said.

"I don't have any."

"Ex-boyfriends, then."

"I've only had one in the past year. He dumped me, although not in a dumpster." Henrietta smiled, a remarkable thing I thought, all things considered. "He said I didn't know how to have fun; such is the price of a sober lifestyle."

"You impress me, Ms. Weller," I said. "Most people I know would have been traumatized by all of this to the point of helplessness, yet you seem to be handling it so calmly."

"I assure you, Mr. Taylor, I am anything but calm. In any case, I've already experienced my emotional meltdown. Now I want answers."

"I don't have any answers yet, but the fact that you weren't physically harmed raises some intriguing questions."

"If you were raped, we get that," Freddie said. "If you were held for ransom, sold into slavery, imprisoned by an ex-boyfriend who can't figure out why you don't love 'im anymore; if you were tortured by some sicko who doesn't like pretty women, yeah, we get that, too. Taken and then let go unharmed without explanation, though..."

"Unless I escaped my captors and hid in that dumpster..."

"Unless..."

"You see my problem, gentlemen. Assuming I didn't do this to myself..."

"The hole in your memory," I said. "From five-thirty-five Thursday evening until you escaped the dumpster at what time was it?

"About ten AM Saturday," Henrietta said.

"Forty hours without a trace of drugs or alcohol in your system at the end of it…"

"Closer to forty-two hours by the time I arrived at the hospital."

"Could you have done this to yourself in forty hours, even with alcohol and drugs and not remember?"

"There were times in my past when I couldn't remember the last drink I had or the last line I snorted or the last guy I fucked, but I always remembered the first. This time, though…"

"My guess—you were either taken by someone you have a personal relationship with or by someone who has a personal relationship with you that you are not aware of. Finding out who could prove very costly."

"Money isn't a problem," Henrietta said. "I have plenty."

"That's good to hear, except I wasn't talking about money."

Henrietta gave it a few beats before she replied. "I need to know what happened to me and why, Mr. Taylor."

"There are contracts to sign. Plus, we'll need to know everything there is about you. We'll start with a questionnaire. After that—do you have some place you need to be?"

"I've already called the office and taken the day."

"Where do you work?" Freddie asked.

"Mother Mercy Community Church."

"Really?"

"Now you know why I dress like my mother. I'm the assistant business administrator. I handle communications plus some accounting and finances."

"How long you been there?"

"Since I found God in the church basement during an AA meeting. I'm not a drunk, gentlemen, even though I've told people I was. 'Hi, my name is Henrietta and I'm an alcoholic.' I can have a drink and walk away easy enough. My addiction is chaos. For the longest time, I wanted to create as much of it as possible by any means that I could. I've hurt people. My mother."

"I understand," I said.

"One more thing, gentlemen, so there's no misunderstanding later—someone threw me away like so much garbage. Someone is going to pay for that."

"I like her," Freddie told me.

"You like her legs, anyway, the way you kept staring at them."

"Her chocolate-colored eyes, too. Don't tell Echo."

"You know I call your wife every night and tell her what you've been doing all day, especially when you're ogling clients."

"I wasn't oglin'. I don't even know what oglin' is."

"Staring in a lecherous manner."

"Oh."

Henrietta had left our offices after submitting to an interrogation process during which Freddie and I learned as much about her life and the people who touched it as she was willing to give.

"She was very forthcomin'," Freddie said. "Told us a lot of shit most people woulda kept to themselves outta embarrassment."

"Except about her family. She was closed-mouth about her family."

"I 'preciate she don't want nothin' to blow back on 'em. 'Can you do this for me and don't let mommy and daddy know?' How many times we heard that? Or somethin' like that? Oh, oh, oh, before I forget. I kinda strolled through her transactions when I was examining her checkin' account. The woman deposits $1,007.16 twice a month from the church where she works, comes out to $24,171 a year after taxes and such."

"Henrietta told us money wasn't an issue," I said. "She claimed she had plenty."

"She does have plenty. Besides what she gets from the church, she's bankin' $8,333.33 the first of the month every month. I'll do the math for you—it adds up to $100,000 a year."

"I have always been impressed by your grasp of numbers, Mr. Fredericks. Tell me—where's the one hundred grand coming from?"

"The Robert T. and Elizabeth R. Hudson Foundation."

"Wait. Aren't those the people who fund all those charities, all those art organizations like the Guthrie Theater?"

"Yeah."

"How does Henrietta rate, I wonder?"

"Maybe she's a poet, and we don't know it."

"She tells us all about the college professor she inflated in exchange for a passing grade, but not this?"

"Like I said—'Don't tell mommy.' Or whoever's writin' the checks."

I gave that a moment to sink in before I asked, "What's on the agenda?"

"There're a couple of subpoenas we need to serve, a couple of skip traces, and Sackett wants us to do 'nother round of background checks for the new plant he's buildin'. God, I love Sackett. Nothin' we can't work around, though."

We divided the labor between us. I would hit the bricks on Henrietta's behalf while Freddie ran the skip traces from his computer, a tool for which he had developed amazing nerd-like skills during the years we'd been in business together. I remembered when he thought a mouse was something you lured into a trap with a dollop of peanut butter.

As I headed for the door, Freddie said, "Listen, there's somethin' we should get settled right now, partner. The girl wants payback. I'm all for helpin' her get it."

"That's why we signed the contract."

"No, no, man. She's payin' us to ID the bad man. I'm sayin' I'm perfectly happy to go beyond that. You feel me?"

"Let's find out what we're dealing with first."

"Why? You think whoever did this had a good excuse? They threw her in a fuckin' dumpster, man."

"Or did they?"

Freddie stared at me for a few beats as if he was trying to see what was inside my head.

"Whaddya mean?" he asked.

"You live in Minneapolis. You tell me."

Freddie stared some more.

"What am I missin'?" he asked.

"She said all this happened Saturday morning, her adventures with the garbage truck."

"So?"

"There is no garbage pickup on Saturdays in Minneapolis."

CHAPTER TWO

Stepping out of my car, the sweltering afternoon heat slapped me in the face like a lover who thought I was cheating. The temperature was shocking. Exactly one week earlier, we had been pounded with the highest April snowfall the Cities had ever experienced—19.8 inches where I was standing at the mouth of an alley in North Minneapolis and only four degrees above freezing. Yet now it was eighty-four degrees and ungodly humid. In April. In Minnesota. We went from winter to summer without even a glance at spring. The ground wasn't just dry, it was parched. Sweat beaded along my hairline and under my arms. I would have removed my black sports jacket, except I didn't want anyone to spot the 9mm Beretta holstered behind my right hip.

Looking down the alley, I could easily see the back of Dillman's on the right, its battered green dumpster not far from the rear entrance. There was a small asphalt lot next to the bar where I had parked. Beyond that, a few single-family homes mixed in with a sandwich joint and a store that sold used sports equipment, all of them facing Lowry Avenue a few blocks west of Lyndale. On the left side of the alley, I found only small houses. Most of them were built in the 1920s and would have been in high demand if they were located in a neighborhood that didn't have the highest concentration of violent crime in the state. Not to mention robbery, drugs, and prostitution.

I wandered over to the dumpster and looked inside. I had no idea what I thought I'd find. Mostly it was plastic trash bags, the majority tied shut, some torn open, their contents spilling out. I tried to imagine being locked in there for any length of time and couldn't.

Standing with my back to the dumpster, I surveyed my surroundings and wondered how easily I could be seen by Dillman's customers and neighbors. Not very, I decided. Especially at night. There was a street lamp near the entrance to the alley, only I doubted its light penetrated this deep.

I thought about canvassing the houses bordering the alley. North Minneapolis was not known to be particularly inviting to the cops, and I doubted a private investigator would be better received. Still, you never know.

I decided my first stop would be the house directly behind the bar. It had a high wooden privacy fence and untrimmed weed trees facing the alley. There was a door with a latch between the fence and the garage. It swung open as I approached. An older African-American woman stopped and stared at me. She was holding a white trash bag.

"Who you?" she asked.

"My name's Taylor. Do you have a minute?"

Her answer was to push past me, cross the alley, glance around like she was doing something illegal, open the Dillman's dumpster, and stash her garbage bag inside. She came back.

"Don't tell anybody," she said. "I ain't supposed to do that."

"Your secret's safe with me."

"You a cop? Course not. Cops don't come around here. What you want?"

I pulled out my cell phone and called up a pic of Henrietta that I took in the office.

"Have you ever seen this woman?" I asked.

She took my phone, looked hard at the image, and handed it back.

"Can't say I have," she told me. "Why you wanna know?"

"I'm looking for her." It was a lie, of course, but it had the virtue of simplicity. "Are you sure you haven't seen her? Friday night perhaps?"

"Sorry. She workin'?"

"What do you mean?"

She snickered at me. "You ain't from around here, are ya?" she said.

"No."

"Didn't think so with that nice jacket you be wearin', unless you a john but then you'd be cruisin' in your car, pullin' up to the bus stop over there on Lowry, woman sittin' on the bench all mornin' long but ain't waitin' for a bus. Roll down your window and the woman says 'You wanna party?' Somethin' like that. You sayin' 'How much?' Then she'd gits in your car and you'd drive, I don't know, maybe you drive over here, pull into the alley, stop in front of my garage and what? Last I heard, a trick sells for thirty to a hundred dollars on the street depending on what you want to do. What would you want to do?"

"Find the woman I just showed you."

"I hope you do; I hope you do."

"Ms…"

"You don't need to know my name."

"Okay."

"I've been livin' in this house near fifty years. One thing I learn, you wanna git along, stay outta other folks' business. Use to be I hear a noise, hear someone shoutin', hear someone cryin', I'd come out and take a look. See if I could help. Now…Couple weeks ago I found a woman—what woman? Was a girl, couldn't be much older than sixteen. She was lyin' unconscious on my front lawn. Someone beat 'er up and dumped 'er there. I knew who she was, too. Called herself Tasha. Sometimes walkin' by she'd stop to pet my dog. I called the po-lice, only I wouldn't give my name. Course, they probably have it anyway, the way them computers work nowadays. 'Cept not giving my name, I didn't use to be like that. The neighborhood didn't use to be like that.

"Was a time, the alley was treated like a border, you know? You'd find condoms and such, see people doin' what they doin' in cars parked here in the alley or behind them bushes over there." She pointed at a stand of shrubs and trees bordering a yard a few houses down. "But that's where it ended. Now it's on my street and the street over and the street over from that one. Now I walk outside I get them cat calls, get them so-lic-it-ations. Old woman like me. You believe that?"

I came *this* close to slipping into my so-called charming mode and saying "Yes, I can" like it was a compliment. Then I thought of Freddie's Chinese wife Echo, who had suffered her share of so-lic-it-ations, and thought better of it.

"The world's going to hell," I said instead.

"Least this part of it," the old woman said. "Walk by here late at night, say around two, not that I would; it's like a scene outta that TV show, the one with the zombies—*Walking Dead*. Prostitutes, drug dealers everywhere, just hangin' around plyin' their goods. They be doin' the same thing during the daylight, walk down Lowry and take a look. Come late night though, it just seems so much worse."

"Did you ever think of moving?"

"That's what my kids want me to do, but you know—this is my home. Been here fifty years. I tell you that? Besides, think I'd get a good price the way things are? Uh uh."

"About last Friday night. Or perhaps Thursday."

"I'm sorry. I know what you're askin', only I didn't see your girl. I don't even look no more. Couple weeks ago, I heard gunshots right out here, pretended it was the TV."

CHAPTER THREE

I tried a few more houses up and down the alley. If people were home, most of them didn't bother to come to the door to tell me. Those who did wouldn't give me the time of day. I ended up standing next to the dumpster again. The name of the waste disposal company and its phone number were stenciled in white on the side. I wrote both down in a small notebook I carry, thinking I might be able to contact the driver of the garbage truck.

While I was doing that, the back door to the bar swung open, and an older woman wearing faded jeans and a Minnesota Vikings t-shirt stepped out. Like the African-American woman across the alley, she was carrying a garbage bag except she was white and her bag was black. She also stopped and stared. An unlit cigarette dangled from her mouth, the cigarette the same color as her long hair. It bobbed up and down when she spoke.

"What are you doin' here?" she wanted to know.

"I'm looking for someone."

"In the dumpster?"

"As a matter of fact, it was the last place she was seen. By the garbage man."

"Garbage man? What are you talkin' about?" I started to explain. She held up a hand. "Know what? I don't wanna hear it. I hear so many fuckin' stories makes my head hurt."

She moved to the dumpster, deposited her garbage bag, and moved away.

I took out my cell phone. "If you would take a look..."

She held up her hand again, said "I don't have time for this shit," and went back through the door. I tried to follow, only she closed it in my face.

I circled the bar and went in through the front door. There were windows facing Lowry Avenue yet no others, so the front half of Dillman's was bathed in sunshine while the back was partially hidden in shadow. There were plenty of wooden tables, chairs, and booths with high backs. All of the furniture seemed as if it had been there since World War II. Customers who looked like they had been hanging around since V-J Day filled a couple of booths. Two women were sitting at a table and staring at a flat-screen TV mounted in the corner tuned to CNN, the sound off. If it was me, I would have checked their IDs and then checked, again.

Directly in front of me, the woman in the Vikings shirt was standing behind the bar. From her expression, I formed the idea that she wasn't a happy person; that this wasn't the life she had wanted, but it was the life she was living, and she was trying hard to make the best of it.

She shook her head when I approached. I pulled a thin leather wallet from my pocket; the one with the ID that says I'm a professional private investigator licensed by the State of Minnesota and flicked it open. Some people are impressed. She shook her head some more.

"Whaddya want?" she asked.

"Booker's." She looked at me like I was deliberately kidding her. "Jim Beam on the rocks."

She poured the bourbon and set the glass on a coaster in front of me. It cost a ten, including a hefty tip, which didn't impress the bartender any more than my ID did. I pulled out my cell phone again, called up the pic and slid it toward her.

"Ever see her around here?" I asked.

The bartender hesitated before taking a long look.

"No," she said.

"Friday night? Maybe Thursday?"

"I don't think so."

"You're not sure?"

"I see a lot of people comin' and goin'. I know it don't look like it now, but it's a Monday afternoon, 'kay? Unless she does something to catch my attention, cut her boyfriend with a broken beer bottle or dance topless on the bar for no particular reason, I ain't gonna remember."

"How 'bout your regulars?"

The bartender spread her arms wide, glanced around the nearly empty bar and said, "Ask 'em."

I did, taking my cell first to the three occupied booths. No-body sitting there knew who Henrietta Weller was, although they all wanted to talk about her—who is she, what did she do? The two young women sitting at the table looked at me with expectation. Both wore more makeup than they needed, but their clothes were casual. When I first started working for the St. Paul Police Department back in the day, I had the impression that prostitutes needed to be attractive, that they had to dress provocatively to attract customers like in the movies. I quickly found out that it's the opposite on the street. Most professionals looked like they had just rolled out of bed. Teenage girls waiting for the school bus dressed sluttier than they did.

"Ladies," I said.

"Anything we can do for you?" the one with the darker hair asked.

"And we mean anything," the one with the lighter hair said.

I showed them the pic.

"Ever see her around, maybe last Thursday or Friday night?" I asked.

They both looked at the photograph, they both shook their heads.

"Let me guess," the one with the lighter hair said. "The family hired you to scoop her up, give her a happy ending."

"Something like that," I said.

"There aren't any happy endings out here," the girl with the darker hair said. "It's just surviving. You're either predator or prey."

"Sometimes, I think I'm a predator, but mostly I know I'm prey," said the other. "Are you sure there's nothing we can do for you? We might even be talked into offering an afternoon discount."

"Thank you for your time," I said.

"I hope you find your friend, take her home."

"Thank you."

"I mean it. Take her home."

I returned to the bar.

"Anything?" the bartender asked.

"No."

"Didn't think so." She pointed at my bourbon. "'Nother?"

I shook my head and finished the drink.

"Come back anytime," the bartender said.

I returned to my Toyota Camry parked in the Dillman's lot. Once inside, I used my phone to call the number I had written down in my notebook. A woman answered, "Markland Waste Management Service, how may I help you?"

Since she asked so pleasantly, I identified myself as a private investigator. However, before I could explain why I called, the woman said, "Is this about the girl that one of our drivers found in the dumpster?"

"As a matter of fact..."

"Isn't that crazy?"

I agreed it was.

"Is she all right? Do you know who she is, what happened to her? The driver said that she was acting hysterical when he fished her out of the container. He said he was hooking up when the top of the dumpster flew off and the woman started screaming."

"He didn't actually lift the dumpster?" I asked.

"Not while she was in it, no. He was moving the dumpster into position and the woman popped up and started screaming is what the driver said. He kept asking if she was all right, if he should call the police. Then he asked how she got into the dumpster in the first place. The woman said 'That's a good question' and just walked away. That's what the driver said. Isn't that crazy?"

Henrietta embellished her story, I told myself, made it sound more dramatic. I wonder why she did that. Did she think we wouldn't believe her unless she made the story bigger?

"I have a question," I said aloud. "Why was Markland picking up garbage on a Saturday?"

"Because of the snowstorm. We have a holiday schedule. Labor Day, for instance. Our drivers take the day off like everyone else, and the schedule gets bumped a day. Monday pickup becomes Tuesday and Tuesday becomes Wednesday and so on 'til Saturday. The snowstorm last Monday was so bad we had to pull our trucks off the road, so we went to the holiday schedule. We called all of our customers with a taped message. Didn't you get it?"

I ended the conversation and dropped my cell into a cup holder.

Okay, I told myself, Henrietta Weller was telling the truth. Kind of. Good to know.

So now what?

I started the Camry and eased it out of the parking lot. I drove around the neighborhood for no better reason than to get a sense of the place. There was plenty of traffic, most of it purposeful. People drove the streets because they took them where they wanted to go. No one was sightseeing. No one was cruising around North Minneapolis searching for a likely spot to dump a woman's body. I decided that whoever put Henrietta in Dillman's dumpster must have known that it was there.

I promised to return to Dillman's later that evening, telling myself that I might have better luck with the late-night crowd. I didn't mind the inconvenience. One of the reasons I liked PI work: it wasn't nine-to-five. I worked weekends and nights as often as weekdays because when you needed to interview someone, you needed to do it according to their schedule, not yours. What I didn't like—free time, empty hours to fill. It reminded me I didn't have much of a life when I wasn't working.

CHAPTER FOUR

Amanda Wedemeyer perched on the front steps of the 100-year-old brown-brick apartment building in the Crocus Hill neighborhood of St. Paul that I shared with her, her mother and eight other tenants. She was wearing shorts and her soccer jersey even though it wasn't soccer season, her elbows propped on her knees, her face resting in her hands. She appeared to be the saddest, loneliest, and most unloved seventh grader in the universe which, I'm sure, was exactly the look she was going for.

"Hey, kid," I said. "What's going on?"

"Nothing."

"Okay."

"Taylor?"

"Mandy?"

"Are you my friend?"

"I am."

"Will you kill my father for me?"

"No problem. Should I do it now?"

"You're joking with me."

"Aren't you joking with me?"

"I guess."

"Is your mom home?"

"She's running late. She said some nit decided to schedule a meeting late in the afternoon. That's what she called him. A nit."

"Come on up. I'll buy you a root beer."

We went inside the building and took the stairs to the second floor. I was in 2A; the Wedemeyers were in 2B. I unlocked my apartment door and swung it open. I used a rubber wedge to keep it from closing. My door is never closed when Amanda is inside the apartment. It wasn't something I ever discussed with the girl or her mother, just something I did automatically ever since Amanda discovered I shared the place with a gray-and-white French lop-eared rabbit.

We both heard his soft thump-thump-thumping before he appeared, running fast, trying to stop and sliding across the hardwood living room floor until he caromed off the bottom of a stuffed chair. Amanda squealed when she saw him, as she nearly always did.

"I love when Ogilvy does that." She knelt on floor. "Do you think he does it on purpose? That he likes to slide across the floor?"

"He only does it when you come over," I said.

I watched her over the counter in my kitchen and for a moment she became the light-haired hooker I had met earlier that afternoon, the one who wanted me to find my friend and take her home. She was what? Five years older than Amanda? Six? Couldn't be much more than that. What events conspired to bring her to Dillman's, I wondered. And sixteen-year-old Tasha whom I hadn't met, did she pet the African-American woman's dog the same way that Amanda petted my rabbit? Tasha who was beaten unconscious and dumped on the woman's front lawn. For a moment, I felt a thrill of fear moving up my spine.

"Jesus," I said.

"What?" Amanda asked.

"Nothing."

I shook the images from my head, went to my refrigerator, found a carrot and a can of A&W that I poured into a glass with ice. I gave both to the girl and returned to the kitchen. Amanda held the carrot above the rabbit's head.

"Beg," she said.

Ogilvy stood on his hind legs, holding his front paws forward, like a dog might.

Next the girl waved the carrot in a circle.

"Roll over."

The rabbit rolled over.

She rested the carrot on the floor.

"Play dead."

The rabbit flopped on his side and sprawled out in front of her.

She slid the carrot along the floor to his mouth. Ogilvy hopped to his feet and started gnawing on it like he was starving.

"He's getting fat," Amanda said.

"That's because there's this strange little girl that keeps feeding him carrots, celery, broccoli, lettuce and whatever other vegetables she won't eat herself."

"How can you get fat eating vegetables?"

"He's supposed to be eating hay and sometimes alfalfa."

"Taylor, do you think I'm fat?"

"No." I wasn't being polite, either. Mandy had a lean and athletic body, having discovered both soccer and a love of running. Sometimes she ran with me early in the morning. I'd tell her I'm deliberately slowing down so she can keep up but really I'm not. "Why would you ask that?"

"My father said I was fat."

"Ahh."

"Not in those exact words. He said I was big for my age, but fat is what he meant."

"When did you see him?"

"Yesterday in Stillwater. For an hour. He's getting out of prison this week. Next week? I don't know. I do know that he has to live in a halfway house for six months."

"He's transitioning from prison to life on the outside—that's what they call it."

"I guess."

Amanda picked up the rabbit and set him on her lap so she could more easily pet him while he ate. Ogilvy didn't seem to mind.

"He wants to see me," Amanda said. "Spend time with me even though he thinks I'm fat."

"Would that be so bad, you spending time with your father?"

"He made my mother cry. That's all I remember about him from before he went to prison. He gambled away all of our money; he gambled away our house, and he made her cry. Mom took me to visit him a couple times, but he was more interested in yelling at her than talking to me. Mom divorced him, and then he wouldn't talk to me at all, not even to yell. His family, my grandparents and aunts and uncles and cousins, they would have nothing to do with us, Mom and me. They disowned us. I wouldn't even get a birthday card. Now he wants to be my father like nothing happened?"

"I don't know what to tell you, kid. Maybe he's a better person than he was. Sometimes prison does that. Not often, but sometimes."

"Mom's afraid he might sue for joint custody."

"Did she say that?"

"I heard her talking to someone on the phone. She's wondering if she should hire a lawyer."

"I know a lot of lawyers, some very good lawyers, as a matter of fact. I work with them all the time."

"Will you help her?"

"Of course I will, kid. Whaddya think?"

"See, you call me kid, and it's filled with affection. He called me kid, and it was an insult. I remember that, too."

"What do you remember?" Claire Wedemeyer said.

She stepped across the threshold into my living room while adjusting the heavy bag that hung from her shoulder. This was not an uncommon scene in my place, mother and daughter chatting. It was something I looked forward to, although the bag—why do women carry such heavy bags?

"I was telling Taylor about Dad," Amanda said.

"Mandy." Her voice echoed with the sound of annoyance. "We do not discuss family matters with strangers."

"Mom…"

"Have you done your homework yet? Don't you think you should get to it? I'll have dinner ready in a minute."

"Mom…"

"Go."

Amanda brushed Ogilvy off her lap, stood, and walked out of the room, trying hard to make each step sound like an obscenity. Claire turned to follow her.

"See you around, stranger," I said.

Claire stopped where she was. Her shoulders drooped.

"I'm sorry." Her eyes were on the floor when she first spoke, but then they swung around toward me. "I really am sorry. I don't know why I said that. You've always been kind to both me and Mandy. Watching out for her…"

Ogilvy rammed her foot with his head, which was what he did when he wanted attention. Claire bent to scratch him between his ears. She smiled; something else that I always looked forward to. Mother and daughter were opposites in appearance. Claire had a dark and brooding appearance while Amanda was all sunshine and wheat fields. Except for their brilliant smiles. Their smiles were identical.

"I tell people you keep a rabbit for a pet and that Mandy loves coming over here to play with him. Some people think it's pretty cool, while others think it's weird. One guy I met said when he was young, his family raised rabbits and then ate them."

"Hey, hey, hey," I chanted. "Not in front of the b-u-n-n-y."

She stood. "I am sorry, Holland."

"Let's not get maudlin about it, using my first name. My friends call me Taylor, remember? C'mon."

"Calling you a stranger. What was I thinking?"

"Like most people, you don't want the world to know your troubles. I get it. So, stop being sorry. You and the kid are always welcome here, you know that. And even though it doesn't need to be said, if there's anything I can do to help you, just ask."

I meant it, too. Claire knew it. She and Amanda were among the precious few people who brought light into my otherwise gloomy life. Okay, maybe I was the one being maudlin. Only I had lost both my wife and daughter to a drunk driver who couldn't tell the difference between red and green ten years, ten months, and eleven days ago—yes, I've kept track—and it kinda messed me up, I'm not afraid to admit it. Then there were a couple of other women who piled on after that. Amanda didn't remind me of Jenny, and Claire certainly didn't remind me of Laura. I wasn't substituting them for the family that I had loved and lost. Yet having them around made me feel happy.

"Taylor knows a lot of lawyers," Mandy said.

She was standing in the hallway and peeking around my doorframe.

"Amanda Wedemeyer," Claire said.

"That's my name. Don't wear it out."

Claire turned from her daughter to me, an expression of shock on her face. I didn't know what to do, so I shrugged.

"She's almost a teenager," I said.

"I thought I still had a couple of years."

"Hey, kid." I pointed at the half-filled glass sitting on the floor precariously close to the rabbit. "Hit the bricks and take your root beer with you."

CHAPTER FIVE

The black woman I had met earlier suggested I should return to North Minneapolis at two AM if I wanted to see zombieland. It wasn't necessary. Most crime takes place at night, and in April in Minnesota, the sun set at about eight PM. By nine, the neighborhood around Dillman's had been transformed into an open-air bazaar dealing in sex and drugs.

Driving down Lowry, I saw plenty of cars idling on the street. Women, five or six to a block, lingered at crosswalks without ever actually crossing the street or strolled against the traffic, trying to make eye contact with drivers. A young woman wearing a rhinestone-studded tank top stood with one foot on the curb and the other in the gutter until a car slowed to a stop. She spoke briefly with the driver and climbed into the car. The driver accelerated down the avenue as if he were suddenly on the clock.

Three cars were lined up at a corner in front of a young man who held a cell phone to his ear. He flicked his thumb toward some place behind him. The first car turned the corner and moved slowly down the street. That left two cars in line until an SUV joined the parade, followed by a Chevy pickup.

The lot next to Dillman's was filled, so I had to park down the street and walk back to the bar. I passed several prostitutes and drug dealers. They gave me head nods, but no so-lic-it-ations. I knew why. It was the sports jacket. It had been a problem when I worked undercover for the SPPD, too. You always wore a jacket because you were armed; you were carrying a concealed weapon. Only when it was summer—or a historically hot and humid evening in April—it looked weird and the more experienced street urchins would automatically mark you for a cop and move to the next block.

Female officers posing as prostitutes had the same problem, even those who went unarmed, who put their safety wholly into the hands of their male backup, because they always carried their badges. Some would tuck them into their shirts. Others wore short-sleeve jackets to hide them.

Dillman's was surprisingly crowded. At least I was surprised. There was loud music, only I couldn't make it out over the much louder voices and the smell of cigarettes, even though it was unlawful to smoke in bars and restaurants in Minnesota.

Many heads turned when I stepped inside, eyes worked me over. Some patrons wondered if I was a business prospect. Others asked if I was trouble, how much, and whether or not they could handle it. Most greeted me with casual indifference, some asshole wearing a sports jacket into Dillman's. Who the fuck does that?

The older woman in the Viking's tee was still standing behind the bar. I couldn't prove that she had wandered ten feet since I saw her last. When I approached, she attempted to attract the attention of a black man who was talking to a young white woman at the far end of the stick without attracting my attention. The black man didn't notice, so she gestured some more. He still hadn't noticed her by the time I reached the only empty stool.

"You're back," she said.

"I missed you."

"What's your name again?"

I hadn't told her when I was there earlier, yet couldn't think of a reason to keep it to myself.

"Taylor," I said. "You?"

"Glynis."

"No kidding? That's a beautiful name."

Glynis seemed pleased by my enthusiasm.

"Whaddya have?" she asked.

"Some more of that Jim Beam with ice."

She went to fetch it. While she did, she tried again to gain the attention of the black man, who remained enthralled by the girl. Glynis set the drink in front of me.

"You wanna run a tab?" she asked.

"I'll pay as I go," I said.

I slipped her a ten. Glynis returned after a moment and dropped the change next to my glass. I ignored it, instead concentrating on the black man, watching him in the mirror behind the bar. He was pushing thirty, tall, his head hair cut short while his facial hair had been trimmed into a thick mustache and goatee. He reminded me a little of Denzel Washington in that movie where he played the most corrupt cop in the history of the LAPD until he smiled at the white girl. Nobody has Denzel's smile. Except for maybe Freddie, only I would never tell him that.

I spun on my stool and took in the rest of the bar. Everyone behaved as if they were safe, as if no harm could ever befall them inside Dillman's including two men who casually exchanged product for cash across a square table and a woman who took the hand of a gentleman at least twice her age and led him out of the back door of the bar toward the dumpster. Certainly, no one was paying any attention to me, sports coat and all, except for the Asian sitting in the booth nearest the door who kept glancing my way while pretending not to.

Before I met Echo, I had no idea how to distinguish Chinese, Japanese, and Korean people from one another. She told me to look at the eyes. She said that the Chinese, her people, have big eyes that tend to angle upwards, Japanese have smaller eyes that angle downwards, and Koreans "have little beady eyes." But perhaps that was her personal prejudice talking—Americans weren't the only racists in the world. From a distance, the Asian appeared Chinese to me. Honestly, though, what did I know about it? In any case, he didn't remind me of anyone I had ever seen in the movies or otherwise.

I swung back and stared at my reflection in the mirror while I sipped the bourbon. By then Glynis had moved down the bar to where the black man sat. She whacked him on the arm. He turned as if he had every intention of hitting her back. She stepped away and gestured toward me with her chin. He said something that made her react as if she couldn't believe she was wasting her time talking to this guy.

I pulled my cell, called up Henrietta's pic, and set the phone face down on the bar.

And waited.

The black guy sent hand signals to the Asian, who moved from the booth near the door to a table near the bar. The two people already sitting there were surprised by his appearance, yet didn't comment when he sat down. After a few moments, they pretended he wasn't there.

The black guy patted the white girl's hand, said something that made her giggle, and left his perch at the end of the bar. He walked past me, went to the far end of the room, turned, and watched me for a moment before coming back.

"Yo," he said.

The two men who were sitting next to me picked up their drinks and abandoned their stools without saying a word, which told me a lot—the black guy, whoever he was, ruled the joint.

He took possession of the stool furthest away, leaving an empty seat between us.

"S'up yo?" he asked.

"Not much," I replied. "You?"

"I hear you're lookin' for someone."

"As a matter of fact…"

"You see her?"

I spun in my stool so that I was facing him and, at the same time, was able to watch the Asian out of my peripheral. The black guy was smiling his non-Denzel Washington smile while his backup displayed all the expression of a marble statue. Inscrutable, all those 1940s and 50s propaganda movies would say.

"I don't see her," I said. "Course I haven't looked that hard yet."

"She's not here."

"How do you know?"

"I know."

"Short blonde, goes about one-fifty?"

"You mean tall brunette weighs closer to one-twenty, don't you?"

I picked up the cell and held it so he could see Henrietta's pic.

"Whaddya know?" I said. "You're right. How is that possible?"

The black guy gestured at the bartender, who had moved close enough to hear us without advertising that she was eavesdropping.

"Glynis told me," he said.

"The woman is surprisingly precise with her descriptions."

"I pay attention," Glynis said.

"I bet." I slipped the cell into my jacket pocket. "Still, you don't object if I look around, do you? Talk to the people?"

"Yeah, I do," the black guy said. "It makes my customers nervous, some PI dressed like a cop askin' questions. They get nervous, maybe they take their trade elsewhere. Business declines. Profits shrink. That's bad. Bad for everyone."

"Especially bad for you."

"You see my point."

"Are you Dillman?"

The black guy and Glynis thought that was funny. The Asian didn't so much as crack a smile.

"Dillman's been dead over ten years," the black guy said.

"I hope he died of natural causes."

"Whatever killed him, it wasn't poking his nose into other people's business."

"Finding the girl is my business."

"Find her somewhere else." He spoke like Hernán Cortés explaining it to the Aztecs. "This is our place."

The Asian left his table and moved to the bar, positioning himself a few steps behind me. I watched him in the mirror while I sipped the bourbon. I set down the glass.

"I'm confused," I said. "Here you are threatening me with bodily harm. Makes me wonder if it's because you want to protect your turf or because you know something about the girl and you don't want me to find out. You are threatening me, aren't you?"

The black guy moved from his stool to the one closest to me, so I could hear him snarl when he leaned in.

"You've got ten fucking seconds," he said. "One, two…"

The Asian picked up a bottle of PBR by the neck.

I reached out with both hands, grabbed the back of the black guy's head, and slammed his face against the bar just as hard as I could.

His head bounced upward and he fell off the stool, his nose and mouth were already bloody.

At the same time, I slid off my stool and pivoted to face the Asian.

He took two steps toward me while raising the beer bottle high above his head with the intention of using it as a club.

That gave me enough time to pull the Beretta from its holster and center the front sight on his chest.

He stopped.

I might have told him to put the bottle down except it was half full and I liked the way the beer splashed out onto his hand, arm, and shoulder.

The black guy had moved into a sitting position on the floor and was cradling his face with both hands.

Neither of them spoke.

I took a couple of steps backward so I could watch both men without turning my head. I was in a Weaver stance like I had been taught at the academy, holding the Beretta with both hands. I must have looked impressive because no one in Dillman's was speaking, not even to ask what was going on. There were no screams, no threats to call the cops. For the first time, I could hear the music. A Minnesota rapper named Dessa was warning a friend to work on her alibi. Not necessarily the song I would have selected, but okay.

Glynis reached under the bar, which made me anxious, until she pulled out a cigarette, stuck it between her lips, and lit it with a plastic lighter. She took a long pull and said, "So, now what?"

I had a speech in my head where I was going to tell them all that if I discovered they had anything to do with the disappearance of the woman I was searching for, I would come back and burn the place to the ground. Only there were too many people behind and around me staring intently. And quietly. Fear was contagious, much more so than laughter. Only I knew it wouldn't last. None of these less-than-innocent bystanders were on my side, and if any of them should decide to make some noise...

A quick glance showed me an unobstructed path to the front entrance. Instead of pretending I was a badass, I backed along it until I reached the door. Again, some heroic movie words came to mind. I left them there and slipped out of the bar.

I half walked, half ran to my Camry, always watching over my shoulder. The black guy didn't come after me. Nor did the Asian. Nor did anyone else, for that matter.

I sat in the car, wondering if I should drop a dime on Dillman's. Smart money would bet that the Fourth District cops knew all about the place. Of course they did. Most likely they were operating under the theory that if they couldn't stop the sex and drugs—and they couldn't—they might at least try to contain it to—what did Paul Simon call it in his song "The Boxer?" *"The poorer quarters where the ragged people go."* Still, there are always things you can do.

I used my smartphone to determine Dillman's was located in the Fifth Ward and looked up the name and number of the man who represented the ward on the Minneapolis City Council. When I was kicked to voice mail, I reported that there was a bar near my house called Dillman's, where they prostituted teenage girls and that "I've called the police over and over again and they never do anything about it except wave when they drive by. I know this is your first term on the Council, so maybe you don't know anything about it, or maybe you do. All I can say is that there's another election coming this November."

It was an utterly childish prank to pull, I know. Only I was angry, getting chased out of a bar by a bunch of punks. I could already hear Freddie giving me the business over it. Besides, you never know what might shake loose when the pressure was put on, and no one puts on more pressure than a politician trying to keep his job.

CHAPTER SIX

While I was busy at Dillman's, Freddie was inspecting the second scene of the crime, Henrietta Weller's apartment. He explained it to me the next morning over coffee after I related my own misadventures.

Now understand, most of our clients demand well-written, precisely worded reports. The law firms, in particular, insist on it. Freddie was as good at delivering them as anybody. Except, when he recounted his escapades to me it could never just be he did this and then he did that, oh hell no. He had to tell his tales as if he were channeling Julie Klassen or one of the many other romance authors hailing from Minnesota. I think he did it to annoy me...

The tall, good-looking black man moved through Uptown as if he owned the place, the hipsters giving him plenty of room to swagger, the yuppies who lived there and the college grads who hung in the oh-so-chic clubs, bars and restaurants caring more about the cut of his fashionable clothes than the color of his skin...

"Fashionable clothes?" I said. "God, Fredericks, you're killing me."

"You don't like what I wear?"

"I think Echo dresses you very nicely."

"I blend in Uptown is what I'm sayin'."

"You blend in North Minneapolis, too."

"Yeah, but you don't. You really wore a sports jacket into Dillman's; you had to dress like a homicide dick?"

"I used to be a homicide dick."

"Emphasis on dick, man, c'mon. You coulda handled that so much better."

"There was nothing I could do. The dude decided he wasn't interested in a conversation long before he even saw my jacket, probably when Glynis told him I was snooping there earlier."

"So now what? You got a plan?"

"Of course I have a plan. But tell me what you got first."

The black private dick that's a sex machine for all the chicks..."

"Stop it," I said.

He drifted deeper into the neighborhood until he discovered an ancient brick building that resembled a small castle. It was located in an oasis of solitude a handful of blocks south of Lake Street, between Hennepin Avenue and the lake.

"I still can't believe they did that," Freddie said.

"Did what?"

"Change the name of Lake Calhoun to—what they call it now?"

"Bde Maka Ska."

"That nobody can pronounce. It was originally named after John Calhoun cuz he was secretary of war when they built Fort Snelling. Couple of hundred years later, they discover he was also a pro-slavery Southern politician from Charleston, South Carolina, so now the name's gotta go. But what 'bout George Washington? Father of the country, he had slaves. Thomas Jefferson? He kept slaves, too, man. Over six hundred I read, the same dude who wrote *'we hold these truths to be self-evident, that all men are created equal.'* Kept 'em 'til he died and then they were all sold off. How many Lake Jeffersons out there? Towns called Washington. Schools? Gotta rename them, too, don't we?"

"You're asking me?"

"You know what really pisses me off? Be-day mah-kah ska," he said, sounding it out. "Is from the Dakota language. They shoulda given the lake an African name."

"What would you suggest?"

"Lake Asha."

"You wanted them to name it after your mother?" She was christened Judith, only she changed it during her militancy days back in the late sixties. Asha meant "lively woman" and she sure as hell was that. "Works for me."

"Anyway..."

The castle contained sixteen apartments. Henrietta Weller lived in a 600-square-foot unit that featured large windows, hardwood floors, arched doorways, beamed ceilings and a gas fireplace that went for a tidy 2K a month not counting utilities. There was a small asphalt parking lot behind the building large enough to accommodate twelve vehicles at an additional cost of $300 per stall. Henrietta was on the third floor with a view of the street, so she couldn't have seen someone lurking in the lot until she walked out there.

The black man circled the block and then the building itself, examining the terrain, deciding that there was no way to enter or exit the lot without risking discovery. He also decided that wasn't necessarily a deterrent. It was five-thirty-five by the black man's Rolex. He had deliberately arrived at the castle at the exact time his client had been abducted to gauge the amount of traffic that had existed. There was surprisingly little, despite its close proximity to Uptown and the lake, leaving him to conclude that there would have been few, if any, casual observers to witness the event.

He stepped into the parking lot itself and searched for Henrietta's vehicle; he had learned the make and model when they had interviewed her earlier that day. The car wasn't present, which meant the client was probably absent as well.

He was considering what gag he could employ to gain access to the castle and interview those tenants with a view of the parking lot when the back door swung open. A thin white woman his mother's age came charging toward him, all five-foot-nothing of her. She was brandishing a sixteen-inch Louisville Slugger with the Minnesota Twins name and logo burnt into the wood.

When she came within swinging distance of the black man, she raised the souvenir bat so that the barrel was about even with his head and shouted, "What are you doing here?"

"Whoa, lady, c'mon, what are you doing?"

"Why are you here, boy? Answer me? I'm going to call the police. You don't belong here."

He considered his options. One of them was pulling his Colt Commander and blowing her cracker brains out...

"You didn't really think that," I said.

Instead, the black man held up one hand to fend off the blows in case the old woman decided to swing on him while he used his other to locate his identification. He held it for her to see.

"Ma'am," he said. "I'm an investigator."

The old woman kept her bat poised in the air, yet stepped forward and squinted as she read the ID aloud.

"Fredericks and Taylor Private Investigations," she said. "Sidney Poitier Fredericks. Oh, I love him. Sidney Poitier, I mean."

"Yeah, me, too."

"You're a private investigator? Private eye? Detective? Shamus? Continental Op?"

"Oh, oh," I said. "Fan girl."

"Don't knock it, man. Kept her from goin' all overseer on my ass."

"I am a private investigator," the black man agreed.

"I read all the books."

The black man made a patting motion with his free hand.

"Could you..." he said.

The woman lowered her souvenir bat.

"It's not about your race," she said. "Uh uh. I voted for Obama. Twice. But you're not supposed to be back here if you aren't a tenant."

"Do you always guard the parking lot so zealously?"

"I live..." She pointed at her basement apartment; her windows were parallel to the ground. "I live over there, so I have a good view of people coming and going. There's a sign—didn't you see the sign? It says no trespassing. Parking for tenants only. People are always sneaking into the lot, though. Sometimes they're visiting the tenants, but sometimes they're people who live around here." She waved more or less at the entire neighborhood. "People who are too lazy to find a space on the street or who think they'll only be a minute. Especially in the winter. I'm not above having them towed, either. People pay extra for these spaces."

"Are you the caretaker?"

"I'm the owner."

"Did you see anyone sneaking into the lot last Thursday?"

"No. Why? What is this about?"

"One of the tenants was involved in an incident in the parking lot last Thursday evening at approximately five-thirty-five PM."

"Which tenant? What incident? Do you work for an insurance company? Is someone threatening to sue me?"

The black man knew he had to offer her something to keep her talking, so he revealed the client's name but not her circumstance.

"Oh no, Henrietta?" the woman said. "What happened?"

"I'm not at liberty to say."

"Is she all right? Of course she's all right. I saw her this morning. She always gives me a wave and a smile. Such a sweetheart. The last time she paid her rent, she gave me a gift card for a flower shop just over there on Hennepin. None of my other tenants ever do nice things like that."

"Henrietta is good people."

"She nothing like her mother, that's for sure."

"Do you know her mother?"

"Don't you?"

"We've never met."

"I've never met her either, but I know enough about her to say that she's a socialist bitch who's all for free speech if it supports her politics but against it if it don't."

"Henrietta's mother?" the black man said.

"Abigail Hudson. Are you telling me you don't know Abigail? She's a member of the U. S. House of Representatives."

"Wait," I said. "What?"

"It gets better," Freddie said.

CHAPTER SEVEN

"Oh, I knew that," Lori Hertz said. "We all knew who Rhett's mom was, even though she changed her name when she decided to go into politics. It wasn't a secret. Some of us, not me, but some of her classmates thought that was how Rhett got into the school of management in the first place."

Several thoughts swirled through the black man's head. The first—"Rhett?" he said.

"Short for Henrietta. You didn't know that?"

The woman leaned back in her chair while she regarded the man across the table from her. He had told her he was Henrietta Weller's friend; that he was trying to help her. Only now she was wondering. If he was a friend, why didn't he know her name was Rhett?

The black man gave her a reassuring smile...

"Echo says my smile reminds her of Denzel Washington," Freddie told me.

"I don't see it," I said.

The black man smiled and said, "We're not that close."

Lori nodded while she glanced nervously around the club as if she suddenly needed to note where the exits were, as if she wanted to determine if help was nearby and if she could count on it. The black man decided he needed to give her a reason to trust him. He took his ID from his pocket and dropped it in front of her. Lori stared at it for a few moments then turned her blue eyes on his; her hand brushed her golden hair behind her ear. He had seen it before, how that laminated card gave him instant credibility.

"Rhett had some trouble over the weekend," the black man said. "She needs your help."

He had said as much when he spoke to the young woman over the phone to set up the meeting, yet repeating the words in person, adding his picture ID and his smile, made a significant difference. Lori leaned forward, clasping her hands in front of her.

"What can I do?" she asked.

Even with her Minnesota eyes and hair, Lori lived on the border between pretty and plain and was tilting south, the black man decided. She had gained at least twenty pounds since she bought the dress she wore into the Uptown club, unless she thought she looked good wearing clothes that were two sizes too small. Perhaps the alcohol had something to do with it. She had two drinks during the half hour she and the black man were together and was ordering a third as he was leaving.

"I've had a stressful day," she said.

"Doing what?"

"I'm a project manager for a biotech in St. Louis Park. My group is attempting to develop an instantaneous anesthetic to be used on the battlefield for a pharmaceutical company that has a contract with the U.S. Army and we are way, way, way behind our timetable, which was arbitrarily established in the first place. They're a bunch of pricks. Big Pharma, I mean. The Army guys are cool."

"Working for a biotech. Isn't that a good thing?"

"Four days out of five it is, even though half my net income goes to paying down my college debt. Rhett and a lot of the other girls I knew in school didn't need to worry about tuition, living expenses. Mommy and Daddy took care of them. I don't begrudge them that. Believe me, I wish I had been in the same

boat. They were all smart, too. You don't get into the Universi-
ty of Minnesota's Carlson School of Management unless you're
a serious student. If you didn't take honors courses in high
school, if you're not in the top ten percent of your graduating
class, if you don't have a 30 on your ACTs or better, don't even
bother applying. Course, they all went to private schools like
Blake, Breck, and St. Paul Academy. That had to help. I went
to a public school, Patrick Henry. That was okay, too. You do
the best with what you have.

"What bugged me was that so many of them didn't seem to
take school seriously. Rhett was the worst, but a lot of the
others, it was like once they got there, they didn't have to work
so hard. It was like they all knew that their futures were secure.
Maybe it was, I don't know. Rhett—she was my roommate for
two years. She spent nearly all of her time partying, barely got
her homework done. It affected me, too. I found myself
spending more time with her than on my schoolwork. Finally,
they kicked her out. I was shocked when that happened,
because of her mother, the congresswoman, you know? On the
other hand, I was furious with her. How could you waste an
opportunity like that?

"I loved her, though. She was kind to me. I didn't see much
of her—heck, I didn't see her at all after she left school. I ran
into her again years later at, well, here—this very club. Was it
two years ago? She had changed. She wasn't nearly the same
party girl. We all grow up, don't we? Anyway, I've seen a lot of
her since then. She's been my good friend."

"You had planned to see her last Thursday," the black man
said.

"We had arranged to meet—not here. At Nightingale up on
Lyndale. Only she never showed. I called her cell, but she didn't
answer. I blew it off thinking, yeah, that's the old Rhett I knew
and loved, only now you're telling me that something happened.
What?"

"I'm not at liberty to say. You'll need to ask Rhett. Tell me,
did anyone else know you and Rhett were getting together last

Thursday?"

"No," Lori said. "*I don't think so. I didn't even know un-til—it was like four-thirty, five when we started texting each other, deciding what to do so, no. Nobody knew.*"

"*Was it unusual for the two of you to meet after work?*"

"*We did it all the time. Well, not every night. Couple times a week. When we did, usually my boyfriend was there, too.*"

"*Was the boyfriend there last Thursday?*"

"*No.*"

"*Where was he?*"

"*What are you asking?*"

"*I'm asking where your boyfriend was last Thursday.*"

Lori leaned back in her chair and crossed her arms over her ample chest. She stared at the black man for one beat, two, three. He knew what she was thinking. She was thinking about her boyfriend's relationship with her girlfriend.

"*I don't know where he was,*" she said.

"*Did he know that you and Rhett were getting together?*"

"*What exactly happened to Rhett?*"

"*Like I said, you'll have to ask her.*"

Lori found a small dot somewhere over the black man's shoulder to stare at while her face took on a worried expression on her face.

"*My boyfriend likes Rhett,*" she said. "*He's always helping her with her car; things like that. My boyfriend thinks Rhett is funny. My boyfriend thinks Rhett is gorgeous.*"

"*What's his name?*"

"*My boyfriend would never hurt Rhett.*"

"*What's his name?*"

"*Sean Worra. I met him at Patrick Henry. In fact, he still lives a couple blocks away from the school. We didn't start dating though until after I graduated. He was with me when I bumped into Rhett that one time.*"

The black man was surprised by how quickly Lori had given up the name until she added, "*I need to know about this*" and then he understood—she didn't trust her boyfriend.

"What do you think?" Freddie asked.

I rested two fingers against my cheek and said, "Hmm."

"Exactly what I thought."

"I'd like to talk to this boyfriend," I said.

"Me, too. I'd also like to chat with Congresswoman Hudson. In case you're wonderin', she represents the Fourth District, which includes all of St. Paul and most of its suburbs. Your district."

"I received some literature in the mail that claims she's running for the U.S. Senate."

"She's runnin' in the Democratic primary that takes place August fourteenth. If she wins, then she'll be runnin' for the Senate. If she doesn't, Hudson will probably go back t' the House. She has no primary opponent in the Fourth and the voters there haven't elected a Republican since 1947. I looked all this up, by the way."

"Abigail Hudson is Henrietta's mother," I said.

"Which might explain the foundation—remember the Robert T. and Elizabeth R. Hudson Foundation? It was set up fifty years ago by Abigail's parents after the Hudson family cashed in the oil refinery and the hundred sixty-three service stations it owned for just shy of ten billion bucks. Course the family had to share the loot with its investors. They only took home a little over one-point-eight billion."

"The foundation is where Rhett is getting most of her money."

"You do remember. Yeah, one hundred stacks a year she gits. 'Cept that's chump change compared to what her family is actually worth."

"I wonder why she didn't tell us."

"You wanna know what I think?"

"Yes, Freddie, I really do."

"I think we should ask her."

* * *

"I didn't believe it was important," Henrietta said.

"Yes, you did," I said. "Otherwise, you would have told us."

Henrietta was sitting in the same chair in our office as the day before, sipping another cup of caramel cream coffee, her pinky extended.

"I was hoping what happened to me had nothing to do with my mother," she said.

"It might not. Still..."

"Henrietta," Freddie said.

"Rhett. Now that we're all friends, call me Rhett. My parents named me Henrietta after my great-grandmother. Since Kindergarten I've gone through a series of nicknames. Henry. Rietta. Etta. Rhetta. By the time I hit college it was mostly Rhett, although there was this one guy, because of him, half my freshman year they called me *Henri*, pronounced like I was French. I hated that one."

"Rhett, we've pretty much decided that the attack on you wasn't random," Freddie said. "You were targeted. Which brings us back t' the same questions we had before—why weren't you robbed, why weren't you raped, why weren't you hurt, I mean besides emotionally? Why were you drugged up so that you'd have nothin' to say about who took you and what happened after?"

"Our theory, such as it is," I said, "is that you weren't the primary victim. That it was your mother. That you were kidnapped for ransom. Or blackmail."

Henrietta sipped more coffee.

"I've hurt my mother. I told you that before," she said. "When I got into trouble, it was never Henrietta Weller. It was always the daughter of Representative Abigail Hudson. I was hoping what happened to me had nothing to do with her. The last thing she needs right now is to answer questions about her screwed up daughter."

"You're not screwed up," I said.

"I was, though. My father—should I tell you my story,

gentlemen? Is that what you want to hear? My father was Jefferson Weller. He was a lawyer, and he died when I was twelve, which is the worst possible time for a girl to lose her father. At least I thought so. My mother dealt with the tragedy—it was a tragedy, too. I mean, he didn't have any health issues. He wasn't a drinker or a smoker or anything like that. I kissed him goodbye before I went to school in the morning. By the time I arrived home in the afternoon, boom, he was gone. Cardiac arrest.

"My mother was always active in the family's charities, things like that. After Dad died, she became political, ran for public office; ran using her maiden name instead of Dad's because people in Minnesota were familiar with it. That's how she dealt with his passing. I just—eh. I already gave you the long version. The short version is that I messed up enough that my mother, my family, finally disowned me. Shock therapy. Probably it was the best thing they could have done since I sure as hell wasn't going to consent to traditional therapy. I learned quickly, though, that when you're on your own, one of two things happen—you either figure it out, or you crash and burn.

"Only that was then. Over the years, I've been slowly readmitted back into the family. Now I get along fine with my mother. We don't talk as much as we should, that's true. I see her on holidays, though, and we get together once in awhile when she's not in D.C. trying to make the world a better place. At least that's what I hope she's trying to do. Some of the votes she casts, I'm not always convinced. Yet even though our views differ politically, we can discuss them without going off the rails. We were never able to do that before. Plus, whenever I see her, she encourages me to get on with it, to go back to the U and get my business degree, find a guy and do something with my life besides counting nickels for Mother Mercy Community Church. I get an allowance now, too. So, it's all good."

"We'd like to speak with her," I said.

"I can't allow that. Besides, if I were kidnapped for ransom or blackmail or whatever, my mom would have gone crazy trying to find me. Wouldn't she? If she had paid a ransom to get me back, don't you think she would've at least called to make sure I was all right?"

"I don't know," Freddie said. "Would she?"

"Can you think of any reason why she might not?" I asked.

Rhett paused long enough to finish her coffee.

"Yes, I can," she said.

CHAPTER EIGHT

I realized that something was terribly wrong almost immediately. After some hemming and hawing, Representative Hudson had agreed to meet with her daughter. Only not at Rhett's apartment or at Hudson's place or at campaign headquarters on Selby Avenue in St. Paul or even at a random coffeehouse down the street. Instead, she insisted the meeting take place in the private offices of her attorney.

"It's not as bad as it sounds," Rhett told us. "I don't think."

"How does it sound?" I asked.

"Like she's going to threaten me with a lawsuit or something."

"We know Charles Boucek," I said. "He's not just an attorney. He's a certified financial manager for the rich and famous. And infamous. His mission in life is to solve their big-money problems both legal and otherwise as quietly as possible, problems that are too complicated or too embarrassing to be entrusted to ordinary law firms."

"He's a fixer," Freddie said.

"He's also my mother's…" Rhett started chuckling as she finished the sentence. "Friend. Let's just say he's her friend. They've known each other since before I was born. He's assisting her as she ramps up for the Senate run and will probably become her chief of staff if she wins. No one is supposed to know that, though, so…" She placed her index

finger against her lips. "Shhhhhh. Course, if I can figure it out...
How do you know Charles Boucek? He's not a guy who
advertises. Instead, his name is whispered from one person to
another at parties that even I don't get invited to."

"We've done business with him in the distant past," I said.

"Doing what?"

"This and that," which was another way of saying "I can't
tell you."

"Dammit." Rhett rose quickly to her feet and began to pace
our office. "I didn't know that when I hired you."

"Know what?"

"That you work for Charles."

"Worked for him," I said. "Past tense."

"If I have to bid for your loyalty..."

"You don't," I said. "You don't have to bid for anything.
We signed a contract in good faith. We will honor it."

"We take that shit very seriously," Freddie said.

"Charles has a way of making people do whatever he
wants," Rhett said. "Including me."

"I suppose he does," I said. "Why is this an issue?"

Rhett stopped pacing and stared out one of our windows
at—I don't know what. When she stopped staring her eyes
flicked from my face to Freddie's.

"I trust you," she said. "I trust you both. Why is that?"

"Damned if I know," Freddie said.

Boucek and Associates took up an entire floor of a glass and
granite building located four and a half blocks from our office.
One of the reasons Freddie and I remained in downtown
Minneapolis despite the high rent was because our office was in
close proximity to so many of our clients. We arrived ten
minutes early and were made to wait for another twenty in the
reception area outside the elevators. I didn't think it was an
exercise of power so much as a show of opulence. We were

expected to be impressed by the plush and tasteful surroundings, and Freddie and I might have been if we hadn't been there before. Rhett didn't seem to care one way or another.

The place was humming with activity. At least half a dozen employees hurried past us, all handsomely dressed, all with expressions that suggested if they stopped moving they would die, kind of like sharks. One who did stop rocked back and forth the way that joggers sometimes do while waiting out a traffic light.

"Hey," he said.

"Mr. Bruce J. Gillard." Freddie stood to shake his hand. I stood as well to be polite. Rhett remained seated.

"Freddie, Taylor, it's been a long time," Gillard said. By a long time, he meant the three years since Boucek and Associates last made use of our services. "What brings you to our humble abode?"

He was fishing for information; neither Freddie nor I would bite.

"We missed you," Freddie said.

Gillard kept glancing at Rhett while pretending not to. It was as if he didn't want us to know he recognized her.

"The old man must be really up against it to draw you two out of the holster," he said.

"Old man?" I asked.

"Charles Boucek."

"The name sounds familiar and yet..."

"Didn't he play safety for the Chicago Bears?" Freddie said.

"Alright, alright," Gillard said. "I get it. They made me an executive vice-president, yet nobody tells me anything."

"That's because you can't be trusted," Rhett said.

Gillard looked down at her like an exasperated parent who couldn't believe his child was acting up in public. I knew very little about Gillard except that he was Boucek's lefthand man—Boucek didn't have a righthand man—and I had no reason to dislike him. Yet the glaring expression and patronizing tone he served my client made me want to slap him.

"Your mother trusts me, Ms. Weller," he said.

"She doesn't know you like I do. Besides, my mother trusts Charles, not you."

"And yet"—Gillard raised both his hands as if to stop himself from saying whatever was on his mind. "We will never be friends again, will we, Ms. Weller?"

She made a low guttural sound I had never heard before. I took it to mean no. So did Gillard. He smiled at us, bowed his head, and said "Gentlemen" before joining the other fish that were swimming by. He stopped midstream though and glanced back at Freddie and me, then at Rhett, as if he was trying to figure out the geometry. For a moment he had a hungry look like a northern pike, thinking he was on to something good just before he finds the hook.

"Congratulations on your promotion," I said. Yet what I was thinking—*friends, again?*

Gillard bowed his head once more and disappeared down the corridor.

Freddie and I sat on either side of Rhett.

"What was that about?" I asked.

"Hmm?"

"You and Gillard."

"He's my parole officer. He monitors my behavior for the family. I need to be a good little girl if I want to keep getting my allowance. You know the story."

"Apparently, not all of it," I said.

"That's why we're here."

We all sat quietly and waited some more. Finally, a tall, slender, and extraordinarily attractive young woman with an impassive face and a nothing-but-business demeanor opened a large wooden door and said, "This way, please."

As we passed through the doorway, Rhett said, "Good to see

you again." She was grinning.

"Ms. Weller," the woman replied.

We followed her down a long corridor flanked by offices where people were busily doing whatever it was they did to yet another large wooden door. She rapped twice, opened it, and ushered us into a conference room. Congresswoman Hudson sat in a chair at the head of a gleaming glass table. Her lawyer stood behind her, the consigliere to her don.

"Thank you, Ms. Jordan," Boucek said.

Jordan bowed her head and left the room. Freddie and I watched her go. I, of course, was way too "woke" in this era of #metoo to harbor sexist thoughts, yet I knew what was going through Freddie's mind. He was thinking, "Yeah, now I'm impressed."

Rhett remained standing in the doorway as if she were unsure what to do. When I see my own mom I always give her a hug, because if I don't, she'll ask "what's wrong?" and hug me. Rhett and her mother didn't seem to have that kind of relationship, despite Rhett's protestations that they got along just fine.

After staring at each other for a moment, Rhett said, "Mom?"

Representative Hudson gestured at a chair. Rhett sat, carefully smoothing her skirt beneath her; her back was straight, her legs pressed together, her ankles crossed, and her hands resting in her lap, as if she was attempting to emulate the lady-like pose that someone taught her. I stood behind her shoulder. Freddie found a chair out of the line of fire.

"I see you brought friends," Representative Hudson said. "Who are they?"

"They're private investigators."

Boucek nodded at us.

"Taylor, Freddie," he said.

"Charles," Freddie replied. I had never heard anyone call him Charlie or Chuck, not even behind his back.

"It's been a long time," Boucek said.

"Do you know these men?" Representative Hudson asked.

"We've had dealings in the past."

"What kind of dealings?"

"You know," Freddie said. "It's been so long ago we forgit."

Boucek smiled. It was exactly the kind of answer he would have expected from us.

"Why are they here?" Representative Hudson asked. "Henrietta? Why did you bring a couple of detectives to a meeting with your mother?"

"Why did you bring a lawyer?"

"Answer me, Henrietta."

"Because mother, four days ago I woke up covered with garbage inside a dumpster, and I had no idea how I got there. I hired Mr. Fredericks and Mr. Taylor to help me find out."

"Oh, my dear."

"They've uncovered evidence suggesting it was because of you."

"What evidence?" Boucek said.

We didn't answer because, well, we didn't have any evidence, just a theory. Of course, Boucek didn't need to know that.

Representative Hudson's reached for his hand, not for comfort, but to steady herself. Her eyes never left her daughter's.

"I—I don't understand," she said.

Rhett rose from her seat and approached Representative Hudson. Her shoulders trembled, and she began to weep, the first time I had seen her behave emotionally despite her trials.

"My clothes were soaked through," she said. "There were wet coffee grounds in my hair. The smell..."

Representative Hudson released Boucek's hand and leapt from her chair. She crossed the room and embraced her daughter. She was also crying.

"I'm sorry, I'm sorry, I'm sorry," she said. "I thought it was you. Oh my God, I thought it was you. Please forgive me, forgive me..."

CHAPTER NINE

Boucek gestured with his head and the three of us retreated to the corridor, closing the conference room door behind us. He tugged at the lapels of his jacket as if he whole-heartedly endorsed the notion that success and failure could be determined by the cut of your suit or how carefully your silk tie was knotted.

"What evidence?" he asked. "Tell me."

"Charles," Freddie said. "We don't work for you this trip."

"I'll double your fee."

"Yeah, that isn't going to work." I patted his shoulder. "Nice try, though."

Boucek was fifty-something and handsome, yet he had a way of narrowing his eyes and sucking in his cheeks that scrubbed the handsome away, leaving a face meant to scare the bejesus out of you. He was giving us that face now.

"I could make your lives miserable," he said.

"At least he's not threatening to kill us," Freddie told me. "Charles, you know how many people have threatened to kill us over the years? Scary."

"I'm trying hard not to become angry. I keep reminding myself this is why I hired you two in the first place, because of your discretion. However, I must insist. What evidence?"

"Is this going to be a cooperative effort, Charles?" I asked. "Are you going to tell us what you have?"

"What makes you think I have anything?"

"Congresswoman Hudson didn't hire you to stuff campaign envelopes."

"I can't divulge information without the expressed permission of my client."

"Now you know how we feel."

We studied each other after that.

"We ran into Gillard earlier," I said. "He said he's been promoted to executive vice-president. Nice step up. What was he when we knew him?"

"Besides pencil pusher," Freddie said.

"Bruce has his uses," Boucek said.

"I'm sure," I said.

"What did you tell him?"

"Even less than we told you."

"Keep it that way."

"Keeping secrets from your veep, Charles? What's that about?"

Boucek didn't reply.

"The receptionist, Ms. Jordan?" Freddie said. "She looks like you hired her off one of them fashion runways they got in Paris."

"She's my personal assistant."

"Nice."

"She has a Bachelor of Science Degree in Business Management."

"Even nicer."

"I don't appreciate your insinuation."

"What in-sin-u-ation?" Freddie asked.

"*In the Spring a young man's fancy lightly turns to thoughts of love*," I said.

"You two disappoint me," Boucek said. "Thinking that of me and Ms. Jordan."

"Thinkin' don't count," Freddie said. "It's the actin' that's messed up."

We studied each other some more.

"Interestin' weather we're havin', ain't it?" Freddie said. "Whenever it gets cold like last week the climate deniers say 'What global warmin'?' and then when it gets really hot, like it is now, and you don't hear a peep from 'em. What's that about?"

Eventually, we returned to the conference room. Mother and daughter were practically sitting in each other's laps at the head of the table; suddenly they couldn't keep their hands off each other. The reconciliation seemed affected to me, though. Mom trying to prove that she still loved her little girl, and daughter wanting Mom to know that she was her BFF. It might have worked, too, if Rhett hadn't been twenty-seven-years-old and Representative Hudson wasn't twice that age.

"I'm embarrassed," Representative Hudson said. "I'm ashamed."

Rhett whispered, "Mom," and rested her head against the older woman's shoulder.

"I'm sure you gentlemen require an explanation."

"If it ain't too much trouble," Freddie said.

"Sit."

We sat, not as elegantly as Rhett had, but still…Boucek resumed his place directly behind Representative Hudson. She reached for his hand and squeezed it. It made me think theirs was not the typical attorney-client relationship.

"First, I need assurances…" Representative Hudson said.

I interrupted.

"Congresswoman," I said. "We work for your daughter, not you."

A slight smile appeared on Rhett's lips before she used them to kiss Representative Hudson's cheek. I think she liked that we had taken her side against her mother.

"I trust them," Rhett said.

"Very well," Representative Hudson said. "Last Thursday evening, I flew home from Washington. The House was not in session Friday, and I wanted to take the long weekend to help organize my campaign office in St. Paul. I don't know if either of you is aware that I am seeking the Democratic endorsement of the U.S. Senate seat from Minnesota this August."

"You got my vote," Freddie said.

Representative Hudson stared at him as if she didn't know if he was kidding or not.

"On Friday morning, I received a Priority Mail Express envelope from the U.S. Post Office with a return address that I didn't recognize," she said. "Or I should say that my assistant received it. After opening the envelope, she insisted I take a look. It contained Rhett's driver's license and a single sheet of paper. The paper claimed that my daughter had been kidnapped. It said that I had until midnight that day to deliver a ransom, or she would be killed. I immediately contacted Mr. Boucek and asked for his advice. He recommended I pay the ransom. So, I did."

"You called your lawyer instead of the police, instead of the FBI?" I asked.

Representative Hudson response was to lower her eyes. Rhett squeezed her shoulders.

"It's all right," she said.

"I thought it was a prank. I thought my daughter was attempting to extort money from me."

"Some prank," I said.

"I don't know if Rhett told you about our past relationship..."

"I told him, Mother," she said.

"I thought she might have regressed..."

That's an interesting word to use when referring to your own child, I decided—regressed.

"I thought that she might have arranged to kidnap herself," Representative Hudson said. "We had argued about money in the past. I'm so sorry…"

Rhett hugged her mother some more.

"It's okay," she said.

"No, it's not okay."

"We'll make it okay."

Tears began to fall, but I didn't want to spend another twenty minutes in the corridor. "How much was the ransom?" I asked to keep Representative Hudson talking.

"Fifty thousand dollars."

"Whoa," Freddie said. "Fifty stacks? You're worth over one-and-a-half-billion bucks, and they only ask for fifty stacks?"

"That's what my entire family is worth," Representative Hudson said. "I only have about two hundred million."

"That makes all the difference."

"You see, that's one of the reasons why I thought it might be Rhett, because the amount was so small."

"How was the ransom paid?" I asked.

Representative Hudson lowered her head again.

"In cash," Boucek said. "My personal assistant made the drop."

Ms. Jordan was beginning to impress me more and more, I thought.

"I'd like to speak with her," I said.

Boucek gestured as if he didn't care one way or the other.

"I was supposed to deliver the money," Representative Hudson said. "That's what the note said. I was supposed to put it in a—in a garbage bag and—I was supposed to drop it in a…in a dumpster."

She started weeping again despite Rhett's hugs.

"Where?" I asked.

"Behind a bar called Dillman's," Hudson said. "Only I couldn't. I couldn't do it."

"Fuck," Freddie said.

"Let me see the letter," I said.

Representative Hudson shook her head.

"The envelope."

She shook her head again.

I found Boucek. "You didn't keep them?"

He shook his head, too.

"You know better than that counselor," I said.

"There was no reason to retain incriminating evidence," he said. "Representative Hudson was not going to have her own daughter arrested and charged."

"Yeah, sure. Congresswoman, who knew you were going to be in town Friday?"

"I don't know. My staff. Members of the media. I did an interview on Minnesota Public Radio Friday morning."

"Except Priority Mail is an overnight service. The envelope must have been addressed to you at your campaign headquarters and posted on Thursday. The kidnappers knew you would be there instead of Washington."

"I don't know what to say."

"Rhett, did you know your mother was going to be in town?"

She shook her head and said "Mom never contacted me."

Representative Hudson moaned as if she felt a sudden twinge of pain.

"I don't know why I didn't call," she said.

"It's alright," Rhett said.

"Time to notify the FBI," Freddie said.

Representative Hudson's head came up like a racehorse at the starting gate.

"No," she said.

"Whoever did this is gonna to do it again."

"No."

"Representative Hudson," I said.

"No. No. No."

"We don't want the publicity," Boucek said. "It'll severely damage Representative Hudson's campaign. Half the voters will think it was a staged publicity stunt; the other half will complain that by paying the ransom she gave in to criminals, that she's weak on crime. Media will seize on it; it's all they'll talk about from now until August. You can see that, can't you? Besides, no one was hurt."

"Speak for yourself," I said.

"I'm okay," Rhett said. "Now."

"Freddie's right, though. This is going to happen again, if not to you, then someone else. It'll all get out eventually, anyway. Then where will you be? Call the Feds, Charles. Call them now. Control the narrative. Isn't that what you said the last time we worked together, how it was so important to control the narrative?"

"Mr. Taylor, Fredericks," he said. "You're off the case."

"Don't know how many times we have t' say it," Freddie said. "We don't work for you."

Rhett spoke with her mother's arms wrapped around her.

"I guess you did what I asked you to do, find out what happened to me," she said.

"Rhett," I said. "We have a suspect, remember? Lori Hertz's boyfriend."

"Even if Sean had something to do with it, Charles is right, the publicity...I can't be responsible for the ruination of my mother's campaign. I can't."

"Honey," Representative Hudson said. She kissed her daughter's forehead.

"Rhett," I said. "Remember what you said in our office? Someone threw you away like so much garbage. Someone is going to pay for that, you said."

"Sometimes people do things for you that can never be paid back except, maybe, by taking what they give you and doing the best you can with it. My mother gave me more than a mother should have to give. I won't hurt her now because of pride."

"It has nothing to do with pride."

"You want to do the right thing," Representative Hudson said. "I appreciate that. Only sometimes it's difficult knowing what the right thing is."

"Not in this case."

"You heard Ms. Weller," Boucek said. "Your job is done. I know we can count on your discretion."

"Rhett?" I asked.

"Thank you," she answered.

I might have made more of an argument except, as if by magic, Ms. Jordan appeared at the conference room door and held it open until Freddie and I passed through it. No one bothered to say goodbye, although, once we reached the reception area, Ms. Jordan did tell us to "Have a nice day," the quintessential Minnesota farewell.

Before we could leave, however, we heard Gillard's voice again.

"Ms. Jordan," he said. He was standing near the reception desk, his arms folded across his chest and looking every bit like a high school vice-principal, the one in charge of discipline. "May I have a moment?"

"No."

Gillard seemed surprised by the response.

"Ms. Jordan," he repeated.

"I answer to Mr. Boucek and to him alone."

"We shall see."

Gillard went one way. His expression suggested that Jordan was in for a long period of detention.

Jordan went in the opposite direction. Her lovely face offered no hint of what she was thinking.

Back on the street and walking toward our own building, Freddie and I stopped at a red light along with a dozen other office workers and shoppers.

"Whaddya think?" Freddie said.

"If we take what we know to the cops, to the FBI, without first receiving our client's permission, if it gets out that we broke client confidentiality, there isn't a law firm in the Cities or anyone else of consequence who will hire us ever again."

"If someone gets hurt or killed and it gets out that we were aware of the criminal activity that hurt or killed 'em and we didn't report it, our licenses could be suspended or revoked, not to mention fines and shit."

"Don't you just love the PI business?"

"Yeah, it's swell. What are we gonna do?"

The light changed, and we started crossing the street with the crowd.

"Why don't you get on Sackett's employee background checks, and I'll start serving those subpoenas," I said.

"So, business as usual?"

"It's what they pay us for."

CHAPTER TEN

Fifteen days later the office landline rang.

I answered "Fredericks and Taylor Private Investigations."

"Whom am I addressing?" a woman's voice asked.

"Holland Taylor. Whom am I addressing?"

"Mr. Taylor, Mr. Boucek requests to speak with you and your associate."

"Put him on the phone."

"He wishes for you to come to his office. Without delay."

I thought of saying something clever to assert my independence, "I'll be there when I get there," something like that. Only I'm a private investigator with services to sell and if Boucek was willing to buy them, why should I be a dick about it just because I didn't like his assistant's tone of voice?

"Ten minutes," I said.

"I will greet you in the lobby. Please, do not keep me waiting."

I kept her waiting. I had estimated that it would take ten minutes to walk from my office to Boucek's, yet it took closer to fifteen. Still, I probably could have made it in ten if I ran. I might have, too, if I had known Ms. Jordan would be standing just inside the main entrance to the office tower, looking at her silver watch and tapping her toe as if she was timing me.

Her nostrils flared when she said "You're late."

The nostril flaring was meant to intimidate, only it didn't work with her lovely face. I came *this*close to telling Jordan that she looked beautiful when she was angry, except I didn't trust her reaction. Instead of smiling or zinging me back, there was a better than even chance she'd punch me right in my big mouth.

"The traffic lights were against me," I said. "And the head-winds, whew."

"Where is Mr. Fredericks?"

"He's been unavoidably detained."

Jordan continued to stare at me.

"He's giving a deposition for one of our other clients," I said. "If you prefer to wait for him?"

"Time is of the essence."

"It often is. Why are we meeting here instead of your offices?"

"Follow me."

She spun around and walked across the lobby, moving in a straight line at a brisk pace, forcing other visitors to dodge out of her way. It took an effort to keep up with her. We passed the bank of elevators and continued on until we encountered a door marked "Authorized Personnel Only." Jordan tapped a security code into an electronic keypad and the door unlocked. Once past it, we followed a narrow and brightly lit corridor to a single elevator. Jordan had to impute another security code into yet another electronic keypad to access it. She pressed the button for Boucek's floor after we stepped inside and stared straight ahead. I watched her blurred reflection in the stainless steel door. There was no Muzak, only the muffled whir of the elevator's cables.

"So," I said. "The scenic route."

Jordan didn't respond.

"Is there a reason why you're smuggling me into your office?"

"Direct all of your questions to Mr. Boucek."

I continued to watch her reflection. I liked her brown eyes

and her brown hair that she wore up. Only I didn't want to tell her that.

"I was told by Mr. Boucek that you delivered the ransom when Rhett Weller was kidnapped," I said. "That took nerve. I admire nerve."

"Your admiration is unimportant to me."

"Yet you have it, anyway."

Her eyes flicked from her reflection to mine and back again. For the briefest moment, I thought her mouth wanted to form a smile, yet she beat it down. I liked that about her, too, although I couldn't explain why.

The elevator stopped, and the door slid open.

"This way," she said.

We followed another narrow and brightly lit corridor to a door that Jordan was able to open without use of a keypad. We crossed into a public corridor complete with wall-to-wall carpeting that reminded me of the Persian rug in my living room. Jordan led me along the corridor until we reached a maple door that she unlocked with a key. She held it open for me, then closed and locked the door behind us. I found myself inside Boucek's inner sanctum. I knew it was his office because of the photographs on the wall, mostly of him posing with rich and famous personages, including Representative Abigail Hudson. The maple door was his escape hatch.

We passed through the inner office to the outer office where Boucek conducted his business, at least the business that he had conducted with Freddie and me. There were high-backed chairs, two sofas, black walnut tables, original paintings on the wall, and soft lights. Boucek was standing next to one of the chairs; his exquisite suit looked as if he never sat down while wearing it.

"Mr. Taylor," he said. "How good of you to come on such short notice."

He shook my hand yet did not smile. I noticed, though, that when he nodded his head at Jordan, he was smiling like crazy.

Jordan smiled back. Both smiles went away in a hurry, however, as Jordan retreated to a spot against the wall.

Boucek gestured at a wet bar.

"May I offer you a drink?" he asked.

I noticed Boucek wasn't drinking, so I answered, "No, thank you. I'm working." When in Rome...

Boucek gestured toward a man sitting on one of the Chesterfields who was drinking, who looked as if he had been drinking for some time. His suit was so wrinkled I wondered if he slept in it.

"I don't think you've met," he said. "This is Brian Haskins."

I didn't need an introduction. I had seen Haskins' name and face on countless billboards and TV commercials for twenty years. He was king of the new and used car business in Minnesota. I had also seen his face lately on the local TV news broadcasts, usually as he was entering or exiting a courtroom. Haskins was currently under indictment for mail and wire fraud.

"Brian Haskins, this is Holland Taylor, the man I was telling you about."

I offered Haskins my hand. He leaned forward on the sofa cushions, reached for it, brushed his fingers against mine, and fell back against cushions again, sighing with the effort.

"What kind of name is Holland?" he asked.

"In my case, it comes from east-central England. It was my mother's maiden name."

"It's a terrible name for a man. A woman I can see, but a man?"

"If you don't like it, don't use it."

Haskins' bloodshot eyes widened, and he glared at Boucek as if he wanted to be told if those were fighting words or not. Boucek changed the subject.

"Will Mr. Fredericks be joining us?" he said.

"I'm afraid he's currently being deposed in a civil matter we've been drawn into," I said. "However, he will be available later if needed."

"Good to know."

"Depositions," Haskins said. "Fucking lawyers."

"Watch your language," Boucek told him.

I didn't know if he was upset about the adjective or the noun.

Haskins said "What did I say?"

I said, "Gentlemen, how can I be of service?"

"Brian?" Boucek said.

Haskins took a long pull of his drink and waved his hand.

"Whatever you think is best," he said.

Boucek crossed the office to a table against the wall where Jordan was standing. They looked at each other, only this time neither of them smiled. Boucek took two sealed, clear-plastic kitchen storage bags off the table and brought them to where I was standing. One bag contained a Priority Mail Express envelope from the U.S. Post Office. The other contained a single sheet of white typing paper.

"Shit," I said.

Boucek didn't correct my language. Instead, he gave me the bag containing the sheet of paper. I read the copy printed there through the plastic.

> We have your niece. You will place $50,000 in cash in a garbage bag. You will take the bag to Camden Central Pond. You will enter the park off Morgan Avenue and follow the path. You will place the bag into the receptacle adjacent to the third park bench. You will do this no later than midnight tonight. You will not inform the authorities. If you meet our demands, your niece will be released unharmed in a timely manner. If not, she will be executed at exactly 12:01 AM. We are watching.

"Niece?" I asked.

Boucek handed me the bag with the mail envelope, turning it over so I could see the driver's license that came with it. It read Carole Robey. Twenty-five. Brown hair, brown eyes, the DMV's camera had been uncharacteristically flattering to her.

"We've made several calls," Boucek said. "She's unaccounted for."

"I don't even like her," Haskins said. "My sister's kid. Judgmental little bitch, thinks life should be fair."

"This is where I'd mention that we told you so," I said. "But it's probably not the best time."

"No, it most certainly is not," Boucek answered.

"Call the FBI, Charles. Do it now."

"Whoa, whoa, whoa, what the fuck, Charles?" Haskins said. "I thought we settled that."

Boucek held up his hand like he was stopping traffic. Once Haskins became still, he turned toward me.

"I'm sure you can appreciate that given Mr. Haskins' current legal difficulties, it would be somewhat awkward to invite the federal government into his life," he said.

"Awkward my ass. What about the girl?"

"Brian will pay the ransom, and she will be released unharmed, just as before."

"Whoa now," Haskins said. "That's a lot of moola. Let's think about this. What if we don't pay? What if we pretend none of this is happening? I mean, who the fuck's to know?"

Boucek moved slowly to where Haskins was sitting and hovered over him.

"Brian, you retained me to take care of you, to help you avoid catastrophic mistakes like the one you just proposed. That's why you brought this matter to my attention in the first place, correct? If you no longer wish to heed my advice, say so. We will terminate our relationship right here and now. We'll shake hands, and I'll escort you to the elevator. You must understand, though, that your life as you know it will be utterly and irrevocably ruined by the time you reach the lobby."

"Whoa Charles, whoa," Haskins said.

"We will not sacrifice Ms. Robey to your avarice."

"Hey, now."

"You will pay the ransom. Do you understand? If not, I will contact the FBI myself and every news media outlet that I can think of. Do you believe the worst that can happen to you is this upcoming court case? I assure you; it is not."

"There's no reason for that kinda talk. I was just thinking out loud. Jesus, Charles."

"You told me you had the money. In cash."

"Yeah, in a safe I keep in a storage unit no one knows anything about."

"Please go get it. Bring it back here. Do it now."

Boucek turned toward his personal assistant, who was standing near the wall. There was a slight, nearly imperceptible smile on her face and in that moment, I understood exactly what Mona Lisa was thinking—all the men around her were idiots.

"Please attend Mr. Haskins," he told her. "He will direct you to his storage shed. Afterward, I expect you to return here. With the money. Given Mr. Haskins' level of intoxication, I suggest that you drive."

Jordan nodded.

Boucek spun back to face Haskins, who had managed to get off the sofa without falling.

"We wouldn't want you to be detained by the police," he said.

"At least we agree 'bout that."

"Ms. Jordan, escort Mr. Haskins out the back way."

Jordan went to the door of Boucek's inner office and calmly waited while Haskins shuffled toward her. His leering smile suggested, however, that fear of a DUI was no longer on his mind if it ever was.

"Contact me immediately if he should deviate from the task at hand or use his phone," Boucek said.

Jordan nodded again.

Haskins lost his leer. He was looking down at the carpeted floor and shaking his head when he said, "I can't believe I'm paying for this shit."

His leer returned, however, while watching Jordan's ass as he followed her out of the same maple door that I had entered. For a moment, I felt protective of the woman and nearly volunteered to take her place. Boucek must have been reading my mind because he rested a hand on my shoulder.

"Believe me," he said. "Ms. Jordan can take care of herself."

Once he was convinced we were alone, Boucek drifted toward his bar.

"Are you sure I can't offer you anything, Holland?" he asked.

"I'm good."

"I hope you don't mind if I indulge myself."

"Not at all."

Boucek poured two fingers of Booker's into a squat glass. I half expected him to toss it down, yet instead he took a sip and sighed as the bourbon hit the spot.

"I apologize, Holland, for having you smuggled here like a courtesan," he said.

"The analogy hadn't occurred to me."

"Perhaps it's a bit more fanciful than accurate."

"I'd like to ask, though—who are you hiding me from?"

"Not everyone needs to know our business."

"When you say everyone, do you mean your staff? Do you mean Bruce Gillard?"

Boucek sipped some more bourbon.

"Confidentiality is of paramount importance," he said.

"Call the FBI, Charles."

"It's not necessary."

"Of course it is."

"Miss Robey will be fine."

"You know this because...?"

"It is obvious we are dealing with professionals, Holland; businessmen who have patterned their activities after the Express Kidnapping rings prevalent in Latin America. The kidnappings are strategically planned. The perpetrators gather intelligence about their victims, concentrating on individuals who can claim a family of means. Once they capture the victim, they demand from the family a reasonable sum that can be both gathered without undue difficulty and delivered in a finite period of time. After the ransom is paid, the captive is released unharmed. In many ways, it's a clever and well-thought-out business model. Kidnapping one person for a hundred thousand, five hundred thousand, a million dollars, is an inherently risky proposition. It takes several days to accomplish, if not longer, and most certainly would involve the authorities. The difficulty in gathering a hefty ransom would ensure that, if nothing else. By kidnapping ten people for fifty thousand dollars each, by confining their activities to those families that are in a position to pay quickly, they greatly minimize their exposure. My question—why not demand that the ransom be delivered electronically?"

"That's your question?"

"It would seem to be a less problematical means of collecting ransom."

"An electronic transfer would alert FinCEN," I said. "The kidnapper's accounts may be well hidden under a secret identity in an offshore bank. Yours are not. The Financial Crimes Enforcement Network is going to wonder whom you're transferring the money to and why. If its agents knock on your door and ask if you're supporting terrorists, what are you going to tell them?"

"I hadn't thought of that, Holland."

It bothered me that Boucek was using my first name so frequently. It wasn't that I objected to what was an obvious attempt to strengthen the personal bond between us so that I would be more willing to go along with his strategy. It was the idea that he thought it was necessary to play me at all that I found distasteful.

"Something else you haven't thought of," I said. "All the families the kidnappers are victimizing, they're your clients."

"We don't know that. It's possible that it's merely a coincidence. It's possible this ring has been operating for a great deal of time in many places, and it has just now touched my clients. Research shows that less than twenty percent of kidnapping incidents are reported."

"In Latin America, maybe. Not here."

"Don't be so sure, Holland."

"Call the cops, Charles. If nothing else, taking Carole Robey proves these guys are not going away. They're not looking for a big payoff, and whoosh, off to Aruba. Sooner or later, it's going to get out, and then where will you be?"

"The kidnappers understand that publicity would be highly detrimental to their activities. If all this reaches the mainstream media, they know their victims will have no choice but to bring in the FBI, and that will put their enterprise at risk. They will take all necessary steps to keep their activities quiet. It's the same reason why I am convinced that they will not injure or kill their victims."

"You're convinced, are you?"

"In any case, Holland, my clients pay me to protect them. That includes minimizing their exposure to both governmental institutions as well as the media. In these two individual cases, it is better for my clients if the authorities remain uninvolved."

"What about the victims? Not just Henrietta Weller and Carole Robey, but those to come? And about Carole—what happens when she tells Mom and Dad and all her friends that she was kidnapped? If she posts it on Facebook or tweets about it? What'll keep her from going to the police herself?"

"Those possibilities will be dealt with."

"What are you going to do, have her served with a restraining order?"

"It's something to consider."

"Charles..."

"Holland, that's a problem for tomorrow. At the moment, I have other concerns. The reason why you're here..."

"I've been wondering."

"Mr. Haskins refuses to make the drop. I'm not sure I trust him to do it, anyway."

"Do you want me to deliver the money?"

"No. Ms. Jordan has already volunteered."

"How gutsy of her."

"I want three things from you. First, to make sure that Ms. Jordan arrives safely at this Camden Central Pond and leaves unmolested. Second, to conduct surveillance. I wish to take steps to learn the identity of these criminals. Make no mistake; you are not to intervene in any way. We will not risk the safety of Ms. Robey. Is that understood?"

"Yes."

"Meanwhile..." Boucek gestured at the two plastic bags filled with evidence that I was still holding. "I want these analyzed for fingerprints, find out about the printing; perhaps learn where the paper came from and whatever intelligence we can glean from the envelope."

"Charles..."

"Holland, will you accept this assignment or won't you?" he asked.

"I like it better when you call me Taylor."

CHAPTER ELEVEN

As it turned out, I knew a guy. I gave him a call after I returned to my office and said that I was on my way. I said I was on the clock.

"Science cannot be rushed," he said.

"I'll double your usual fee."

"Science cannot be rushed," he repeated. "However, it can be hurried along."

Next, I contacted Freddie, getting the voice mail on his cell phone. I told him to call me, that if he had plans with Echo and his son that evening, he should cancel them and put it on me. I told him that it was going to be a long day.

Paul Dimeski had been a Forensic Science Supervisor specializing in Criminalistics and Crime Scene Investigations for the Minnesota Bureau of Criminal Apprehension before retiring to hunt, fish, and play golf. Only it turned out that for some people, hunting, fishing and playing golf could become pretty boring if that's all they did. Especially, I thought, for those who have spent a lifetime seeking answers, reasons, and explanations for everything around them, who demanded facts no matter how bitter while rejecting opinions no matter how comforting, who wanted to know the truth whether it made them happy or not unlike, say, politicians and their most ardent groupies. So now Paul supplemented his government pension and filled his hours by selling his skills and experience on a freelance basis to guys like me.

I met him at his home on the Shoreview side of Lake Owasso. After greeting me at his front door, he led me through the house to the redwood deck he had built on back that had a splendid view of the lake, the dock protruding into it and the boat tied at the dock. My first thought—it was postcard gorgeous. My second—it's hard to get too excited when you realize that we have so many postcard-gorgeous lakes in the Twin Cities that I doubted anyone had ever bothered to count them. Instead, we compiled lists—Top Ten Lakes in St. Paul, 15 Best Lakes in the Twin Cities; Top Ten Lakes in Minneapolis plus Nine More You'll Want to Visit.

Paul offered me a Leinenkugel, and I accepted it.

We sat at a round, white patio table with a giant umbrella sticking out of it. The umbrella was open, guarding us from the sun. I was grateful for the shade because once again I was wearing a 9mm Beretta beneath a black sports coat and once again the weather was ridiculously warm.

"What do you think?" Paul said. "Do you think this is the new normal?"

"What do you mean?"

"It's the Sixteenth of May in Minnesota. The average historic temperature is sixty-nine degrees. Today we'll top off at eighty-seven or higher."

"What's the record?"

"Ninety-four degrees set in 1934."

"Either it's an anomaly or a harbinger of doom."

"The climate models suggest doom."

"What was it that Mark Twain said? *Everybody complains about the weather, but nobody does anything about it.*"

"Actually, it was the essayist Charles Dudley Warner who originally said it. Twain merely repeated the line in a lecture. But that's the problem, isn't it? We're so reluctant to do anything about it. In any case, you didn't come here to discuss the weather. So, tell me, Holland, what have you got?"

I set the beer bottle on top of the table and retrieved the plastic-enclosed ransom letter and envelope from the briefcase I carried. I gave him both. As he examined them, I took another pull of the beer.

"What the hell are you doing with this?" Paul asked.

"My client doesn't want to take it to the cops."

"Jesus Christ, Taylor. This is a federal crime."

"I've explained that. My client wants to handle the matter quietly."

"Then why bring this to me? Why did he even hire you?"

"My guess—to prove to his insurance company and the authorities that he acted in a reasonable manner if it should all go sideways."

"Sounds like a lawyer."

"Besides," I said. "There's no law that says you have to report a crime. You know that."

"What about a moral obligation?"

"There are moral obligations and ethical requirements. Sometimes they're in conflict."

"I could make the call if you like," Paul said.

"Whatever you do with the information I provide will be on me, whether my name is mentioned or not."

"Okay, but what if you don't get the girl back?"

"Then I'll make the call. I promise."

"Drink your beer, Holland."

I did.

"What exactly do you want?" Paul asked.

"Whatever you can tell me."

"It'll take a while."

When Paul stood, I did too.

"Where are you going?" he asked.

"With you."

"I hate it when people hover over my shoulder while I work.

There're more Leinies in the fridge, and I have fishing equipment in the boat down on the dock. Go wet a line if you want. The northerns are hitting pretty well this spring. And if Alyce should come home before I've finished, you're on your own."

Alyce was Paul's wife, a vibrant free spirit to his serious scientist. I had socialized with both of them. That was before Laura was killed, though. Afterward I didn't see the point. Last time I saw her, Alyce gave me a lecture about it. She even called me a couple of names that only friends can get away with. She was right, of course.

Paul abandoned me on the deck while he went inside. I knew he had built a lab in his basement, only I had never been allowed to see it. I doubt Alyce had seen it, either.

I finished the Leinenkugel, went to get a second, and drifted down to the lake. There was a bench mounted on the dock and I sat there and watched the boats flying across the water and the birds that soared above it. It wasn't long before the sun forced me to remove the jacket and drape it over the back of the bench. I rolled up my shirt sleeves and opened an extra button on my shirt.

Most people would have enjoyed the moment. Laura, for one, would have stripped down to a two-piece swimming suit and sprawled across a beach towel. I would have volunteered to apply the suntan lotion, and she'd agree, but only if there was no one else around to see us. Otherwise, she'd say "Catch me later, Copper."

Copper.

My life that was.

I drank more beer.

Freddie called. He said he had just finished listening to his voicemail.

"A long day?" he said. "What's that supposed to mean?"

I told him.

"Do we wanna git involved in this shit? I mean we told 'im, didn't we? We told Boucek. Now we're supposed to do what?"

"He wants us to protect his personal assistant while she makes the drop."

"The model, what's her name, Jordan? She's worth protectin' but c'mon? You know sooner or later this is gonna end bad."

"What are you worried about?"

"That we're the ones it's gonna end bad for."

A few hours later, Paul Dimeski summoned me. We met beneath the umbrella on his deck again. The original letter and envelope had been returned to their plastic bags, but shiny photographic enlargements of each were resting on the table. BCA pointed at the envelope.

"There's nothing remarkable about this," he said. "Standard Priority Mail Express flat rate envelope. It has a self-adhesive flap, no saliva, no DNA. It was postmarked at the main post office building in Minneapolis, so it has God knows how many fingerprints, far too many to classify, anyway. The label was addressed with a common inkjet printer. Could have been a Cannon, could have been a Dell. Uniformed letters. There are no broken *Rs* or worn *Os* like with the old-fashion typewriters. Sometimes I hate the so-called technological age."

"Me, too."

"For the kidnappers to address the label and print it out themselves, though, requires an account with the U.S. Postal Service. Probably they created an account and funded it using a prepaid credit card or one that's attached to a fake name."

"Probably a fake name, probably tied to the return address on the envelope," I said. "I ran it before I came over. Don't give me that look. I am a semi-professional private investigator, after all."

"I keep forgetting," Paul said. "The address—was it a ghost?"

"No, it belongs to a Mail Box Store."

Paul nodded because he knew what I knew. One result of the Patriot Act is that the Postal Service now requires citizens to present two forms of ID and a verifiable home address in order to rent a P.O. box. Commercial stores not so much. What they sold besides a convenient place to send phone, cable, Internet, utility, and bank statements is privacy. Managers were always tight-lipped about giving out renter information. At least they were to me. I've always found it extremely difficult to find someone who was hiding behind a series of drop boxes. On the other hand, people invariably rented boxes in the same zip code where they lived or close to it, which is why Paul asked "Where?"

"55411," I said. "North Minneapolis."

"We don't have the resources to take it any further. However, both the FBI and the Postal Inspection Service do—in case the thought hadn't occurred to you."

"We've already had this conversation."

"Yes, we have. Alright. The letter was also printed using an inkjet on standard copy paper. You can buy reams of it in any office supply store. There is only one set of fingerprints. I'd bet the ranch they belong to whoever received the letter. Unfortunately, I can't tell for sure unless I have that person's prints to match."

I was considering Haskins' legal problems when I said, "They're probably already in the system."

"Which we don't have access to," Paul said. "What interests me most, though, is the language. The ransom note is written in short declarative sentences. Consider—the kidnapper wrote 'receptacle adjacent' instead of 'trash can next to,' 'inform the authorities' instead of 'call the police,' 'released unharmed in a timely manner' as opposed to 'we'll let her go,' 'executed' instead of 'killed.'"

"What does that tell you, besides whoever wrote the note might have gone to school?"

"My experience is that the people who use the English language most carefully are from out of town."

"A foreigner? English is his second language?"

"I'm merely speculating."

"Someone else speculated that all this resembles the Express Kidnapping rings found in Latin America."

"Another reason to make a call."

"Swear to God Paul, if I could I would."

"Want another beer?"

I did, but it was already approaching mid-afternoon and, as I told him earlier, I was on the clock.

"Rain check," I said.

"I'd give you one, Holland, except you never cash them in."

CHAPTER TWELVE

Freddie spread out a large print of a satellite photograph on a black walnut table in Charles Boucek's outer office. The four of us gathered around it.

"What am I looking at?" Boucek said.

"Camden Central Pond," Freddie said. "It's up here in a neighborhood called Webber-Camden, better livin' than where Dillman's is located, but still considered North Minneapolis."

"Is that significant?"

"We don't believe in coincidences," I said.

"You think the kidnappers are operating out of North Minneapolis?"

"A possibility."

"Minneapolis has an anti-crime campaign," Freddie said. "Kinda copies the one Homeland Security uses—if you see somethin', say somethin'. Except on the north side, people don't always see or say much of anything, you know?"

"I understand."

"'Kay, here's the pond located on Forty-Second Avenue North between Penn Avenue North and a service road here. It's a big pond. In some places, it'd be called a lake. In Minnesota, unless you're 10 acres or more, you don't measure up, so it's a pond. You can see the walkin' trail that circles the pond. There's an entrance here on Forty-Second and Morgan Avenue and another here on Forty-Second and the service road. We blew up the photograph so you can see the benches—one, two, three. Do you see it?"

Freddie was speaking to Jordan. She was standing straight and still next to the table.

"Ms. Jordan?" Freddie said.

The woman nodded.

"You don't need to do this," I said. "I'll be happy to make the drop."

"I can handle it," she said.

"I know you can. That's not the issue."

"I'll do it."

"That will free you up to conduct surveillance," Boucek said. "Make sure she's safe."

Jordan brushed her hand along Boucek's arm before letting it fall to her side.

"I'll be fine," she said.

Boucek looked at her hand like he wanted to take it in his and never let it go.

"Directly across the street is the Victory Memorial Ice Arena," Freddie said. "The parking lot for the arena is facin' the pond. That's where Taylor will be in his car. We checked, and the arena is hostin' a men's hockey league t'night; the last teams go on the ice at eleven PM, so there'll be plenty of traffic. Taylor will be hidden in the crowd. If he's noticed, he's a white dude playin' hockey or waitin' on his buds. Not too many brothers play the game, even in Minnesota."

"What's this?" Boucek moved his finger over what looked from outer space to be a large, tree-laden park directly behind and running alongside the western border of the pond.

"It's a cemetery," I said.

"That's where I'll be," Freddie said. "The plan is to drive through the cemetery, park on a road here—you see it? We'll hang at one of the gravesites for a few minutes and then leave, 'cept instead of leavin' I'll move to this stand of trees right here." Freddie tapped a spot on the photograph. "It should give me a good view of the bench and the trash can. Just hunker down with a camera and wait."

"For how long?" Boucek asked.

"As long as it takes," I said. "We have no doubt that the kidnappers will have the area staked out, too. We hope to get into position before they do, or at least go unnoticed by them. They'll be watching for the money, after all. The kidnappers will wait awhile after it's dropped off. Eventually, once they think it's safe, they'll recover it. Freddie will take photographs. When they leave, I'll follow; try to at least get a license plate number. If I think I've been made, I'll peel off and let them go."

"What about Ms. Jordan?"

"We'll watch to make sure that she's not followed when she leaves the area. If she is, we'll move to protect her. She won't be followed, though. The only thing the kidnappers will care about at that point is retrieving the fifty thousand dollars. Once Ms. Jordan has delivered it, they'll forget about her."

"Where is the money?" Freddie asked.

Boucek gestured at a canvas tote bag with an illustration of a raccoon inside a crimson heart. Below it was printed #MPRRACOON *Minnesota Public Radio*. The bag was celebrating a female raccoon that spent two days scaling a twenty-story skyscraper next to the MPR building in downtown St. Paul a couple years ago.

"The bag is mine," Jordan said.

"I don't doubt it," I said. "Except the kidnappers wanted the money placed in a trash bag."

Jordan went to the tote and pulled out a white kitchen-size trash bag sealed with a red tie.

"Fifty thousand dollars," she said. "Half in fifties, half in twenties. I watched Mr. Haskins count it out. For some reason, I thought there would be more bills than this. I don't think there are enough to fill a shoe box. The weight..." Jordan bounced the bag up and down. "It's only about three and a half pounds. My purse weighs more than that."

I was staring at Jordan and wishing I could get inside the woman's head.

"I want you to be more frightened than you appear," I said.

"Would you prefer that I swoon into your arms?"

"Look, lady," Freddie said. "This is our work, Taylor and mine. We do shit like this all the time. We carry guns when we do it. And we're frightened. Fear is good. Fears keeps you focused. Fear keeps you from doin' stupid, 'kay? You wanna be Wonder Woman, that's cool. But be a little afraid. It'll make us feel better."

Jordan nodded as if she understood what Freddie was trying to tell her, only I wasn't sure that she did.

"We'll be in constant contact using two-way radios," I said.

I went to the bag that I had brought from our office and opened it. Inside were three hand-held radios, each with twenty-two channels and a range of thirty-fives. I gave one to Jordan.

"We'll start at channel three," I said. "If there's interference, we'll keep moving up the dial—four, five, six—until we find an unoccupied frequency. Use these as well." I gave Jordan an earpiece and a tiny microphone attached to a thin wire. "The ear bud goes into your ear, obviously. The mic is plugged into the radio. There's a clip that lets you attach the microphone to your shirt near your mouth.

"It's now four-twenty-three," I added. "Ms. Jordan, you'll leave here at exactly seven PM. Traffic should be light by then. The sun will still be up. Get on I-94 going north. Exit at North Dowling Avenue and follow it west to Penn Avenue. That will take you along the south side of the cemetery. Hang a right on Penn, follow the cemetery to Forty-Second Avenue, hang a right. The Victory Memorial Ice Arena will be on your left. You can see it on the map. Morgan Avenue is here. The entrance to the trail that circles the pond is here."

"I know."

"You won't have the map with you."

"I'll remember. It'll be all right."

"Park on Morgan or in the lot, whatever is easiest. Do not look for me. I'll see you. So will Freddie."

Jordan nodded.

"You do what the kidnappers demand. Take the money to the trash can, drop it inside, turn around, leave the park, go to your car; drive away. Do not talk to anyone. Someone says something, you just keep walking. If there's a problem"—I tapped my chest with both hands—"we'll take care of it."

Jordan nodded some more.

I gestured at the radio.

"Make sure it's hidden in your coat or under your clothes. We'll be listening in case there's a problem, but don't talk unless there is a problem."

"We don't want people to think you're nuts talkin' to yourself," Freddie said.

"How about screaming?" Jordan asked.

"Now you're gittin' int' the spirit of things."

"I don't know," Boucek said.

"You wanna call the game, ump? Fine with us."

"No. It's just...No. We—we need to get Carole Robey back."

"Well, then," I said. "Let's get to it."

A few minutes later, Jordan led Freddie and me out the back door and down to the main floor. We probably could have managed it ourselves, except she didn't trust us with the security codes, although she didn't actually say that.

What Jordan did say surprised me, though—"If the police discovered what we're doing, would we go to jail?"

"No," I said. "It's perfectly legal to pay ransom to kidnappers. It's your money and you can do whatever you want with it. If you have good reason to believe that the ransom demands will be honored, paying the kidnappers could be seen as a reasonable choice. On the other hand, if Carole is killed...Even if she isn't hurt, if everything works out as planned and the authorities still find out what we've done...It's an example of what happens when you place the individual above everyone else. Society will argue that by paying the criminals, you're encouraging kidnapping, that you're putting the rest of us in danger. The backlash will be catastrophic."

"Do you think Mr. Boucek's business will suffer?"

"Oh, yes. Everyone with a reputation to protect will flee with flags furled."

"You afraid of losin' your job or endin' up in an orange jumpsuit?" Freddie asked.

Jordan shook her head solemnly.

"I graduated summa cum laude with a degree in business management," she said. "I can get a job anywhere. Plus, I look fabulous in orange."

I believed her, and because Jordan laughed, I laughed. Freddie merely grinned, though, as if he wouldn't believe it until he saw it.

By then we had arrived at the "Authorized Personnel Only" door that led to the lobby of the office tower. Jordan held the door open for Freddie and me to pass through.

"Remember what I said," I told her. "Don't look for us."

"We got you," Freddie added.

We told her goodbye and turned toward the lobby.

And saw Bruce Gillard, who clearly saw us.

He was standing in front of the bank of elevators, carrying a briefcase, a paper cup from Caribou coffee, and the shocked expression of a man who found a raccoon digging in his underwear drawer. He mouthed the words "What the hell" or maybe he said them aloud and we were too far away to hear.

"Darn it," Jordan said.

She closed the door. Freddie and I quickly crossed the lobby toward the exit as if Gillard wasn't there. He watched every step we took.

CHAPTER THIRTEEN

As hot as it was outside my Camry, it was considerably warmer inside. The windows were rolled up because it was easier to hide behind the reflections bouncing off the glass. My engine was off along with my air conditioner for fear that passersby would wonder what I was doing sitting in a parked car idling for hours at a time. The result was that I was sweating profusely in what I estimated was one hundred degrees or more. I complained about it.

"It's always 'bout you, ain't it, Taylor?" Freddie spoke just above a whisper into the radio microphone. "Bitchy, bitch, bitch."

"Yeah? How are you doing?"

"It's really comfortable out here in the shade under a tree, a nice breeze comin' offa the pond. You'd like it."

Freddie and I had arrived in Webber-Camden two-and-a-half hours earlier. Our first stop was the cemetery. We drove along the narrow roads until we reached that part of it with a clear view of the Camden Central Pond and parked. We moved to a rectangular marble headstone that marked the grave of a man named Joseph Allen Gensmer and pretended to stare down at it like close relatives paying their respects while we inspected the grounds.

"Whaddya think ol' Joe died of?" Freddie asked.

Along with his name, the headstone listed the years of his

birth and passing. I did the math.

"Old age," I said.

"Best way to go. Die in bed in the arms of a beautiful woman. That would be Echo in my case. How 'bout you? Still seein' the professor?"

"I can't see anyone in the cemetery or lurking around the edges."

"Me, neither. Nothin' comin' or goin' on the road. There's a lot of trees and brush between us and the pond, though, 'specially along the fence line. Black chain link, whaddya think? Four feet high?"

"High enough to deter the casual vandal without annoying the neighbors by making the place look like a prison."

"You didn't answer 'bout the professor."

"What makes me nervous is that the kidnappers might already be in place. They could be dug in along the fence line and watching the trash can. If we think it's a good idea, why not them?"

"They'll be watchin' for dudes look like cops, not us."

"You don't think we look like cops?"

"I don't."

"You used to be a cop."

"I was with the U.S. Air Force Police, completely different thing. About the professor—Dr. Alexandra Campbell, right? Tenured professor in the Department of Horticultural Science at the University of Minnesota with a Ph. D. in Agronomy and Plant Genetics."

I had known Sidney Poitier Fredericks for many years; we had been partners for nearly six and a half of them. He rarely surprised me anymore. This time, he did.

"You know all this because...?" I asked.

"I'm a seasoned private investigator. Whaddya think I didn't look 'er up?"

"Alex was fine the last time I saw her. Thank you."

"When was that?"

"A couple weeks ago. Freddie, let's keep our eyes on the prize, shall we?"

"If anyone is hidin' along the fence line, they're doin' a good job of it. I haven't seen any movement since we got here. You and the professor goin' at it hammer and tongs for a while there."

"Oh my God."

"I don't care myself. Was Echo wanted to know. She has this friend from work..."

"You're worse than a teenage girl."

"No need for that kinda talk."

"How about we get back to work?"

"Trees by your Toyota," Freddie said. "We'll stroll back to the car, and I'll make like I'm gettin' inside. You drive slowly. When we pass the trees, I'll peel off behind them. You keep drivin'. When you git to the turn, beep your horn. Anyone watchin' will be distracted long enough for me to go from them trees to the ones over there. You see 'em?"

"I do."

"From there, I'll work my way close to the fence. When I'm in position, I'll call on the radio."

"Sounds like a plan."

"What about the neighbor woman? The one with the little girl? If you and the prof are quits..."

"Let's go."

We returned to the Camry. The driver's side was facing the pond. I opened the door and slipped inside. At the same time, Freddie circled the car, opened the passenger door, grabbed the camera off the seat, ducked down like he was getting inside, and closed the door. He squatted alongside the vehicle, his head below the windows. I started the car and edged forward. When we reached the trees, Freddie let the car move past him until he was even with the rear bumper. He dashed toward the trees; I caught him in my side-view mirror while I kept driving the narrow cemetery road. When I reached the gentle curve, I hit my horn hard for a few seconds. At the same time, I watched the reflections in my mirrors. I couldn't detect any movement behind me. Course, I wasn't supposed to. I continued driving until I reached the cemetery's exit and hung a right on Dowling Avenue.

I didn't travel directly to the Victory Memorial Ice Arena, choosing instead to meander through the neighborhood streets until I was certain I wasn't being tailed. There was very little traffic even around Patrick Henry High School. Finally, I hopped onto Forty-Second Street and followed it until I reached the hockey rink. I pulled into the parking lot and halted the Camry in a stall facing the street and the pond beyond. There were plenty of cars in the lot and I was lucky to get a spot with the view I wanted.

I left the car and wandered into the arena. I wanted to be seen walking into the arena, yet did nothing to draw attention to myself.

There was a large sitting area just inside the door with vending machines serving candy, pop, and energy drinks. Mounted above the machines was a TV tuned to ESPN. On one side of the sitting room were metal doors leading to locker rooms A and B. On the other side was the manager's office. There was a large sign next to the door that read "There will be a $5 fine for whining." I walked past it to yet another metal door, this one with a window that revealed the ice rink beyond. There were two teams on the ice, one dressed in white jerseys, the other wearing colors ranging from yellow to black.

I stepped through the doorway. The temperature went from livable to well below freezing. There was a high, arched ceiling above the ice sheet, bleachers arranged along one side of the rink, and a lighted scoreboard against the far wall. Home was beating Visitors 3-0. I watched the hockey players for a few minutes, the sound of sticks, skates and the puck caroming off the boards echoed around me. Two women, their heads angled close together yet watching the ice, were sitting on the bleachers. They wore winter coats and gloves. As far as I could see, they were the only people in the arena who weren't on the ice or sitting on the bench.

I returned to the sitting area and hung around, waiting to see if anyone came or went. No one did. While I waited, I watched ESPN. A couple of commercial breaks later, I slipped out of the arena and made my way back to the Toyota; taking a circuitous route so I could detect if there was anyone in a vehicle facing the pond that was doing what I was doing. There wasn't.

I climbed inside. Going from the chilled ice arena to the hot Camry came as a shock to my system.

Freddie called on the radio.

"You didn't git lost, did ya?" he asked.

"I'm here."

"I've been scannin' the fence using the zoom on the camera. I do believe I am alone."

"I've been in and around the ice arena. I think I'm alone, too."

"Means the kidnappers are bein' careless, or they have a way better plan than we do."

CHAPTER FOURTEEN

We didn't have much to say to each other after that. The sun arched across the sky and began its slow descent. The temperature in the car rose to unbearable levels.

Surveillance was stressful. You sit, you watch, your mind wanders. You can't do much stretching and moving while hiding beneath a tree or locked inside a car, but you can play mind games to keep alert. You try to activate all your senses, asking yourself what you smell, taste, hear, and feel instead of just what you see. You plot world domination or at least the sudden demise of your enemies. You think about sex—the professor came to mind—decide what you're going to do if you're attacked, chew on something unhealthy like, I don't know, a bullet, count the number of people you see and make up stories about them, punch yourself in the face. Or, if you have a partner, you could chat from time to time if for no other reason than to reassure yourself that you were not alone.

Freddie said "Shouldn't we be hearin' from sweet cheeks 'bout now?"

"Why would you call her that?"

"Cuz she's got the nicest ass I've ever seen."

"You know she can hear you, right?"

"How 'bout it? Are you on the move, sweet cheeks? You listenin'?"

A half minute passed before we heard a reply.

"I'm driving north on I-94," Jordan said. "Yes, Mr. Fredericks, I'm listening to every word."

"You angry? You sound angry. Got the ol' adrenaline pumpin'?"

"Are you deliberately attempting to antagonize me?"

"Are you antagonized?"

"Mr. Fredericks, do you think it's easy being pretty?"

"I think it's a damn sight easier than being not pretty."

"My looks have definitely opened doors for me, both figuratively and literally. I admit that. I have never interviewed for a position I didn't get. However, being beautiful also means being hated. Mostly by other women. Women have made me cry my entire life. They don't trust me. They don't want me around their husbands and boyfriends. They exclude me from conversations, lunches, parties, after-work get-togethers. I've had women conspire to get me in trouble in college, get me fired from jobs, lying to my teachers and bosses about, ahh, it doesn't matter."

"Yes, it does," I said. "Keep talking."

"Throughout my life, other women, especially women who are attractive, wealthy, and entitled have really hated me for being the prettiest girl in the room. More often than not, they treat me like I'm either stupid or a whore or a stupid whore. The men haven't behaved much better. They all get flirty when they're around me. Or jealous when someone else gets flirty. The men I've actually dated, many of them treat me like I'm an accessory, like I'm a nice suit and tie or an expensive sports car."

"First time I saw you, I thought Ferrari," Freddie said.

"You saw how Brian Haskins looked at me. I always have to be on my guard; I'm constantly worried about my safety. I get catcalls and honked at walking down the street. The other day, I took a ten-minute walk from the office to City Hall to retrieve a file for Mr. Boucek, and I was honked at twice. A guy got out of his car at a red light and asked if I needed a ride. Random guys will stop me on the street and ask if I want to get coffee or a drink. Men follow me around in stores and try to talk to me, invade my personal space. Once I left my laundry in the dryer at my apartment building; one of those community washer and dryer setups. When I came down later to retrieve it, some of my lingerie was missing."

"Have you ever found out who stole it?" I asked.

"No, but there was this creepy old man living on my floor who was always trying to talk to me, always trying to get me to come to his apartment…Are you gentlemen attempting to distract me?"

"Whatever gave you that idea?"

"I assure you; it is unnecessary. I am not nervous."

"You're talkin' a lot like someone who's nervous," Freddie said.

Jordan had no answer for that.

"It's okay," I said. "It's often easier to vent to strangers than it is to your friends."

"I don't have any friends except for a woman I went to school with. My closest friend is a gay man I met in college. He's never jealous of me, and he doesn't want to get laid. His might be the only pure friendship I've ever known. I'm taking the North Dowling Avenue exit off I-94 now."

"Is there anyone taking the same exit behind you?"

"A single car. I'm turning left, though, and he's going right."

"What kinda car?" Freddie asked.

"I don't know cars. It's red. The light is turning and I'm going left…I'm on Dowling now, driving straight ahead. There's no one behind me. Is that a castle? Oh, no, it's an old church. It looks like it belongs in England."

"In the cemetery?" I asked.

"Yes. Must be a chapel. It looks very nice. I'm coming up to Penn Avenue. There still isn't anyone behind me."

"Good."

"I'm turning right…I'm on Penn."

"Forty-Second will be your first right."

"I see it."

Jordan didn't say anything after that. I watched her turn onto the avenue, slow her car, and finally turn into the same lot where I was parked. I didn't tell her that, though, because I didn't want her looking for me. She parked in the line behind me and a few stalls over.

"Here I go," she said.

"Stay frosty, sweet cheeks," Freddie said.

"Mr. Fredericks, the next time I see you, I'm going to slap your face."

"He'll deserve it, too," I said. "Be careful."

I watched Jordan, first with my mirrors and then through the windshield of my Camry. She paused at the curb, adjusted the MPR tote bag she carried over her shoulder, looked both ways, and crossed Forty-Second. She moved with purpose to the mouth of the hiking trail and started following it around the pond. She did not look right or left, only straight ahead. I could hear the pad-pad-pad of her soft-soled shoes on the gravel over the radio. I could hear her breathing. It wasn't labored or unusually fast. You would not have guessed that Jordan was carrying $50,000 in cash to a kidnapper who was probably watching every step she took; a kidnapper who was threatening the life of a woman the same age as she was.

Jordan had changed out of her office attire into jeans and a loose-fitting soft-green pullover with sleeves that ended below her elbows. She had fixed her soft-brown hair into a ponytail and hid her brown eyes behind sunglasses. There was nothing overtly sexy about her appearance, yet it was difficult to take your eyes off her just the same. Perhaps it had something to do with the way she moved. A couple walking a small dog passed her about the time she reached the first bench. The man smiled broadly, nodded, and said, "Good evening." The woman stared at the man like he had committed treason.

A younger man who was dressed as if he was jogging but who was not jogging passed Jordan as she approached the second bench. He gave her a Minnesota wave, lifting his hand to upper-waist level and extending his index finger like he was flashing a half-hearted peace sign, but with only one finger instead of two. I couldn't tell if Jordan acknowledged him or not.

She reached the third bench without encountering anyone else. She did not sit, nor did she look around. Instead, Jordan set the raccoon tote on the bench, reached inside, and pulled out the white trash bag. The "adjacent receptacle" was one of those green metal jobs with evenly spaced steel slats and a polyester sleeve, the sleeve containing its own plastic trash bag. The receptacle had a narrow opening, and it took some effort before Jordan was able to stuff the money through it. Once she did, she retrieved her tote, turned around, and retraced her steps without hesitation.

The jogger who wasn't jogging had hovered near the mouth of the hiking trail. When he saw Jordan coming his way, he started stretching like he was about to go for a hard run. Once she was in shouting distance, he smiled and strolled toward her. I heard his voice over the radio.

"Beautiful evening, isn't it?" he said.

Jordan's response was to stroll past him as if he wasn't there. He fell in step with her. My hand gripped the handle of my car door as I watched.

"Do you live around here?" the jogger asked. "I was thinking of getting a drink. Would you like to join me?"

Jordan refused to look at him. She kept walking. The jogger stopped and watched her leave the trail.

"What a bitch," he said. "I was just trying to be friendly."

"Asshole," Freddie said. "He's lucky I don't shoot 'im."

Jordan chuckled loudly and kept chuckling until she reached the curb. Once again, she looked both ways before crossing Forty-Second Avenue and walking directly to her car. She slipped inside; I heard her lock the doors. She started the vehicle and put it in gear.

"Gentlemen," she said. "I believe my work here is concluded."

"Very calm, very cool, Ms. Jordan," Freddie said. "You did good. My advice; go home, have a glass of wine and take a bubble bath. That's what my wife does when she's had a rough day."

Jordan drove out of the parking lot and hung a right on Forty-Second and a left on Penn Avenue, heading back to I-94. I could hear traffic sounds over her radio. No one followed her that I could see.

"Somehow I can't picture you married," she said.

"It's worse when you meet Freddie's wife," I said. "Beautiful Chinese woman called Echo. Smart. Funny. You wonder what she sees in him."

"Maybe she sees a friend. I'm turning onto Dowling. There's no one behind me."

"I think you're good."

"Should I turn off the radio?"

"Unless you want to hear some more of Freddie's sexist remarks."

Jordan paused before responding.

"I've heard worse," she said. "Goodnight gentlemen."

The traffic sounds stopped.

The sun continued its slow descent and the area around the pond became engulfed in dusky shadows. Streets lamps that were made to resemble antiques flicked on even though they were not yet needed, including one set very near the third bench.

No one went anywhere near the garbage can and all that cash.

"Look for someone walkin' his dog around the pond," I said. "He'll stop for a rest on the bench, casually look inside the trash can, pull out the bag, and walk away. If the cops stop him, he'll plead innocence. He'll say 'I was just going to call you. I was taking Rover for a stroll when I found this bag filled with cash. Can I keep it?'"

"That's one way of doin' it." Freddie continued to speak just above a whisper. "Except there's no po-lice presence."

"Just us."

Dusk gave way to darkest night. Twice the ice arena emptied out two teams of hockey players, only to be replaced by another two teams while we waited.

No one used the trail that circled the pond whatsoever, probably thinking that it was too late, too dark, and too scary to walk through the park at night.

"I like her," I said.

"Who? Jordan? I like her, too. I like the way she walks."

"You can't help yourself, can you, Freddie?"

"No, no man, the way she walks. Like she owns them mean streets, yo. Like she's sayin' you can take the girl outta the hood, but you can't take the hood outta the girl, so be careful."

"You think Jordan is from the hood?"

"Maybe not the hood, but she's gotta be from someplace that'd make her fearless enough to do ransom drops and such. Girls from Edina, from Lake Minnetonka, they'd faint dead away."

"Or resign their jobs before they get their manicured finger-nails dirty."

"Is what I'm sayin'."

"The way she sits quietly while the drama unfolds around her, too."

"Bet she knows plenty about Boucek and all his works. Bet she wouldn't give up a word of it, either, without what did Charles call it? Expressed permission?"

"I don't know, Freddie. You hear about the captain going down with his ship all the time. Have you ever heard about the first mate going down with it, too?"

"Somethin' to consider should the SS Boucek start listing."

"Which might happen if the Feds or Boucek's clients catch

on to what been happening lately."

"Should I tell you what I think?"

"When don't you?"

"There are times."

"Really?"

"I think once we finish this gig we should run, not walk, to the nearest exit."

The final hockey teams were on the ice, and I was becoming concerned about staying in the parking lot after all the other cars departed. I considered moving the Toyota to Morgan Street, hoping to get a spot near the intersection with Forty-Second so I could still have eyes on the pond ,if not the third bench.

I mentioned it to Freddie. He thought nearly any intersection would do.

"Just hang 'til I give you the heads up," he said.

I said I would do that after the last of the hockey players took off. An hour later, they were getting close to doing that.

Freddie said "Did I ever tell you 'bout my vacation to Charleston, South Carolina?"

"Yes, you did."

"Tell you 'bout tourin' the plantation?"

"No. What plantation?"

"Middleton Place outside the city, what made its money harvesting rice, not cotton or tobacco like I would've guessed. Yellow rice. Carolina Gold, they called it. Anyway, Echo is big into the ancestry thing; wants to know where it all began, 'kay? She sits down with Asha, and they work it out that the slave ships that brought my people t' the land of the free and the home of the brave came through Charleston. No surprise there. Half the slaves brought over from Africa came through Charleston. They also determined that my great great granddaddy, I don't know how many greats; that he mighta been sold to the Middleton family who owned something like twenty-two-hundred slaves between 1738 and the end of the Civil War. So, we went over there t' take a look, me and Echo and the boy. I didn't really want to go, but you know Echo. Big fuckin' place; musta been somethin' back in the day. Now it's a tourist attraction. Got a restaurant, an inn, museum, gift shop, these incredible sprawling gardens, emerald green lawns that reminded me of my football days. They recreated the stables, too; slave quarters, mansion house, all of that. It was—I was going to say 'cool.' It wasn't that, but it was illuminating. Yeah, that's the word. I thought it would make me angry t' be there, only it didn't."

"How did it make you feel?"

He didn't reply.

"Freddie?"

No answer.

"Are you still with me, Freddie?"

I didn't take the time to lock my car, just slammed the door shut, and that was only because it was in my way. I dashed out of the parking lot and across Forty-Second Avenue without bothering to look for traffic. I ignored the gravel path, running instead at a diagonal along the edge of the pond and across the field, moving as fast as I could toward the stand of trees where I knew Freddie had been hiding. The four-foot black cyclone fence blocked my path. I leapt, grabbed the top rail, hoisted myself up and vaulted over. I was running again before I hit the ground.

When I reached the trees, I pulled my Beretta from its holster and the smartphone from my pocket, accessing the flashlight. I shone the beam carefully over the ground until I found Freddie's sprawled body.

I called his name and knelt close to him.

Someone had smashed the back of his head with a tree branch.

CHAPTER FIFTEEN

It took forever to get an ambulance into the cemetery. First, I had to convince the 911 operator that I wasn't putting her on, that I wasn't a drunk pulling a prank. It took some doing, and I'm afraid I raised my voice more than once.

The operator said "Sir, you're talking loud enough to wake the dead."

Under normal circumstances, I would have laughed.

Finally, she dispatched both an ambulance and the MPD. The ambulance arrived silently. It seemed unsure where to go once it hit the narrow cemetery road. I managed to flag it down using the light on my smartphone. The police squad roared into the cemetery with bar lights flashing and siren blaring as if it were the cavalry riding to the rescue. I think the officer liked the narrow roads because it gave him a chance to spin his tires.

The EMTs wasted no time at all, rushing to Freddie's side and taking care of business. They didn't seem to care about the how and the why, only the what. The Minneapolis Police Officer, on the other hand, was very much interested in the how, the why, and the who, his hand resting on the butt of his Glock while he barked his questions.

I barked back my answers. He didn't like any of them which, admittedly, were a little sketchy when it came to explaining what we were doing in the cemetery in the middle of the night. I thought my PI license might cut me some slack, except it didn't.

I would have dropped Charles Boucek's name, only I knew he wouldn't like it.

The EMTs loaded Freddie onto a stretcher with wheels and dodged headstones as they pushed it to the ambulance. I noticed that there wasn't any blood on the back of his head, I said, "That's a good thing, right?"

They didn't reply. Instead, they shoved the stretcher into the ambulance. The EMTs asked if I wanted to ride with my friend. I asked where they were taking him. They said North Memorial Hospital in Robbinsdale, a suburb northwest of downtown Minneapolis. That wouldn't have been my first choice. Google reviews gave it only two-point-eight stars. But it was only eight minutes away.

I told them I would be right behind them. The MPD said no I wouldn't. I said "Watch me" and started running toward my car. I hopped the fence at the Camden Central Pond again and moved swiftly along the gravel path. If the MPD had followed, he never got past the fence. Nor did he shoot at me which, given the temperature of the country these days, took admirable restraint.

Just for fun, I paused at the receptacle adjacent to the third park bench and looked inside. The $50,000 was gone.

The folks at North Memorial wouldn't give me the time of day. It didn't matter that I was Freddie's business partner. I wasn't a relative. I didn't even learn that Freddie had suffered a skull fracture until Echo arrived and they told her.

The way the emergency room personnel kept glancing at me, I suspected they thought I was somehow responsible for his injuries. It didn't help that they witnessed an officer from the Minneapolis Police Department arriving to take my statement. He wasn't the same cop from the park but someone he must have contacted, someone who didn't feel the need to get badge heavy with me. We spoke quietly. He didn't like my answers anymore than the first officer, especially when I told him that Freddie was "attacked while performing confidential services required of him as a licensed private investigator in the State of Minnesota." Instead of getting all large and emphatic about it though, he said "Have it your way." Tone of voice matters.

He left just as Echo arrived, coming in direct response to my phone call. I moved to embrace her, only she wasn't in the hugging mood.

She set a hand against my chest and said, "Where were you?"

I tried to explain, only it turned out to be a rhetorical question. She really didn't care to know.

I led Echo to the emergency medical specialist who caught the case. Suddenly, he was all smiles and soft morning sunshine. I decided Freddie was correct about what he had told Ms. Jordan—it is better to be pretty.

After assuring Echo that her husband was going to be all right, he led her to him. No one seemed to mind that I followed along. We stepped into the private room. Freddie was sitting up, pillows piled behind his back. He must have seen me first.

"Well, we fucked that up," he said. When he saw his wife, he changed his tone. "Messed up, I mean."

There was a needle stuck in the back of Freddie's hand that was attached to a thin hose that was connected to a heavy clear-plastic bag with the words "lactated ringer's" printed on it. Other than that, he looked as if he was waiting for breakfast in bed.

Echo moved quickly to his side as if she wanted to hug him and paused to glance at the doctor.

"It's all right," he said.

Echo proceeded to hug her man even as Freddie said, "Whaddya askin' him for? I'm the one what needs lovin'."

"What you need is rest," the doctor said. "You have a linear skull fracture, what we also call a closed fracture. It's actually quite common. There is a break in the bone, however the bone hasn't moved. There's considerable swelling and tenderness around the impact area, yet the skin remains unbroken. There's no bleeding and no need for stitches or bandages."

"I woke up in the ambulance," Freddie said. "Then I threw up. Then I went out again. Now my head hurts like crazy and I feel nauseous."

"Those are the symptoms, yes. However, the computed tomography scan..."

Freddie looked at the doctor as if he was speaking Swahili.

"CT scan," the doctor said. "The big white tube we strapped you down and ran you through."

"'Kay."

"It produces highly detailed images of the bone, tissue, and other structures of the head. We use it to check for possible injuries to the brain. There were none. We've determined that surgical intervention is not required."

"What is required?" Echo said. She was sitting on the edge of Freddie's bed and holding his hand.

"Rest, like I said. Most skull fractures will heal by themselves, especially when they're simple fractures like this one. The healing process might take some time. As long as a couple of months for a man your age."

"I think he's calling you old, Freddie," I said.

"Yeah, I git that."

"The pain, however, will usually disappear in a few days, maybe a week," the doctor said. "We'll give you some medication..."

"No opioids," Echo said. Her tone of voice implied that she would not debate the issue. The doctor heard it, probably had heard it from others who were frightened by the wildly addictive nature of the painkillers.

"We have substitutes we can provide," he said.

Freddie squeezed his thumb and index fingers together and made a puffing gesture.

"Little medical marijuana?" he asked.

"I think you qualify," the doctor said.

"Now, we're talkin'," Freddy said.

"In the meantime, we'll maintain close observation here in the hospital for a day or two. After that, you'll be free to go about your business. One thing we are concerned about is concussion symptoms. Headaches, of course. You might also have problems with concentration, memory, balance, coordination..."

"I used to play college football, Doc," Freddie said.

"Then you know what I'm talking about."

"Had the bell rung a couple of times, yeah."

"We'll talk again before you're discharged. At present, I'm anticipating a positive outcome."

No one had anything to say to that.

"All right, then." The doctor was looking at Echo when he smiled and said, "I need to deal with some sick people."

"Thanks, Doc," Freddie said.

After the doctor left us alone, Freddie asked, "Where's the boy?"

"With his grandmother," Echo said. "Asha is being calm about all this, so I thought I should try to be calm, too, only I'm not. I'm very, very angry."

"Be angry at Taylor. He's the one who fuuuu-screwed up."

"Don't tell her that," I said.

"Nah, I'm just foolin'." Freddie squeezed Echo's hand. She was not reassured. "This is on me. Instead of talkin', I should have been listenin'."

"Stakeouts are long and boring," I said. "You need to do something to keep from falling asleep."

"Yeah, well, I didn't fall asleep, but I might as well have. Unprofessional."

"Is that all you care about?" Echo wanted to know. "Being professional? You could have been killed."

"Echo…"

"Don't Echo me." She looked in my direction. "Where were you, Holland?"

"I was…"

"It's not on Taylor," Freddie said. "Like I said. What happened…"

"I don't want to talk to either of you," Echo said. But she didn't let go of Freddie's hand, and she didn't leave.

"What about the ransom?" Freddie asked.

I brought my fingers together, kissed them, and let them fly open while adding a "Poof" sound.

"Shiiioooot." Freddie glanced at Echo even as the word became warped in his mouth. Freddie rarely cursed in front of his wife.

"Shit is right," Echo said.

"They probably had the spot scoped out since they sent the express mailer," Freddie said. "Could even have set up a camera; a drone hoverin' above the trees watchin' a couple of dipwads pretendin' to be PIs. We should post all this on our website—how not to conduct surveillance. Gotta boost business."

"No one was killed," I said. "That's the main thing."

"We're gonna git paid no matter what, right?"

My cell phone rang. At three AM I figured it could only be trouble.

The caller ID read Boucek and Associates. I swiped right.

"Yes," I said.

"Mr. Taylor?" Jordan said.

"Ms. Jordan."

The sound of her name caused Freddie to sit up straighter on the bed.

"Would you please hold for Mr. Boucek?" she asked.

"Sure."

"Mr. Taylor, I'm sorry about your partner's injury. I hope he's alright."

"Freddie'll be fine."

"Speak for yourself, man," Freddie said.

"Maybe I won't slap him now."

"You're very kind," I said, even as the alarm bells sounded. How did she know about Freddie?

While I waited for Boucek, I told Freddie what Jordan said.

Echo asked, "Why would she want to slap you?"

Freddie shrugged, the epitome of innocence.

Boucek took up the phone.

"I apologize for calling so late, or early, if you prefer," he said. "I was sure that you would want to know—Carole Robey has been recovered unharmed."

"Recovered?"

"An officer with the Minneapolis Police Department found her asleep on a bench near the playgrounds at Jordan Park less than ninety minutes ago."

"Jordan Park is in North Minneapolis, two miles from the pond, a half mile from the dumpster where Henrietta Weller was found."

"That is my understanding as well," Boucek said. "The officer thought Ms. Robey had passed out from alcohol or drugs. She was revived and transported to the Fourth Precinct. Her parents were contacted, and she was taken home."

"So, she's in the system."

"Taylor, please, I do have my connections. Calls were made. The event was deemed by higher authority to be little more than a family matter. An incident report was not filed."

"So, you're going to get away with it again."

"Mr. Taylor, the young lady has been returned to the loving embrace of her family. That is what matters. Nothing else."

"It's going to happen again, Charles. Sooner or later, someone is going to get hurt."

"Which brings me to the second reason I called. What can you and your partner tell me? Can you identify the kidnappers?"

I was staring at Freddie when I answered "I'm sorry. We missed the opportunity."

"That's unfortunate. However, I assume the ransom had been delivered, otherwise Ms. Robey would not have been released."

"The ransom was delivered."

"Yes, and Ms. Robey is safe and sound."

"I would like to speak to Ms. Robey."

"Certainly not."

"Charles…"

"Taylor, I consider this matter to be closed. May I assume that you agree?"

I tried mightily to think of an argument that Boucek hadn't heard before and came up empty.

"Mr. Taylor?" he repeated.

"Yes, I agree."

"Good. I thank you and Mr. Fredericks for your efforts. I was, of course, informed by the MPD of Mr. Frederick's injury…"

That's how Ms. Jordan knew about it, I told myself.

"I wish him a quick recovery, and please feel free to add his medical expenses to your invoice. Goodnight."

I ended the call.

"Yeah?" Freddie said.

"Case closed."

"Figures."

"Until the next kidnapping."

"As long as it doesn't have anything to do with us. And what do you mean 'Sooner or later someone is going to get hurt?'"

"Quit your whining you big baby. You're lucky to be alive."

"That's not funny," Echo said.

CHAPTER SIXTEEN

I drove to my apartment in St. Paul, marveling at how little traffic there was. Four million people lived in and around the Twin Cities, and it seemed like half of them were using our 758 miles of freeway at any given time. The American Transportation Research Institute claimed we had more bottlenecks than Chicago, LA, or New York. Except at three-thirty AM, I had the roads virtually to myself.

The lot behind the building was first come first serve, and I assumed all the slots would be taken, so I parked on the street. There were several streetlamps not unlike the antique replicas at Camden Central Pond. Nothing moved beneath them, not even a stray cat on the prowl for whatever felines prowled for late at night.

I admired the lights. I could imagine F. Scott Fitzgerald leaning against one, sipping gin from a flask while waiting for a young lady to sneak out of one of the Victorian mansions that dotted the neighborhood. Together, they would walk hand-in-hand past the grand mansions located along a quiet Summit Avenue, stopping to neck in the shadow of the St. Paul Cathedral. Or maybe I was just having romantic delusions. When you're exhausted, your partner has a fractured skull because of a botched stakeout, and you're anxious about becoming involved in the cover-up of a federal crime, your mind tends to seek relief.

I followed the sidewalk to the apartment building and used a key to unlock the main entrance. I tried to make as little noise as possible, not because I was concerned with disturbing my neighbors, but because I didn't want them to mark my comings and goings.

There was a soft light above each landing, so it wasn't hard to find 2A at the top of the first flight of stairs. I unlocked the door, stepped inside, closed it, and immediately realized that there was an intruder hiding in the darkness. I don't know why I knew this. There was no movement, no sound of breathing that would have given away my guest, and yet...

Caution is a habit. Practice it long enough, and it becomes muscle memory. Longer still, and it becomes instinct. I didn't try to talk myself out of the feeling or tell myself that it was Ogilvy. I had learned the hard way to always trust my instincts. So, I remained motionless, my back to the closed door. My Beretta was gripped in both of my hands, the right pushing out slightly and the left pulling in to steady it. As my eyes adjusted to the dark, I swept the sights over the living room and kitchen, pausing as I peered down the corridor that led to my bedroom and bathroom.

After a moment, I moved closer to the wall, found the light switch, and flicked it up. A lamp in the living room flashed to life. Beneath the lamp and curled on my sofa was Amanda Wedemeyer. Ogilvy was lying on top of her. They had both been sound asleep; however, the sudden light caused them to open their eyes.

"Mandy?" I asked.

"Taylor?"

I walked toward her, the Beretta leading the way. It wasn't until she called my name a second time that I had the presence of mind to slip the gun back into its holster. I knelt next to the girl but didn't ask how she got in; I already knew the answer: I had given her a key over a year ago after eliciting her promise to take care of my rabbit when I was out of town.

"Mandy," I said again. "What are you doing here?"

"I'm hiding."

"Hiding from whom?"

She shook her head as if she was unable to answer the question. Her face was swollen, and her eyes were red from crying.

"Do you know what time it is?" I asked. "Your mother must be terrified."

"She knows I'm all right."

"How does she know?"

"I sent her a text."

"You sent your mother a text? What did she say?"

"She's been trying to find me, but—she doesn't really care."

"The hell she doesn't."

Both the sharpness and volume of my voice caused Amanda to sit up. Tears were forming in her eyes again when I stood and looked down at her.

"Don't shout," she said.

"Are you kidding me?"

"What are you going to do?"

"What do you think I'm going to do?"

I didn't wait for a reply. Instead, I moved to my door, passed through it, and marched across the landing. I hesitated for a moment outside 2B and knocked three times. The door was flung open as if Claire had been standing on the other side with her hand on the knob.

"Amanda?" she said. "Taylor?"

I flung a thumb over my shoulder at my opened doorway. Claire followed the gesture. Her eyes were wide and alert, yet there was a puffiness around them that suggested she had been weeping, too.

"Thank God," she said.

Claire crossed the landing in a dead sprint, stopping just outside the doorway as if she were attempting to compose herself. Two deep breaths and she allowed herself to enter my apartment. I followed her. Amanda was still sitting on the sofa;

Ogilvy had moved to her lap. Claire walked toward Amanda and lowered herself to the carpet in front of her. I closed the apartment door and watched.

"Are you alright?" Claire said.

"Why wouldn't I be?"

That's about the time I might have taken her over my knee. Fortunately, Claire was made of sterner stuff.

"I know you." Her voice was soft, like she was reciting a lullaby. "I know all about you. You're a stubborn child, willful and impetuous. You don't always consider the consequences of your actions, preferring a more spontaneous approach to life. I've always liked that about you."

Claire reached up to brush the hair out of her daughter's eyes. Amanda waved her hand to make her stop but didn't actually try to slap her mother.

"You're also very smart and extremely kind," Claire said. "I have never known you to deliberately hurt anyone, not even the person you are the angriest with in the entire world."

"I'm not angry at you."

"I didn't think you were."

"Why didn't you make him go away? Why didn't you tell him to leave us alone?"

"That wouldn't have solved the problem."

"I don't want to be his daughter."

"You are, though, whether we like it or not."

Claire reached to move her daughter's hair off her face again. This time Amanda let her.

"Dad—I don't even like saying the word," she said. "Can he really take me away from you?"

"No. That will never happen. That's not what he was talking about, anyway. Joint custody doesn't mean you have to live with him. It means you will live primarily with me and visit your father. Mandy, you can't run off like you did. I was so frightened that something might have happened to you. You've got to promise me…"

Claire was trying so hard to hold on to her emotions, and for a moment, I thought they might get away from her. She rested her face in both hands.

"God, Mandy," she said.

Amanda leaned forward and draped her arms over Claire's back. She rested her head next to Claire's.

"I'm sorry, Mom."

A moment later, they were hugging. They weren't crying, though. I think by then they were both cried out.

"I didn't mean to frighten you," Amanda said.

"Well, you did. You can't do anything like this again."

"I won't. Mom? Did you call the police?"

"No, I didn't call the police."

"Did you call any of my friends?"

"I didn't want to embarrass you. Besides, I kind of guessed you were hiding over here when you texted you were with your friend."

"I heard you knocking on the door before, only I...I'm sorry."

"It's okay now."

"Sometimes I think Ogilvy is the only one who understands me."

Claire scratched Ogilvy between his ears.

"He is one smart rabbit," she said.

"I've been teaching him tricks," Amanda said. "Do you want to see?"

"Not now. We need to go home. Taylor, I am so sorry for all of this."

"Hey, I keep telling you both that you're always welcome here any time, day or night."

"Thank you."

"Do you want to tell me what's going on?"

Claire moved from the floor to the sofa and sat next to her daughter. She draped her arm around her daughter's shoulders and drew her close. Ogilvy remained in the child's lap.

"Mandy's father, Douglas, called me at work," Claire said. "I have no idea how he got my number. He asked if he could come over to the apartment after dinner so he could visit with Amanda and me. He told me how much he had missed us; he sounded so sincere that finally I agreed. When he came over and he was charming. As usual. He kept telling Mandy how beautiful she was and smart and how beautiful I was and smart. I waited for the shoe to drop because I've been a victim of his charm before.

"Anyway, he talked about his plans to regain his CPA; the State Board of Accountancy took it away from him when he was convicted of embezzling from his employer. He talked about going to work for his uncle who owns a construction firm, working in the front office. He talked about how he was going to make it up to us and his family and his friends for all the pain and suffering he put us through. Douglas then talked about how he wanted Amanda to spend weekends with him once he was discharged from the halfway house and moved in with his parents.

"When we were divorced, I was granted sole custody of Amanda," Claire said. "Douglas was serving the first year of his sentence at the time and didn't contest it. Neither did Mandy's grandparents or anyone else on his side of the family. Now he says he wants to have the court order modified because he claims he's a changed man. He says having joint custody of Amanda means he won't be defined solely by his crimes anymore. It would give him the opportunity to live an honest life.

"It's also means, he says, that Mandy will now have grand-parents who will care about her, uncles and aunts and cousins that I can't give her because I have no extended family. The same grandparents and aunts and uncles and cousins that disowned us when I divorced him. Douglas said that once he moves in with his parents, Mandy can visit him there, sur-rounded by his family."

"That's when I ran out of the apartment," Amanda said. "Taylor, can he do that? Can he make me visit him?"

"I don't know. The court will consider your feelings on the matter, of course. At the same time—Mandy, one out of every fifteen adults in this country will serve time in prison, and the courts are becoming more and more keen on upholding a parent's right to participate in a child's life. If your father hasn't abused a child in the past or he's not deemed to be a violent criminal..."

"Like an embezzler?"

"Yeah, like an embezzler—he might be able to convince the court to grant him visitation rights. What'll happen, the court will try to get your mom and your—get Douglas to resolve their custody issues through mediation. The mediator will talk to them—and you—in the hopes of reaching a compromise. The mediator is not a judge. He can't decide anything. He can influence a judge's decision though, so..."

"What should we do?" Claire asked.

"Wait and see what Douglas does. This is a long process. He has to file a lot of paper just to get started. Right now, it's all on him. He has to prove that he's turned his life around. He has to prove that he successfully completed treatment for the gambling addiction that led him to commit his crimes. And he has to prove that he has stable employment and that he has the ability to provide a safe environment for Mandy. My point is, this isn't going to happen tomorrow. Or next month. Or the month after that. You have plenty of time to decide on a course of action."

Claire nodded as if she already knew all this, but didn't trust her understanding of the situation. Amanda yawned and stretched.

"Do I need to go to school?" she asked. "I'm really tired."

"Yes," I said. "Amanda—from now on you are going to be the most pleasant, most obedient, most respectful little girl in the known universe."

"Why?"

"It'll help prove to the court that your mother is doing a magnificent job raising you."

A big, bright smile formed on Amanda's face as she looked at Claire. She kissed the woman's cheek and said, "That won't be hard."

Claire kissed her back and mother and daughter left the sofa and moved toward the door. Claire thanked me again. I held her back as Amanda crossed the landing toward 2B.

"Okay, you're not going to like this," I said.

"What?"

"From this moment forward, you must live a life that's above reproach."

"What do you mean?"

"You cannot have arguments with Mandy in public. You can't threaten her; you can't discipline her in a way that someone else might think is unduly harsh. You must show up at all the parent-teacher meetings and all the school events, and the PTA is also a good idea. Forget about dating because whatever your boyfriend has ever done in his life—drugs, sex crimes, whatever—will be visited upon you. Doug's lawyers will make it seem as if they're your crimes or that you at least endorse them. Do you understand?"

"No, I don't."

"One of the arguments that people use to gain custody of a child is to tell the court that the other parent is worse than they are. Your ex might try to convince a judge that you're the one who is raising Amanda in an unstable environment. That granting him custody is in her best interests."

"How could he do that?"

"Ms. Wedemeyer, you have an interesting relationship with your neighbor, do you not?"

"What?"

"You've been seen coming and going from his apartment quite often. In fact, you seem to spend a lot of time at his place."

Claire stared for a moment while she wrestled with what I was attempting to tell her.

"Sometimes we have coffee," she said. "Sometimes I bring him leftovers from the meals I make for Mandy and me."

"He's your friend?"

"Yes."

"A special friend?"

"What do you mean?"

"You're single. He's single. It would be natural for you to have an affair with him. Tell the court—does your daughter know you're having sex with him? Has she been in the apartment at the same time?"

"That's crazy."

"Claire, I am not proud to tell you I've done this kind of work for clients in the past, digging up dirt that can be used to obtain an advantage in a divorce case or a child custody hearing. Some of that dirt—it's all about context, explaining to a jury that an innocent hug between friends is much more than an innocent hug between friends. I'm not saying Douglas will do this. He might, though. Especially if he gets desperate."

"I understand what you're telling me, Holland, but I will not change my life one iota because of him."

"Yes. You will. You're not Mandy. You *do* consider the consequences of your actions. You must."

"Yes," Claire replied softly. "I must."

She looked up at me with moist eyes and then did something I didn't expect. She kissed me. She wrapped her arms around me and pulled me close and she kissed me hard on the mouth, kissed me hungrily. I should have stopped her, yet I didn't.

When she finished Claire stepped back and said "I've wanted to do that since the first month we met, since that time you helped me get my car started in the snow, only I knew you wouldn't let me because you've convinced yourself that you're damaged goods because of Laura and the other women you've known. I was willing to be patient because I didn't want to frighten you anymore than you already were. Now I want to kiss you again. I want to keep doing it. But you say I can't because my sonuvabitch of an ex-husband might use our relationship to take my daughter away from me. This is unacceptable. I will not allow my life to be dictated by stupid, stupid men."

She spun around and left my apartment, stomping across the landing and slamming her door like she didn't care who heard her.

I gently closed my own door and turned to face Ogilvy. He was still sitting on the sofa and probably wondering if anyone was going to bed anytime soon.

"I am a stupid, stupid man," I told him.

CHAPTER SEVENTEEN

The first week of June and the weather hadn't improved one bit. It was eighty-seven degrees outside. A week earlier, we hit one hundred, a good twenty-seven degrees above the historic average. Yes, I was wearing a black sports jacket.

Freddie stepped into the office late, as usual. He was smiling, probably the result of the joint he was smoking. It wasn't the first time he'd been in the office since his injury, just the first time that he looked high.

"Nice of you to drop by," I said.

"I thought so."

"How's the head?"

"Fine."

"No pain?"

"Not since I left the hospital."

"Concussion symptoms? Headaches? Memory loss? Problems with coordination?"

"Not anymore."

"Yet…"

I gestured at the joint. Freddie's response was to take a deep drag.

"Just following doctor's orders," he said.

"Is that cherry? It smells like cherry."

"It's cherry flavored, yeah. Black cherry."

I made a gimme gesture. Freddie shook his head.

"I'm sorry," he said. "Do you have a letter from a licensed healthcare practitioner prescribing this course of treatment for a qualifying medical condition?"

"I don't."

"I'm afraid I must refuse your request. Don't give me that look. Sir, I do not make the laws. I can hardly be blamed for refusing to aid and abet criminal behavior on your part."

"I can't believe it was opioid addiction Echo was afraid of."

Freddie took another hit.

"I can quit anytime I wanna," he said, which was difficult to do because he was attempting to hold his breath at the same time.

"Okay. I'm leaving."

"Where are you goin'?"

"To serve a subpoena."

"For who?"

"David Helin."

"He's talkin' to us again? Stanislav, Kennedy, Helin, and DuBois is sendin' business our way, again?"

"Apparently, the PI firm that promised them lower rates also gave them inferior service."

"We are irreplaceable."

"What are your intentions, Freddie?"

"I thought I'd take a whack at all those backgrounds checks that have been pilin' up."

"Are you sure?"

Freddie took one last drag from his joint and snuffed it out against the heel of his shoe.

"I am down to stems and seeds, sir," he said. "My prescription has expired."

"Like you couldn't walk down the street and stock up for the winter."

"Nah, I'm done."

"What's the first step according to AA? Admitting you're powerless over, well, in your case, grass?"

"Let's just say I've decided to end my vacation and get back at it."

"Echo kicked you out of the house, didn't she?"

"She did suggest that I was spendin' way too much time eatin' Doritos and watchin' the Weather Channel, yeah."

"Will you be offended if I check your work?"

Freddie thought that was funny.

"Will you be offended if I kick your ass?" he asked.

"Why, yes. Yes, I would."

"I'm good, Taylor. Don't go worryin' 'bout it."

"Then I won't. I was getting tired of carrying your weight, anyway."

Freddie tapped his stomach. "I have been eatin' a lot of munchies lately."

Patricia Johanssen was a nice woman, kind and considerate. Everyone told me so. Her friends couldn't believe that she had somehow become involved with JD Heggman; although they admitted they hadn't seen much of her lately. Not since Heggman's business partner had been indicted on a charge of money-laundering, anyway.

The partner denied the charges, of course. It wasn't him, he said, it was Heggman. Heggman, on the other hand, was outraged by the scurrilous accusations made by a man who he had once considered his friend. He claimed it was his partner who was using their real estate business to hide a drug dealer's illicit gains, and the company's computers seemed to favor his version of events. The drug dealer, who was serving 158 months in Oak Park Heights, had nothing to say about the matter one way or another.

The indictment was handed down a couple of months ago; the trial was set to begin in one week. Sometime in between, Johanssen disappeared. David Helin, who was defending the partner, was convinced that she was ducking a court order compelling her to testify. The subpoena had been issued, he told me, because she was an accountant well-versed in IT and because she had been sleeping with Heggman.

"An unlikely coincidence," Helin said. "Besides, if Johanssen doesn't know anything, why is she in the wind?"

Except she wasn't running. Johanssen was hiding in an Airbnb in Stillwater Heggman was paying for. It took me a day and a half to find her. She had canceled her cell phone and probably cut up her credit cards since there had been no activity on any of them in the past forty days. Unfortunately—or fortunately, depending on your point of view—she couldn't kick her addiction to social media. Instead of deleting her accounts, she merely changed her settings to private. I couldn't see her posts, but her friends could. It was a simple matter to skip down Johanssen's Friends list until I found one who was willing to help me help her.

Nothing in her posts hinted at her location. However, the friend let me study several of the pics that Johanssen had uploaded. One was a dead giveaway—she was blowing a kiss at the camera with the iconic lift bridge in the background that hovered above the St. Croix River and connected downtown Stillwater, Minnesota, with Wisconsin. Once I knew where to look, the other photos became puzzle pieces I was able to manipulate until they eventually led me to the Airbnb. Sitting in my parked Camry on the other side of a tree-lined street and half a block down, I found myself wondering why Helin's cut-rate PI firm had been unable to locate her.

"Bunch of numb-nuts," I decided.

My watch said it was high noon. Maybe Johanssen was inside, maybe she wasn't, I told myself. The only way to know for sure was to knock on the door and ask. Before I could shut down the Camry, though—yes, it was running; yes, the air-conditioner was on—a woman stepped outside. Johanssen was slender and pretty and fast approaching sixty-one, according to my research. Why she would involve herself with a man who was literally half her age and not all that good looking, if you ask me, I couldn't say. Maybe she had a mother-son fetish. Maybe she was in love.

Johanssen left the property, gained the sidewalk, and strolled toward downtown Stillwater. She seemed happy and for a moment I felt a wrench of guilt because in a few minutes I intended to make her very unhappy, indeed.

I stayed in my car until she was out of sight. Afterward, I drove the side streets, following her from a distance until she reached her destination, a café on St. Croix Trail and Chestnut Street. It took me a few minutes to find a place to park. By the time I returned to the café, Johanssen had already ordered her burger, fries, and Diet-Pepsi. I paused inside the door and took a deep breath before I shouted.

"It's you," I said.

I pointed at Johanssen, who was sitting at a small table against the wall, so there would be no doubt who I meant. She seemed flummoxed. So did the twenty other people inside the café.

"It's you," I repeated.

"Me?"

"Yes, you. Why were you talking to Brian?"

"Brian? I don't know any Brian."

"Don't give me that. I saw you. You stay away from my boyfriend, Sarah. Do you hear me?"

"Sarah?" Johanssen stood and raised her hands as if she was surrendering. "No, no, no, you have me confused with someone else. My name is Patty Johanssen."

"What?"

"Patricia Johanssen."

I probably should have felt a thrill of euphoria. Johanssen had just identified herself in front of two dozen witnesses. Except I didn't. I felt that wrench of guilt again as I reached inside my pocket and withdrew the envelope that contained the subpoena.

"This belongs to you," I said.

Johanssen took the envelope without realizing what it was. And then she did.

"What have you done?" she asked.

"You've been served."

Again she chanted the words "No, no, no" and slowly sat back down. She began to weep.

You can't take it personally, I knew that. These people, these clients, they weren't my family, my friends. They were my work. It wasn't healthy to identify with them or care about their problems. You do the job and move on. Sometimes, though, sometimes...

I knew I should get my sorry ass out of there as quickly as possible, only I couldn't resist one last word.

"All of your friends say that you're a nice woman," I said. "It's time to be that person again."

"If I was that person, I wouldn't be here."

I returned to my Camry. Instead of starting it up and driving off, though, I completed a Proof of Service form, the court paper used as evidence that a process server presented the witness with the subpoena he was instructed to serve.

I had just finished it when my cell phone rang. The caller ID read Boucek and Associates. I swiped right.

"Holland Taylor," I said.

There was no preamble at all. Ms. Jordan said "Please hold for Mr. Boucek" and immediately handed the phone off.

"You can't go to the police," Boucek said.

"What are you talking about?"

"You know exactly what I'm talking about. You cannot go to the police. It would be a violation of privilege. I will ruin you in this town. You and your partner."

"Okay, Charles. You've threatened me. I promise I'm suffi-ciently intimidated. Now will you tell me what's going on—

what the hell?"

"Are you saying you don't know?"

"Know what?"

Boucek took a long pause before he said, "I apologize for my outburst. I would appreciate it if you and Mr. Fredericks would call upon me at your earliest convenience."

"I'm in Stillwater. It'll be at least a half hour."

"Ms. Jordan will greet you in the lobby."

I was going to say "What, again?" except Boucek ended the call before I could.

CHAPTER EIGHTEEN

Ms. Jordan was standing in the same spot inside the main entrance to Boucek's office tower as she had been when I met her a few weeks earlier, tapping her toe and appearing just as impatient.

"You're late," she said.

"You say that like you're surprised," I said.

Her scowl became an expression of benign curiosity when she saw Freddie, though.

"Mr. Fredericks," she said.

"Miss me, sweet cheeks?"

Jordan's hand went to Freddie's face, but instead of slapping him as promised, she merely tapped him.

"I was going to inquire as to your health," she said. "However, I can tell that you're your old self again."

"Good to see you, too, Ms. Jordan."

"Gentlemen, if you would accompany me."

Jordan spun around and headed off past the elevators.

"Is this subterfuge really necessary?" I asked. "If no one else, your executive vice-president knows we're doing business with your firm."

"Gillard knows nothing," Jordan said. I noticed she left off the "Mister" part.

She continued to lead us to the service door. We followed close behind. Halfway there Jordan said, "Enjoying the view,

Mr. Fredericks?"

"Yes, ma'am."

I whispered to him, "How do you get away with this crap but I can't?"

"Charm," Freddie said.

We entered Boucek's inner office through his escape hatch and followed Jordan into the outer office. Boucek was sitting straight up in one of his comfy chairs. The hem of his unbuttoned suit coat was tucked beneath him so that it wouldn't rise up in the back and give his shoulders an uneven line, although there was no one else in the room to appreciate his appearance. His sartorial grandeur was compromised, however, by the exhaustion I saw in his eyes.

"Mr. Taylor, Mr. Fredericks," he said.

He didn't stand and offer his hand, so we didn't stoop and offer ours. Nor did he propose that we share a drink. I could have used one. Freddie, whose own eyes were not nearly as shiny as they had been earlier in the day, probably would have accepted one as well.

"I apologize for bringing you here today," Boucek said. "Of spiriting you up the back passage as if I were afraid to be seen with you. I realize it demonstrates a certain lack of trust on my part that you do not deserve. In your previous dealings with me, as well as your dealings with those acquaintances we share, you have proven yourselves time and again to be the souls of discretion. However, you have both voiced your disapproval of the way I have handled the past kidnappings and I have concluded that I would feel more comfortable if I stressed once more, in person, that you have an obligation to remain silent regarding those activities involving me and my clients."

"You're not going to threaten us again, are you?" I asked.

"You are both aware of the formidable powers I can bring to bear."

"We are." I turned toward Freddie. "Aren't we?"

"Charles," he said. "What the fuck, man?"

"Events have transpired recently that—Ms. Jordan," Boucek said. "If you please."

Jordan gestured at a Chesterfield across from Boucek. We sat; a low coffee table between us. It might have been the most comfortable sofa I had ever parked my fanny on.

Jordan perched on the edge of a stuffed chair where she could watch both Freddie and me and Boucek at the same time. She was as colorful as storyteller as Freddie:

Tracy Burrell had always been a rebellious, defiant child, or so her father claimed.

"I raised her to be independent," he said. "I raised her to be fearless. I raised her to stand up for the things she believed in. That's what fathers are supposed to do. Am I right? But goddamn, I didn't think she'd actually do it."

David Burrell had been angry at his daughter ever since she blew off a job working for his real estate development firm and instead became an advocate and lobbyist for Humans for Human Rights, a non-partisan non-profit that investigated and exposed human rights violations. There were several organizations beneath the HHR umbrella. One represented immigrants and refugees seeking asylum, which Burrell despised even though several construction companies he controlled had been fined for hiring undocumented workers. He tolerated another that advocated for laws protecting women from human trafficking, sexual assault, domestic violence, and sexual harassment in the workplace was acceptable as long as they didn't go too far. Tracy worked mostly with the latter from offices located on University Avenue between Marion and Rice Streets in St. Paul, down the road from the Minnesota State Capitol building.

"Every time I'd see her, I'd offer her a job," Burrell said. "She could make a good living working for me, I'd tell her;

maybe step into my shoes one day. But oh no, that's not going to change the world. I figured one day, she'd get tired of tilting at windmills, but oh no. The only good thing about what happened, maybe now she'll listen to me."

What happened was that late yesterday afternoon, Tracy Burrell was assaulted in broad daylight in Little Mekong, a neighborhood located just west of her office building where many Southeast Asian restaurants, businesses and cultural entities congregated.

Ms. Burrell lived on the Green Line, the high-speed train that ran down the center of University from downtown St. Paul to downtown Minneapolis. It was her habit to board the train at the station near her apartment in Prospect Park and ride it to the station nearest her office unless she had appointments scheduled that required a car to reach. It was also her habit, since she hated to cook just for herself, to grab takeout on her way home. More often than not, this meant patronizing one of the many Thai, Vietnamese or Chinese restaurants in Little Mekong.

Her favorite was Pattaya City Deli where she nearly always ordered shrimp pad see ew with rice noodles. The main entrance to Pattaya City was inside a narrow passageway between two other businesses you couldn't see from University Avenue. Unless you were a dedicated foodie, you might not even know that the restaurant was there.

Ms. Burrell went to Pattaya City and ordered her dinner with the expectation that afterward she would walk to the Western Avenue Station and take the Green Line home. However, when she stepped out of the deli into the passageway, a man seized her from behind. He wrapped his left hand around her mouth, pulled her close against him, and attempted to inject her with a hypodermic syringe held in his right hand.

"Hypodermic syringe?" Freddie said.

"Yes," Jordan said.

"Is she sure?"

131

"Most of our information is coming to us through second-hand sources. We cannot be confident of specific details."

"What happened?" I asked.

Jordan resumed her story.

Ms. Burrell not only advocated in favor of punishment for those who would commit violence toward women, she practiced it over and over again at a gym near the University of Minnesota. According to sources, she dropped her bag and her food the moment she felt her attacker's hands on her. Before they even hit the ground, she spun inside the attacker's embrace and drove her elbow deep into his rib cage. Ms. Burrell followed up by punching him in the groin at least three times. The attacker released her and doubled over, dropping the syringe.

She used the opportunity to escape down the narrow corridor toward University Avenue. However, a second man appeared at the mouth of the passageway to block her path. He held a knife in his hand. He said "Don't make me hurt you." Ms. Burrell ignored both the knife and the threat. Instead, she lowered her shoulder and launched herself against his chest. He fell backward out of the passageway onto the sidewalk, collapsing in front of a trio of young women. Because she was startled, one of the women began to scream.

Ms. Burrell lost her balance yet managed to regain it again without falling herself. She neither called for help nor halted to explain herself. Rather, she continued to run in a straight line across University Avenue. Cars were forced to slam on their brakes to avoid hitting her; it was the height of rush hour, after all.

Unfortunately, she tripped on the curb of the Green Line's track bed in the center of the avenue. This time, she did lose her footing. Her momentum sent her sprawling across the rails in front of the train. The driver was forced to initiate a panic stop, engaging all four of the train's braking systems at once. The high-piercing screeching sound was nearly deafening. Passengers of the train were jerked and jolted forward. Some fell out of their seats. Most of those who were standing fell on their faces. There were many minor injuries.

At the last possible moment, Ms. Burrell was able to roll herself off the rails and under the black chains of the fence that separated the westbound train tracks from the eastbound. She managed to regain her feet and run again, this time pausing until traffic was clear before completing her trek across University.

There she stopped. Her first thought was to call the police, only her cell phone was in her bag in the narrow passageway across the street. She didn't need to worry, however. By then, several St. Paul Police vehicles were on the scene. The officers surrounded the train and fanned out on both sides of University. Several witnesses pointed at Ms. Burrell.

The first officer to reach her shook Ms. Burrell by the shoulders and asked, "What the hell did you do?"

Explanations were made, and the officer became less accusatory, but just barely. The trio of young women had been able to verify that a man had fallen directly in front of them, yet they could not testify that he had a knife or that he had actually threatened Ms. Burrell. In any case, he was long gone by then. Nor had they seen anyone else in the passageway. The hypodermic syringe that Ms. Burrell claimed had fallen from her assailant's hand could not be found. No other witnesses came forward to corroborate her story.

By then several members of the media had arrived, along with a squadron of ambulances and an army of EMTs, to document the light rail crash, the word "crash" being much more colorful than stoppage. One of the reporters recognized Ms. Burrell and knew of her work. He began to interview her. She related her story clearly and without hesitation. This caused the police officers, who had been seriously contemplating taking the young woman into custody for interfering with public transportation, to reconsider their position. Her description of the events soon became the accepted narrative, adopted by the media and the authorities.

Both daily newspapers, and all four local TV news programs, reported that an official investigation was opened by the St. Paul Police Department into the violent assault of a young woman who had dedicated her professional life to combating violent assaults against women. We don't know if the authorities considered the incident to be an attempted kidnapping. We do know the FBI has not yet been contacted.

Burrell was grateful for that but only up to a point.

"You know how it works," he said. "As soon as the investigation starts petering out, the media will start looking at me, wondering out loud if the controversy over one of one my building projects might not have instigated the attack on my little girl. Then they'll start guessing which project it might be. We can't have this. We need to make this go away."

"You said you can't guarantee specific details. Yet you quote Burrell's words..."

I had directed my remarks at Jordan, yet it was Boucek who answered.

"We spoke to him less than an hour ago," he said. "He's concerned that all of this publicity might cause someone to take a closer look at some of his projects."

"He's one of your clients?"

"Yes."

"Long-time client?"

"Yes."

"Then it is your people who are being targeted."

"That has not been proven."

"Did you tell Burrell about the other kidnappings?"

"No."

"Even though the attack on his daughter was probably a kidnapping attempt gone awry?"

"That hasn't been proven, either."

Freddie stood abruptly and moved away from the Chesterfield. I thought he might have been heading for the bar. Instead, he stepped behind the sofa, putting more distance and obstacles between him and Boucek. He thrust his hands into his pockets and sighed dramatically. Boucek pretended not to notice.

"I brought you here for a number of reasons," Boucek said. "The first was to remind you that the previous kidnappings are no one's business but ours. The second was to invite you to determine if the incident involving Ms. Burrell was, in fact, another event orchestrated by the Express Kidnappers or an isolated incident. And finally, I'm offering you the opportunity to prove that my client roster has been specifically targeted or that these kidnappings are part of a grander scheme that has only a tangential connection to me personally and professionally."

"Prove to who?" Freddie said.

"Whom, prove to whom." Jordan spoke without emotion from her perch on the stuffed chair. Freddie's glare made her change her tone, though. "I apologize," she added.

"You were employed by the St. Paul Police Department," Boucek said. "You still have contacts there, do you not?"

"One or two," I said. One being Anne Scalasi, my former partner when I worked homicide, who was now an Assistant Chief currently in command of Family and Sexual Violence, Property Crimes, Homicide and Robbery, Youth Services, Special Investigations, Gangs, Narcotics and Vice, and the Safe Streets Task Force. Only we had two standing agreements between us. The first was that she wouldn't use police department resources to assist me in my investigations. The second was that we wouldn't resume sleeping together again until after her divorce was final.

"Find out what St. Paul knows," Boucek said. "Add it to what we know."

"Then what?" I asked.

"I'm not sure I understand your question," Boucek said.

"Let's say for argument's sake, that Freddie and I are able to link the attack on Tracy Burrell to the kidnappings of Henrietta Weller and Carole Robey. Let's say we're also able to link them directly to your firm. Then what?"

"If the evidence is conclusive and sufficient in quality and quantity to lead to the actual arrest and incarceration of the perpetrators..."

"Charles."

"Gentlemen, it had become increasingly clear that the only way to stop these men is to catch them."

"That's right," Freddie said.

"So, catch them."

His words caught me by surprise. It took a few beats before I was able to come up with a response.

"Excuse me, what?" I asked.

Freddie, on the other hand, was quicker on the uptake.

"You want us to arrest the bad people?" he asked.

"If we can bring these criminals to justice, we'll be able to control the narrative," Boucek said. "Burrell's bad publicity will become good publicity. Instead of capitulation, Congresswoman Abigail Hudson and Brian Haskins' stories will become examples of selfless heroism."

"We're private investigators, not law enforcement," I said. "We don't catch criminals. We can't arrest anybody."

"Law enforcement agencies partner with private investigators quite often."

"Yeah, but usually they know about it up front."

"Identify the criminals to the satisfaction of law enforcement and let law enforcement do the rest."

"I have an idea," Freddie said. "Why don't we eliminate the middleman? You wanna keep all this quiet or at least make your clients look good if it gets out, I get that. So whaddya say we load the three women into a limo, drive them up to the field office in Brooklyn Center, and set them down in front of a special agent to tell their stories. No media. No local cops. You don't think the FBI can keep a secret?"

"I believe that course of action is premature at best," Boucek said.

"Bullshit."

"Mr. Fredericks, if your conscience forbids you from accepting this assignment, I will entrust it to someone else."

"Sounds like a plan to me." Freddie moved toward the door. "You comin'?"

I held up an index finger to keep him in place, but spoke to Boucek.

"I remember an offer we made to Henrietta Weller about finding the people who threw her in that dumpster. You took it off the table. Are you telling me it's back on?"

"Yes," Boucek said.

"Taylor, c'mon," Freddie said.

"We demand complete access," I said. "We will wish to speak at length with both Carole Robey and Tracy Burrell, as well as Rhett Weller again, and any other of your clients that might provide us with pertinent information. We will be as discreet as possible, but our interviews will require that we reveal facts you might want hidden."

"No names," Boucek said.

"No names. Also, if the kidnappers are targeting your client roster, that would suggest someone from inside your organization is likely supplying the intel. Will you allow us to investigate your employees?"

Boucek hesitated before he replied "Within reason."

"Let me put it to you this way," I said. "We will do what we think is best. If you say no to us just once, we'll walk. If something goes sideways"—I was pointing at him now—"I'll call the FBI, and I won't give a fuck what it costs you or me."

Boucek hesitated again.

"I understand," he said.

"I don't," Freddie said. "You mind if me and my partner talk privately?"

"You can use my office," Boucek said.

Freddie moved to Boucek's inner office. I rose from the Chesterfield and followed him. Once inside, he closed the door and grinned.

"What?" I asked.

"Pointing your finger at Charles Boucek like you were going to shoot him, fuckin'-A, man."

"I wanted him to know we meant business."

Freddie threw a thumb at the maple door.

"It'd be easy, man," he said. "We just walk out the door and keep goin'."

"I get that you're pissed off about all this, Freddie. So am I. You want to know what pisses me off more? They threw Rhett Weller into a dumpster. They caved your head with a tree branch. We can't let that slide, can we? They—whoever they are—they gotta pay for that, don't you think?"

"What I think is that sooner or later, it's all gonna go to shit, and when it does, we're the ones gonna be left holdin' the bag. You honestly think Boucek's got our backs? Way he's been sneakin' us in and outta here? Hiding us from his own people? C'mon."

"We'll protect ourselves. Document everything. You know how it works."

"We have other clients, too. I hardly got to the background checks this afternoon because the phone kept ringing."

"I'll take lead on this case and only bring you in when I need backup."

"Needin' backup is one of the things that's got me worried."

As if to prove his point, Freddie brought his hand to the back of his head and massaged it.

"I hear you, Freddie," I said. "Look—we're partners, right? If you say we should pass this up, then we'll pass and no hard feelings. We'll go back inside and tell Boucek to find someone else. He'll stop sending business our way, which is fine. He's never been a big part of our income, anyway. Like you say, it's not like we don't have work. All those backgrounds checks for Sackett."

"Yeah, what fun. Dammit, Holland. I'm the one says we

should never turn down a job, but man..." Freddie thought about it for a few beats. "Just promise me...Nah, man, you don't need to promise me anything. I'm in. I gotta tell ya though, things start goin' bad—I'm gonna put the FBI's Special Agent in Charge, what's her name? I'm gonna put her phone number on my contact list and first sign of disaster, I'm the one who's gonna be droppin' a dime, not you."

"That is so archaic, you know—drop a dime."

"What are you talkin' about?"

"When was the last time you saw a pay phone? Besides, when we were kids, it cost at least a quarter."

Boucek's phone rang while we were in his inner office. It was answered by the second ring. When we stepped back into the outer office, we could hear Representative Hudson's voice over the speakerphone set on a table near where Boucek was standing.

"You know I can't become involved in any of this," she said.

Boucek's head came up when we entered the room. He was staring at Freddie and me when he said, "There's no reason why you should. There is no connection whatsoever between Tracy Burrell and Henrietta."

"I don't believe that, and neither do you. If the media should put them together—all I need is for Henrietta to revert to her rebellious self."

"I assure you, Abby, the situation is under control."

"I hope so. If it's not—Charles, you know what will happen. If this gets out, I'll be forced to sever relations with your firm. I'll be forced to publicly denounce you; perhaps even ask for a federal investigation to prove that I'm not complicit in any of this."

"I understand."

"Please don't make me do that. It would kill me if I had to do that."

"I understand."

"Is Bruce Gillard aware of what...?"

"He knows nothing."

"Perhaps he should know. He does control a portion of my estate."

"He controls nothing. He merely monitors..."

"Charles, you're not listening."

Boucek kept staring at us.

"That's a conversation for another time," he said.

Freddie was right, I told myself. If Boucek was willing to throw his executive VP under a bus, he certainly wouldn't hesitate to do the same to us. The difference, of course, is that Gillard would never see it coming. We would.

"I wish I was there with you," Representative Hudson said. "Or that you were here with me."

Boucek turned his head as if he were suddenly embarrassed.

"I wish that, too," he said.

"I have a thing tonight, but I should be home by ten. Will you call me later?"

"Yes."

"Goodnight, Charles."

"Goodnight, Abigail."

Boucek ended the call.

"You heard," he said.

He didn't ask exactly what we heard, so I took a chance.

"The congresswoman isn't involved," I said.

"Do you accept the assignment?"

"We expect you to complete and sign our standard contract."

"Yes," Freddie said.

"Of course." Boucek gestured at Jordan. "Ms. Jordan will serve as my liaison. She will provide you with whatever you require."

I nodded at Jordan. She did not nod back. Instead, she remained silent and still while seated on the edge of her stuffed chair, her hands folded in her lap.

CHAPTER NINETEEN

David Helin was pleased I had solved his problem so quickly. He said as much in the first of three voicemails that we heard when we returned to the office, each hinting at a different assignment that he wanted us to complete for his law firm as soon as possible. I told him when I returned his calls that, due to a prior commitment, I'd have to pass them off to Freddie. Helin was fine with that. He said the jobs probably required a lot of computer work and he knew that Freddie's skills were superior to mine.

"Vastly superior the man said," Freddie reminded me.

"We're in competition now, are we?"

"Nah, man. I've always figured you were, you know, the junior partner."

"Always?"

"Ever since we named the place Fredericks and Taylor Private Investigations, anyway."

"You won a frickin' coin toss."

"You've been sulking about it ever since, too. 'Kay, I got Helin and the others. What you got?"

"Carole Robey first, I think, followed by Tracy Burrell, assuming the police aren't hanging all over her. Then Rhett Weller, again. After that, we'll compare notes; see if we can find a common denominator that'll lead us to the kidnappers."

"You mean besides Boucek?"

"Yeah, besides Boucek. You know, he might be right. Could be the kidnappers going after the children of three of his clients is just a coincidence. Maybe they've snatched a dozen more and no one's heard about it."

"Wanna bet?"

"No."

"Too bad. I was gonna offer you another coin toss."

Carole Robey couldn't remain still. She'd stand behind her desk, pace the half-dozen steps of space she had back there, sit, stand again, and repeat the process. The door to her office was wide open, and she'd watch intently whenever someone walked past.

I hadn't had any experience questioning kidnapping victims yet more than my share of interviewing women who'd been sexually assaulted. I decided my best course of action was to let her talk.

"My problem is that I have no memory of what happened to me," Carole said. "Almost none. I remember walking. I remember someone grabbing me from behind and putting their hand over my mouth to muffle my screams. I remember being pushed to the ground and I remember feeling a—a pinprick. No, not a pinprick. Something like a, a…"

"A shot in a doctor's office?" I asked. "Like someone stuck a needle in your arm?"

"Yes, yes. That's exactly right, except it wasn't my arm. It was my neck." Carole rubbed a spot between her collarbone and her throat. "Right here. Next thing I remember is waking up on a bench in Jordan Park—I've never been there before, didn't even know where it was—and a police officer shaking me and saying 'Miss, miss, you can't be here.' That's all I remember. In my nightmares, I hear shouting, only I don't recognize the voices, and I hear myself chanting, 'Help me, help me,' but no one does.

"Sometimes I'll be walking—not along the river; I'll never do that again. I'll be walking down the street, walking to my apartment, walking down the corridor of the office building, and I'll stop. Freeze in place. My breathing will become labored and my heart will start beating a hundred times a second and my hands will shake and I can't—I won't be able to move and then it stops and I'm left wondering what the hell just happened and why did it happen and—and I feel if I could only remember, but I can't.

"I know it's affecting my work. I'm a business analyst. I'm supposed to find technological solutions for all of our client's cost of labor problems, yet when I sit in the meetings, I don't hear a word they're telling me.

"I want to tell people what happened, but what would I say? I was walking along the river in St. Paul and then I woke up on a park bench in North Minneapolis and I have no memory of what happened in between only now I no longer trust the people around me and I don't feel respected by those I've known my entire life and I don't feel safe?

"People, my family—they say that nothing bad happened to me. I wasn't raped, I wasn't tortured or beaten, I wasn't humiliated—how can you humiliate someone who's unconscious? So, I should be able to get over it. And I say yeah, yeah, I should be able to get over it only I can't.

"Something else. I feel guilty as if somehow this was my fault because—because I was walking after work, which I always do to get some exercise and unwind. Where I was walking—Mississippi Boulevard in St. Paul near the Shriners Hospital for Children. Do you know the area?"

"Yes."

"It's not isolated. There are plenty of people walking and jogging and biking and skating and driving. It was still daylight. Why didn't I see them? Why didn't I hear them coming? Why didn't I fight back? Why didn't I—it wasn't my fault. I know I'm not responsible for what those people did to me. Yet I feel guilty. And confused. I'm so—it's been sixteen days, and I'm just as confused as I was when I woke up on that park bench, the cop wondering if I was an alcoholic or a drug addict. I've been tempted to do both since this happened, too, have a drink, do a line, except I figured that would only make things worse. I've been tempted to—there are men who would love to spend time with me. Do you know what I mean by spending time?"

"Yes."

"I've never been that woman, though. I don't even know why I've been thinking about these things."

"Post-traumatic stress disorder," I said.

"Is that what it is? How can that be what it is? I don't remember any stress. I'm not stupid, Mr. Taylor. I know I should talk to someone, get professional help. God, I hate the sound of that. It sounds like I'm crazy—get professional help. My family, though, my uncle, they're like no, no, no. They don't even want me to talk to them. Don't make a big deal out of it, they say. It'll be bad for business. Bad for my uncle, what with his legal problems. Half of my family makes its living working for my uncle. More than half. I did, too, up until I earned my BSB from Carlson…

"I'm shocked my uncle even sent you here, him and that man Charles Boucek, scary-looking man I met for the first time standing next to my uncle in the interview room at the police station nodding his head while my uncle said 'Don't talk, don't talk, don't talk' and who is now saying it's okay to talk. At least to you. I don't know what to do. Tell me what to do."

"My advice," I said. "It's not my place to offer you advice, but my advice—make a big deal out of it. Screw your uncle's business and his legal problems. Make a really big deal of it. Carole, what happened to you; maybe you weren't hurt physically, but it's like an earthquake happened in your brain. So, get help. That's why it's there. Have a good long talk with a caring professional. That alone might make you feel better. If it doesn't, well, at least it'll be a first step in the healing process."

"Do you know anyone?"

"As a matter of fact, I do. From when I worked with the police department."

I listed a couple of names. Carole sat behind her desk and wrote them down.

"Should I start with you, Mr. Taylor?" she asked. "Talking to you?"

"If you like."

"What do you want to know?"

CHAPTER TWENTY

Carole and I spoke for a long time. It was well past business hours when we finished, and I walked her to her car. After she unlocked it, she turned toward me.

"Mr. Taylor," she said.

"Holland. Or just Taylor. Most people call me Taylor."

"Taylor. I know you didn't come here to make me feel good, but I do. Talking like we did make me feel better than I have since—since it all started."

"Call one of the numbers I gave you. Make it permanent."

"I will. Thank you." Carole kissed my cheek and brushed it with her hand to remove the lipstick she left there.

"Thank you," she said again.

She climbed into her car and drove away. I watched her go.

I had to admit that I was feeling pretty good myself.

I kept feeling pretty good until I reached my apartment. As I unlocked my door, I saw Amanda Wedemeyer bounding up the stairs with a man behind her who was trying to keep up and doing a poor job of it. I knew that the man was her father and suddenly I felt—jealousy? No, it couldn't be that.

"Taylor," Amanda said.

"Ms. Wedemeyer."

"I like it when you call me Ms. It makes me feel older. This is my father."

"Hey," I said and gave him a chin nod.

He nodded back. He was shorter than I was, which I liked, and carried about twenty more pounds, which I liked even more, and his hair was thinning on top which caused me to smile brightly.

I knew that Douglas Wedemeyer had taken no steps to alter the court order granting sole custody of their daughter to his ex-wife since the night I found Amanda curled up on my sofa. Of course, I didn't think he would until he was discharged from the halfway house, and I knew that wouldn't be for the better part of two months. I also knew that he had been allowed to visit Amanda at least twice since then. I didn't know that he had been permitted to roam freely with her, though.

"Can I show him Ogilvy?" Amanda asked. "I told everyone about Ogilvy, but no one believed me."

"If it's no trouble," Wedemeyer said.

"No trouble at all. Although, what's not to believe?"

"Sometimes children exaggerate."

"Less than adults, I think."

I unlocked the door and propped it open as I always did when Amanda was there. I turned on all the lights and drifted to my kitchen.

"Can I offer you anything?" I asked. "Mandy? Root beer?"

Wedemeyer answered for her—"No thank you. We won't be here that long."

Amanda went to the center of the living room, knelt on the floor, and called "Ogilvy." Wedemeyer walked three steps into the apartment and not an inch more. He stood with his hands on his hips as if he were a restaurant patron waiting for the maître d' to escort him to a table.

"Ogilvy," Amanda said again.

The rabbit came running, tried to stop, and slid across the hardwood floor right into the girl's lap.

"He's so cute," she squealed.

"Oh." Wedemeyer shrugged as if it was the fifth rabbit he had seen that day and the least interesting. "So, there he is."

Amanda waved her hand above his head.

"Ogilvy, beg," she said.

The rabbit didn't move.

"Ogilvy, beg."

Nothing.

"Beg Ogilvy."

Still nothing.

"It's okay, Amanda," Wedemeyer said.

"No, it's not," she said. "Ogilvy, I told people you could do tricks. You're making me look bad."

"It's all right."

I went to the refrigerator; found a floret of broccoli from a takeout stir-fry I had left over, and gave it to the girl.

"Try this," I said.

Amanda held it over Ogilvy's head. Before she could continue with the trick, however, Wedemeyer said "What do you say?"

Amanda's entire body tensed. She spoke between clenched teeth.

"Thank you, Taylor."

"Mr. Taylor," Wedemeyer said.

"Taylor is my friend. I don't have to call him mister." Her head jerked up and her eyes caught mine. "Do I?"

"Never," I said.

"Amanda, I think it's time to leave."

"Not yet," she said. "Beg."

Ogilvy stood on his hind legs and held his front paws forward, waving them a bit to maintain his balance.

Amanda used the floret to draw a circle in the air.

"Roll over."

The rabbit rolled over.

She set the floret on the floor.

"Play dead."

The rabbit flopped on his side and sprawled out in front of her.

"See," she said. "I told you he could do tricks, can't you Ogilvy?"

Ogilvy hopped to his feet, and Amanda fed him the broccoli out of the palm of her hand.

By then, Claire had joined us.

"There you are," she said. "I was getting worried."

"Why?" Wedemeyer asked.

Claire ignored him.

"Ms. Wedemeyer." I emphasized the Ms. "I let your daughter play with the rabbit, again. I hope you don't mind."

"Of course not. So, Amanda, did you have fun at your grandmother's house?"

"One of my cousins pushed me down because I play soccer better than he does. Other than that..."

"The boy was disciplined," Wedemeyer said.

"They told him not to do it again, if that's what you mean. On the other hand, they called me a hot-headed little bitch because I pushed him back." She hugged the rabbit. "Ogilvy, I have to do my homework. I'll see you soon."

She released the rabbit, stood, and made for the door. As she passed me, she said, "Thanks, Taylor."

"Anytime, kid."

She was halfway across the landing when Claire said. "You called my daughter a bitch?"

"I didn't," Wedemeyer said. "My brother, you know my brother. It was his son that did the pushing. A fight was about to break out and he stopped it. My nephew was going to retaliate after Amanda pushed him and my brother stopped it."

"Lucky for your nephew."

Wedemeyer smiled. He had one of those smiles that made everyone else want to smile, too. I was really starting to hate this guy.

"She's a fierce little thing, isn't she?" he said. "I like what you've done with her. She's wonderful. Listen, I'm sorry. I'm sorry Amanda is so good at sports that she embarrassed all of her boy cousins. But the girl cousins love her. And the boys will come around, too, when they get to know her like we do. I'm sorry, Mr. Taylor, if I seemed rude before. But you really shouldn't interfere when a man is trying to teach his daughter good manners."

"Is that what you were doing? I thought you were trying to embarrass her in front of me."

"I'm sorry if it seemed that way. I wouldn't hurt Amanda to save my life. We're just—I'm just going through a period of adjustment. And I am sorry if I seem like the ass you take me for. It'll get better. I promise. I need to go now. They're pretty strict at the halfway house. It's good to meet you, Mr. Taylor."

"Taylor. Just Taylor."

"Taylor. Claire, a great pleasure to see you as always. I'll call in a couple of days. Goodnight."

Wedemeyer stepped out the door, caught the staircase, and hopped down the steps as if he was enjoying the trip. Neither Claire nor I said a word until we knew he was out the door and down the street.

"So," I said. "That's your ex-husband."

"I keep trying to remember him the way he was when we first met, when I fell in love with him, only I can't. I get glimpses sometimes when he smiles and then...Oh, Taylor. Is this going to be my life from now on? Even if I retain sole custody, and my lawyer is convinced I will, he's still going to be given visitation. I'm still going to have to deal with this guy and his lousy family."

"You don't strike me as a woman who'd let some jerk screw up her life."

"Yet I did."

"You're letting him spend unsupervised time with Amanda?"

"On advice of counsel. There's no reason to change the court order if there's no reason to change the court order, if you get my meaning."

"I do."

"My greatest concern is Mandy. I feel as though I'm throwing her to the wolves."

"It'll be okay. You'll see."

I hugged her then, which was a first for me. If there was any hugging to be done in the past, it had always been Claire who initiated it. We were standing inside my open doorway, so Amanda got a good view of us when she opened her own door across the landing.

"What are you doing?" she asked.

I felt Claire tense in my arms, yet she did not pull away. I probably should have stopped, too, only I didn't.

"I'm hugging your mother because she's feeling a little sad," I said.

Amanda smiled as brightly as I had ever seen her.

"I'm feeling a little sad, too," she said. "Can I have a hug?"

I waved her forward. She crossed the landing in a hurry. I had just released her mother in time to catch her in my arms.

"My cousins are idiots," she said. "I can't believe I'm stuck with them. My father—if he thinks he's going to teach me good manners all over again...It nearly killed me the first time." She lifted her head off my chest and glared at her mother. "Well, it did."

Claire smoothed her daughter's hair while I continued to hug her.

"Taylor said it's all going to work out and I'm going to hold him to that," she said.

"You mean Mr. Taylor? Geez."

CHAPTER TWENTY-ONE

Prospect Park was easily the most desirable neighborhood located on the Green Line. It had plenty of Colonial Revival and Queen Ann-style homes, moneyed residents, a low crime rate and the iconic Prospect Park Water Tower, which a lot of people argue is the highest point in the City of Minneapolis. Tracy Burrell lived in an apartment building not far from the tower constructed to resemble the surrounding century-old castle yet didn't.

I parked on the street in front of the building and walked the narrow driveway to the asphalt lot in back. There were spaces for two dozen cars, less than a third of them filled. The lot was surrounded on three sides by a wooden privacy fence; the second floor of several single-family houses peeked over the top.

It was just past noon, and there was very little traffic meandering through the neighborhood. I didn't think it would get much heavier at any given time, day or night. It made me conclude if I was going to take Tracy, this was the place I would have taken her from, either first thing in the morning or when she arrived home from work like they had done with Henrietta Weller. There was a possibility someone glancing out of a window in the surrounding houses or the apartment building might catch sight of me, only I figured the chances of getting caught were a helluva lot less than snatching her off what might have been the busiest street in St. Paul at the height of rush hour.

Or grabbing Carole Robey off a well-traveled boulevard along the Mississippi River.

What were the kidnappers thinking? I wondered. Did they want to get caught?

I returned to the front of the building, entered the foyer, and used the telephone that I found attached to the wall to call Apt. 305. The phone was answered after three rings. A woman's voice said, "Yes?" She could have asked, "Who is this?" and it would have sounded the same.

"Holland Taylor to see Tracy Burrell," I said.

"Who sent you?"

"Charles Boucek, an associate of David Burrell."

"What is the name of Boucek's secretary?"

"His personal assistant is Ms. Jordan"—I couldn't bring myself to think of her as a mere secretary.

"What is her first name?"

"I don't know."

"It's Quinn. Her friends call her Q. If I know that, why don't you?"

"Because I'm not her friend, merely an acquaintance," I said.

At the same time, I wondered why Jordan, first name Quinn, aka Q, hadn't mentioned Tracy was her friend when she recited the long story of what happened to her. Was it that easy to divorce her personal feelings from the facts at hand? Was she that much like her employer?

I waited for Tracy to buzz me up. When that didn't happen, I said, "If you like, I could contact Ms. Jordan and have her call you to verify my identity. If it would make you feel more comfortable, I could ask her to come over and hang around while we talk."

"What do you want to talk about?"

"This is where the conversation becomes complicated," I said.

There was another long pause. Her reluctance to speak with me didn't come as a surprise. When she was first contacted,

Tracy said she couldn't think of a single reason why she should spend time with a private investigator. We needed her father to call at Boucek's urging to beg her to "At least talk to the man. For me?" Finally, the woman said, "I guess it'll be all right. Come on up."

The sound of a buzzer releasing the door lock quickly followed. I opened the door before it ceased. There was an elevator, except I didn't bother with it, climbing the stairs to the third floor instead. The even number apartments were on the right side of the corridor and the odd numbers were on the left. Tracy's was in the exact center. I knocked on the door. I was surprised by how long it took for her to respond.

"Mr. Taylor?" she asked behind the door.

"Yes."

"Hold your ID up to the peephole, please."

I did as she requested.

The door opened abruptly, yet only a few inches; the chain was still attached. Tracy stared out at me through the crack.

"I apologize for intruding on you," I said.

"Then why are you?"

"I was hired to help find the men who assaulted you."

"The police are doing that."

"Only until a crime is committed that they rate as a higher priority and then you'll become a cold case, something they'll pursue when they have the time."

Tracy shut the door, and I thought—that went well. A moment later, though, I heard the chain being removed, and the door opened again, this time wide enough for me to pass though. I did. Tracy backed away, watching me as I approached, as if she was afraid that I would bum-rush her.

"It's kind of you to see me," I said.

"Close the door," she said.

I did.

"Lock it."

I did.

As I stepped deeper into the apartment, Tracy stepped further away, making sure there was plenty of distance between us. She was wearing a gray form-fitting business dress with a high collar beneath a black jacket with matching gray pinstripes and black pumps. Her hair was brown; it fell to her shoulders. Her eyes were the same color; they looked as though they had never read the word "sleep." I smiled at her, yet she didn't smile back.

Glancing around the apartment, I couldn't help but notice all the plants that were stacked on tables and racks in front of her windows. I recognized one.

"You keep gardenias indoors?" I asked. "That takes ambition."

"Why do you say that?"

"You need a sunny window yet can't let the plant stay in the sun all day. You need to keep the humidity around fifty, sixty percent. You must avoid drafts. Plus, you don't want to move them around because they don't like to be moved around."

"Do you keep plants?"

"I know a woman who keeps plants."

Tracy took a deep breath.

"I'm behaving irrationally, I know," she said.

"I don't think so."

"I've become very suspicious of just about everything recently. I'm Tracy Burrell, by the way." She held her hand for me to shake. Yet it was like someone with an extreme fear of heights peering over the edge of a cliff—she was doing it to prove that she could.

"Holland Taylor."

I shook her hand and released it quickly. Tracy seemed relieved.

"What you said about becoming a cold case resonates with me," she said. "What I do—do you know what I do? For the HHR?"

"Yes."

"I'm well aware police departments consider rape to be a

low priority crime. An officer once told me to my face that they didn't like to waste resources on rape investigations because the conviction rates were so low; fewer than ten percent of all rape cases result in a conviction. That's because the police refuse to allocate those resources. The Minnesota *Star Tribune* discovered that the police in this state don't even bother to assign an investigator to a quarter of the rape cases that are reported to them. Half the time, they don't interview potential witnesses. In a third, they don't even interview the victim. Seventy-five percent of the cases won't be forwarded to prosecutors. So, of course the conviction rate is low.

"That doesn't even begin to address the way police treat victims, either; the mocking, insulting, harassing attitudes; the undue skepticism. Do you know how many rape kits go untested in this State? Thousands. I wasn't raped, of course. I was harassed. That's what an officer told me after I explained what had happened. He was incredulous. 'You stopped a high-speed train because you were harassed?' he said. How dare I?"

"I know," I said.

"Do you?"

"I'm ashamed to admit that when I was a kid starting out with the St. Paul Police Department, I believed only half of the stories rape victims told me. It took a few years before I realized I was an idiot. That ninety-eight percent of the women were telling the truth. It haunts me even now knowing that there were so many I could have helped that I didn't, so many I failed because—because of what? Gender bias? That's the polite way of saying I was a misogynist asshole."

"What changed your mind?"

"Marriage, I guess. Having a daughter, I guess."

"The train is what made it a story," Tracy said. "Me stopping the train. If I hadn't, there wouldn't have been any media coverage; there wouldn't even be the appearance of a police investigation. Should I tell you what my father said? If anyone on the train decides to sue, I'm on my own. Thanks, Dad. Can I offer you something, Holland? I don't have much alcohol in the apartment, just wine."

"I'm good."

"Coffee? I've been subsisting solely on coffee for the past two days."

"I've never turned down a cup of coffee in my life."

Tracy went to her kitchen and poured two mugs, both adorned with wildflowers. She gave me one. Afterward we sat; her on the sofa and me in a chair across from her.

"Why are you here, Holland?" Tracy asked. "What do you hope to accomplish? My father was—vague."

"I'm looking for information about you and what happened to you. As much as I can get."

"Why?"

"Hang on to yourself, Tracy."

She set her coffee mug on the table and sat straight.

"We don't believe it was about rape or sexual harassment or anything like that. We believe those men were attempting to kidnap you and hold you for ransom."

"Why do you believe that?"

"Because it's happened at least twice before that we're aware of."

"Jesus, Holland. Jesus. You tell me that?" Tracy was on her feet and moving through the apartment as if she was looking for a safe place to hide. "I can't get out of the house as it is. I'm not joking. Look at me. Look at me, Holland. I've been dressed for work since seven-thirty this morning, yet I can't get out the damn door. I can't even force myself to open the door. Now you tell me this? Jesus, help me."

"I know it's hard."

"Oh, you know that, do you? That it's hard? Kidnapping? Why? Why kidnap me? For what?"

"For the money."

"What money? I work for a non-profit."

"Your father's money."

"Oh, yeah? My father's money? God knows he has plenty. Dammit. You're here to protect Daddy's bottom line, aren't you?"

"I don't give a damn about your father, Tracy. I care about you. I care about the women who came before you, and I care about the women who will follow if we don't stop these guys. That won't help you get out your front door, but...Tracy, I was a police officer for a long time, like I said. Once I wised up, I tried the best I could to help women who were hurt by men. I know saying 'I'm sorry' is inadequate. I know promising to get the guy, even those few times when I was able to keep my promise; it didn't seem to make much difference."

"What did?"

"Listening to them. Believing them. Not pretending that I knew how they felt, not minimizing the trauma or, just as bad, making it seem as if the world was coming to an end. Making the vic—I'm sorry. Making the woman understand that she has value that no asshole can ever take from her. That's just a guy talking, though. What do I know?"

"It seems you know a lot. Tell me about the kidnappings."

I did. While I told Rhett Weller's and Carole Robey's stories without using their names, Tracy retrieved her coffee mug and sat across from me again. She was leaning forward and holding the mug with both hands when I finished.

"You want to call the FBI, but they won't let you," Tracy said.

"Apparently, it's not in the best interests of the parties involved."

"You mean the parties who are paying the ransom, not the actual victims."

"Yeah."

"You won't tell me who they are?"

"No."

"Not even if I say pretty please?"

"No."

"In my experience, the only progress that has ever been made for women was made by women who came forward, who insisted on standing up and being counted."

"That's not for me to say. Or you, either, in this case."

"Don't worry, Holland. I would never out a woman. A man, though...What do you want of me?"

"I'm going to ask you a lot of questions, first about what happened to you, and then about your life in general. Afterward, I'll compare your answers to the other women."

"To see if there's a common denominator that made us all victims."

"That's not quite the way I would put it, but yeah."

"All right, Holland. Ask your questions."

"You might want to put on another pot of coffee."

I had my notebook out as well as my phone, making sure I recorded Tracy's remarks as accurately as possible.

"The man who grabbed me from behind was Asian," she said. "He seemed to be around my height and fat. No, not fat. Stocky. I have a friend who's stocky and his build reminds me of my friend. I didn't see his face very well. It was roundish. Beyond that—I doubt I could identify him in a lineup. I told the police this, too. I was never taught the difference between someone from China, Vietnam, Korea, Japan; any of the Southeast Asian countries. How American of me."

"I was told you need to look at the eyes."

"He was wearing sunglasses."

"Okay."

"The African-American man was tallish. Taller than me, anyway, and I'm five-eight. He had a mustache and a goatee." Tracy used the fingers of one hand to draw them on her own mouth and chin.

I kept my voice even because I didn't want to excite her.

"Are you sure?" I asked.

Tracy hesitated—maybe she did hear something in my voice—before answering "Yes, I am. It's the same as before, though. I doubt I could recognize him if he...I remember the knife. It was black and double-bladed and the way he held it, I could see that it had four round holes in the hilt."

"It took some courage charging him the way you did."

"All it took was muscle memory. I take self-defense classes along with Q. They teach you how to react if you're attacked. Without thinking about it. Without asking yourself if you're brave. The bravery part comes later when you have time to reflect on what you did. I'm so brave I can't get outside my front door."

"What about the hypodermic syringe?"

"It looked like a regular hypodermic syringe no different than what they use to give you a shot in the doctor's office. It was filled with some kind of knock-out drug, wasn't it?"

"That's our guess."

"I still see the needle just as plain as can be, too."

After finishing with her account of the kidnapping attempt, I asked Tracy questions about her life from the same questionnaire that we had used when we first interviewed Henrietta Weller and later Carole Robey. The coffee pot was empty long before we finished. Afterward, I thanked Tracy for her time. We shook hands again, only this time it didn't seem to faze her.

Tracy walked me to the door and through the door and down the corridor to the staircase. It was a typical Minnesota goodbye—one party announces they have to leave and then we talk for another half hour while we head for the exit.

"So, what happens now?" Tracy asked.

"It's as you said earlier, now we'll match what you told me against what the other women had to say and see if we can find a common denominator."

"Did it ever occur to you that this has nothing to do with us and everything to do with the people paying the ransom?"

"Yes, it has."

"Will you tell me what you find out?"

"Yes."

"In my experience, women who are assaulted nearly always ask the police to keep them informed and yet the police rarely do."

"I will keep you informed."

"Thank you, Holland."

We shook hands again. This time I held on to hers long enough to say, "Look at you."

Tracy didn't look at herself, but at her surroundings. She was standing in the corridor, at the head of the stairs, five doors down from her apartment.

"How 'bout that?" she said.

CHAPTER TWENTY-TWO

Freddie was finishing up a few tasks at his desk when I arrived back in the office. Instead of greeting me he said, "Guess who called today?"

"Denzel Washington. He wants you to return his smile."

"Really? That's the best you got?"

I sat behind my desk so we could shout at each other across the room.

"Give me a minute," I said. "It's been a long day."

"Might git longer. Wink, wink."

"Wink, wink?"

"The person who called—Dr. Alexandra Campbell. Seems she hasn't heard from you for a while. Says every time she tries your cell there's some kinda malfunction; she can't get through."

"What did you tell her?'

"Whaddaya think I told her? I said you was a pathetic excuse for a human bein', and I encouraged her to rescue you from yourself. You know, you were a lot more fun to work with when you and her were together. What happened between you two, anyhow?"

"If you must know, she cheated on me."

"Yeah? So? You guys were friends with benefits, man. The woman can't have more than one friend?"

"I don't mind a woman who's sleeping around as long as

162

she's not sleeping around on me."

"You are so fuckin' narrow minded."

"C'mon."

"Were you exclusive with her? Were you thinkin' of puttin' a ring on it?"

"No, but..."

"But what? If you weren't exclusive with her, why'd you expect 'er to be exclusive with you? Fuckin' fair is fair, man. So what, anyway? She's a nice person. She's fun to be around what I saw of her. Seems to me unless you're ready to take it up a notch with somebody else, you ain't gonna do no better. You ready to take it up a notch?"

For some reason, I flashed on Claire Wedemeyer's brilliant smile.

"No," I said.

"So, give the lady a call, would ya? If nothin' else, do it to protect our professional relationship."

"What are you talking about, professional relationship?"

"Think it's fun comin' in everyday to see your miserable face all the time mopin' around, wonderin' why the whole wide world is pickin' on poor Holland Taylor."

"It's not that bad."

"If you don't call the professor, I'm gonna tell Echo."

"Please, don't do that."

"Not only will she slap you upside your head, she'll start bringin' her single friends 'round, parade 'em through the office. There's this one named Shirley. She has a nice personality, man."

"Alright, alright, I give. God, Freddie, when did you become my fucking mother?"

"Hey, hey, hey—you talk to your momma that way?"

"Not exactly."

"Not exactly. Do it again, I'm gonna tell 'er. I got her number on my contact list."

"I'm surprised you're not giving her daily reports as it is.

Freddie—as I was saying when I walked in..."

"You were saying something?"

"Are you free tonight?"

"Why? You lonely? You wanna go t' the movies; share a bucket of buttered popcorn? Call the professor, Taylor."

"I will call the professor, dammit."

"What about tonight, then?"

"I think a return visit to Dillman's in North Minneapolis is in order."

"You gonna wear your black sports jacket?"

"I thought I might."

CHAPTER TWENTY-THREE

I stepped through the doorway at exactly nine PM as promised and was immediately mugged by a combination of loud music and rowdy voices. Dillman's was exactly as I remembered it, except the Asian was not sitting near the entrance and the black man with the goatee was not chatting up a young woman at the bar. Believe me, I looked.

It was the Asian and the African-American who brought me to Dillman's. The way I had explained it to Freddie in the office, Tracy Burrell was sure that it had been an Asian who attempted to stab her with a hypodermic needle in Little Mekong, and it was a black guy with a goatee and a knife who tried to block her escape. I was excited when I heard the news yet tried not to show it when I interviewed Tracy. First things first, after all. Now...

"Helluva a coincidence, don't you think?" I asked.

"Given the racial makeup of the Twin Cities, no, not so much," Freddie said.

"That an Asian and a brother are working together?"

"You and I work together."

"Yeah, and that's like a frickin' miracle."

I made my way to the bar. I noticed Freddie sitting at a table as I passed, yet he didn't seem to notice me. Instead, he was deeply involved in conversation with the two young professionals I had met earlier, both dressed in clothes that were enticing and loose-fitting at the same time. I decided it was a good thing, him pretending not to notice me, until I had a moment to think about it. What if he wasn't pretending? There was a time, and not so long ago, Freddie's attention to detail would have easily been compromised by the girls, by any girl. Course, that was pre-Echo.

I found an empty spot at the bar. Glynis worked behind it looking exactly as she had the last time I saw her, except that she had swapped her Vikings t-shirt for the Minnesota Wild. She didn't notice me until I called her name. She turned her back to me. I thought I saw her mouth the word "fuck" in the mirror behind her. She spun around and walked slowly toward me.

"What do you want?" she asked.

"Good evening to you, too, Glynis. Jim Beam on the rocks if you would be so kind."

"You shouldn't be here."

Glynis poured my drink. I paid for it.

"You're lookin' for trouble," she said.

"I'm looking for information."

"Same goddamn thing. Is this about that girl you were trying to find?"

"No. It turns out the girl wasn't lost after all. Just misplaced. She's fine, by the way, and ready to get on with the rest of her life. Thanks for asking."

"What then?"

"Where are the boys tonight?"

"They'll be around."

"Mind if I wait?"

"Are you crazy?"

"Opinions differ."

"They want to kill you. I'd like to see 'em do it, too, after what you did."

"That was the result of a simple misunderstanding. I'm sure we can all put it past us and walk hand-in-hand toward a bright and shining future."

"I don't like trouble in my place."

"Your place?"

"I run it."

"You don't own it."

"What do you know?"

"Something most people aren't aware of, property tax information is public record," I said. "I went to the Hennepin County Property Tax website and ran the address of Dillman's. Michael C. Dillman is still listed as owner even though I was told that he's been dead for over a decade. His name is still listed under taxpayer, too, and so is his address, this address. How is that possible? Makes me think Dillman isn't really dead. Or maybe, just maybe, someone is pretending that he isn't dead and is running an illegal business in his name. A little far-fetched, am I right? Still, it could happen if all the bills were paid on time, if you represented yourself as Dillman's employee to the restaurant supply companies and such. Why would anyone check?"

Glynis' mouth moved as if she was trying to speak, yet no words spilled out.

"That's what I thought," I said.

"What do you want?"

"Nothing."

The way Glynis pulled out a cigarette, lit it with a plastic lighter, took a long drag, and exhaled the illegal smoke over the heads of her clientele, I didn't think she believed me.

"If you think you can put the arm on me..."

"Would I do that?" I asked. "Besides, between the cops, the pimps, and the health and liquor inspectors, you're probably already paying out enough in bribes."

"The pimps pay me," Glynis said.

"I stand corrected."

Glynis moved down the bar to serve her other customers and take several drink orders from a woman I identified as a waitress solely by the waist apron she wore and the round tray she carried. Otherwise, she looked like a babysitter my brother had a crush on when he was nine. The waitress served the drinks and took additional orders that she didn't bother to write down. She didn't seem to mind at all that several men patted her fanny while she worked, although the one woman who gave her a squeeze was rewarded with an expression that was a mixture of both terror and curiosity.

Freddie bought a round for his table. He gave the waitress a nice tip and a big smile, but no ass-slap. I thought good man. Then I thought, really? That's what constitutes a good man these days, keeping your hands to yourself?

I ordered a second Jim Beam Glynis served without comment. Her cell rang when she stepped away, and she spoke into it. I had no idea if she was talking about me, yet I started to get nervous waiting in that bar for two men who would just as soon shoot me as say good evening.

"Freddie," I said, even though neither he nor anyone else could hear me. "I hope you're paying attention."

I was halfway through the second bourbon when the boys finally arrived. They came through the front entrance and marched straight toward me as if they knew exactly where I'd be sitting long before they got there. The Asian went to my right. He was wearing a long blue shirt with a stand collar and Chinese buttons; his sleeves rolled to his elbows. The black guy settled in on my left. Glynis moved as far away from us as she could and still remain behind the bar.

"Good evening," I said.

"Yo man, I'm gonna fuck you up," the black man said.

I spun on my stool so that my back was against the bar and I was facing the door. My companions turned with me. Together, the three of us made a nice picture, which of course, was exactly what I was looking for.

"Can't we all just get along?" I asked.

"You broke my nose," the black man said.

"It's healing so nicely, though. Besides, it gives your face character. The chicks dig that. Character." I turned toward the Asian. "What about you? Do you have any character?"

His response was to undo the bottom buttons on his shirt and pull it open wide enough to show me the butt of his handgun.

"Oh, I don't care about that," I said. "I'm interested in hypodermic needles. Do you have any?"

He didn't say if he did or didn't. I turned to the black man.

"Knives, too," I added. "You wouldn't happen to be carrying a knife, would you—doubled-bladed black anodized steel with a Full Tang hilt?"

"What are you playing at?"

"I'm going to make a deal with both of you this one time only. Tell me where you were at approximately five-thirty PM the day before yesterday; that would be Monday. Give me an alibi that would appease the Federal Bureau of Investigation, and I'll never set foot in this joint again."

"I don't know what the hell you're talkin' about," the black guy said.

The silent Asian remained silent. Course, action speaks louder than words, so when his hand moved beneath his shirt...

"Don't do that," I said. "There's no need for that. If you pull your piece, my partner will pull his piece, and God knows where it'll end."

That caused the Asian to hesitate. Both he and the black guy started glancing about. The expressions on their faces suggested they thought I was bluffing until their eyes fell on Freddie. He had moved the girls out of the way so that he had a clear field of fire toward the bar. One hand was beneath the table. He gave us a gentle wave with the other.

"I understand that you're upset over what happened before," I said. "I made you look bad in front of your people, but that's on you. You came at me, remember? This time, we can settle our differences, and no one has to see or hear."

"What's your story, bitch?" the black man asked. "What you come here for? What you want?"

"I already have what I want. Out of curiosity though, do either of you have an alibi for five-thirty PM last Monday? Yes? No?"

Neither of them had an answer for me.

"Alright, I'm heading for the door. My partner will cover me. When I get to the door, I'll cover him until he joins me. Afterward, we'll both leave. With a little luck, we'll never see each other again."

"Oh, you'll see me again, Taylor," the black guy said. "Count on it."

I wasn't surprised he knew my name. I had shown Glynis my ID the last time I was in Dillman's. The thing was, I didn't know his name. I decided that put me at a distinct disadvantage.

"Here we go," I said.

I left the bar and moved in a straight line to the entrance. When I reached it, I turned my back to the door and slid my hand under my black sports jacket and rested it on the butt of the Beretta. Freddie rose from his chair, stopped for a quick word with the girls who were all smiles—Jesus, Freddie, I told myself—and moved quietly next to me. We could have been invisible as far as the other customers were concerned.

Freddie waved at the girls and stepped out. I waved at the boys and followed him.

Five minutes later, we were in separate cars heading south on I-94 and talking on cell phones.

"Did you get their pictures?" I asked.

"Yes, I did."

"Send a couple of close-ups to my phone. I'll show them to Tracy and the other women tomorrow."

"It couldn't possibly be this easy, you know that, right?"

"Bet you a dime, Freddie."

"Hey, man. You know how much money I take home. Make it a nickel."

"So, where are you headed?"

"Where do you think? Home to see my beautiful wife and handsome son. You?"

"Just home."

"You didn't listen to a word I said before, did you?"

"What do you mean?"

"Take a refresher course on good livin', God Taylor, from the professor."

CHAPTER TWENTY-FOUR

Dr. Alexandra Campbell answered her phone on the fifth ring. Her voice had a breathless quality, and for a moment, I thought that she might have actually missed me.

"Hi, Taylor." She knew I didn't care for my first name. "I wasn't going to answer—no one calls with good news after ten PM in Minnesota. Then I saw your name on the caller ID."

"I'm sorry. This was the first chance I've had to return your call from this morning. But you're right, it's late. I'll try again tomorrow."

"Don't you dare hang up."

I didn't.

"Would you like to talk?" I asked.

"I would very much like to talk."

"Should we meet? I could come over."

"Yes. No. Umm, meet me—do you know The Parlour on West Seventh Street?"

"I can find it."

"Meet me there."

"Okay. When?"

"Fifteen minutes."

"Okay."

"Actually, make it twenty. I need to get dressed."

* * *

The Parlour in St. Paul was one of those joints that want you to feel as if you had stepped off the street into a Prohibition-style speakeasy, except the wide-screen HDTV tuned to ESPN ruined the effect. I found a table, ordered my customary bourbon on the rocks, and watched the door. A few minutes later, Dr. Alexandra Campbell walked through it. She was wearing a black dress that hugged her contours and three-inch heels. The heels surprised me. She rarely wore them. It made me think she was playing up to me, trying to impress me with her feminine strut and sculptured lines, something she had never done before.

I rose when she approached, and we hugged. The moment I took her in my arms and felt her body pressed against mine, I decided Freddie was right—I was a pathetic excuse for a human being. I took a long sniff of her damp hair.

"Lavender," I said.

"New shampoo."

"I like it."

We sat. A waitress appeared, and Alex ordered one of the bar's signature boozy milkshakes, with chocolate no less; what I call an "ambush drink" because you can't taste the alcohol. She drank it like a milkshake, too, with a straw and a spoon.

"How are you, Taylor?" she asked.

"Overworked, underpaid, and not appreciated nearly enough. You?"

"The same, except school is out, as they say. I'm taking the summer to work on a high-paying research project for one of those biotech companies that's plotting to take over the world."

"Anything that should make me nervous?"

"We're attempting to develop a biochemical marker that will serve as an index for freshness of fruits and vegetables during postharvest handling."

"That sounds important."

"There's important, and then there's important. The instant a crop is removed from the ground or separated from its parent plant, it begins to deteriorate. We call it senescence. The function of postharvest handling, besides the cooling, cleaning, sorting, and packing of fruits and vegetables in ways that will delay deterioration and maintain overall taste and appearance, is to determine whether a crop should be sold for fresh consumption in grocery stores or instead used as an ingredient in a processed food product. I'll be working with a team that's attempting to create an indicator which will accurately measure freshness. If we succeed, we'll be able to improve the selection process, directing those crops with a higher shelf life and greater marketability to the stores, thereby reducing waste and increasing profits. This would be of some value to the food industry, but I'm not curing cancer. I'm not alleviating the effects of Alzheimer's. Besides, I haven't figured it out yet. Others have tried and failed. Heck, it's not even my field. I was invited to participate because the company wanted a different perspective."

"I thought biotechs were basically in the drug business," I said.

"A lot of them are. The difference is pharmaceuticals produce medicines with artificial materials while biotechs use live organisms such as bacteria or enzymes."

"I've always been impressed by your scientific mind."

"I don't know about scientific mind. I've always maintained that what we do isn't all that different."

"It isn't?"

"We're trying to find answers to what often seem to be very simple questions."

"Like why I haven't called even to tell you why I haven't called?"

"I know why you haven't called," Alex said. "The problem is you not calling or taking my calls has made it impossible for me to apologize."

"You don't need to apologize."

"Yes..."

"No. I asked to see you tonight because I'm the one who should apologize. I should not have tried to store my moral baggage in your closet."

Alex snorted into her drink. When her head came up, she had a dab of whipped cream on the tip of her nose.

"I'm sorry, that was rude," she said. "Although, honestly Taylor, that was one of the worst metaphors I've ever heard."

I reached across the table, brushed the whipped cream off with my thumb, and slowly licked my thumb.

"I liked that one much better," Alex said.

"Alex…"

"She was your client. She was only eighteen."

"She was the oldest eighteen I had ever met, and she wasn't my client. She was the woman I was hired to find."

"You asked me to keep an eye on her while you worked her case, not take her to bed."

"She hit on you, as I recall. She was troubled, and she needed comfort. What were you going to do?"

"Say no."

"Now you're taking my side of the argument," I said.

"It's only fair since you seem to be taking mine."

"I'm saying that I don't hold you responsible."

"I am responsible. I was the adult in the bedroom. It wasn't the first time I allowed my libido to get the best of me."

"She was happy when she left you."

"You weren't."

"I was conflicted. Unless you're talking to Freddie, in which case I was being a jerk. I have no right to make demands of you."

"I wish you would, though. Then I could make demands of you. I missed you, Taylor. I missed, well, I missed the sex. You weren't just a fuck buddy, though. I also missed talking to you. I missed hanging out and doing nothing with you. All the men and women I know, we never hang out and do nothing and they rarely have anything to say that I want to hear. I know I'm not conventional. Albert Einstein said, 'The woman who follows the crowd will usually go no further than the crowd. The woman who walks alone is likely to find herself in places no one has been before.' I bought into that philosophy a long, long time ago. That's doesn't mean I wouldn't favor a little companionship from time to time. Real companionship."

"I've been alone," I said. "I've made myself be alone, and you know why and yet—Alex, you've always..." I paused because I didn't want to get this wrong. "You've always amused me. You've always made me smile. You always made me feel as if the world wasn't a tremendous shit hole which let's face it, mostly it is. I like you."

Not love, I told myself—like.

"I like you, too," Alex said. "So where does that leave us?"

"When I called earlier, you said you needed time to get dressed, only you weren't in bed were you?"

"Yes, Taylor, I was in bed. With someone I didn't find nearly as interesting as you. Does it matter?"

"I shouldn't have asked. I'm being a jerk again."

"I kicked him out so I could come running to you. That makes me a jerk. I can live with it if you can. Taylor, we both know what's right and wrong. We also know that in between there's a lot of gray. Can you live there with me? In the gray?"

I didn't know if I could live there, but sure wouldn't mind visiting.

"Yes," I said.

"You need to tell me when I do something that you don't approve of, though," Alex said. "You can't just walk away, again."

"Don't worry, Alex. If nothing else I've learned that Mark Twain was right about at least one of the steps he thought was necessary to finding true happiness—*a sleepy conscience.*" I pointed at her drink. "Would you like another ice cream?"

Alex gave me a modest grin and a slight head shake.

I stood.

She stood. Her heels brought her eyes to about an inch below mine.

"Just so you know," she said. "My house is a mess."

CHAPTER TWENTY-FIVE

Alex had parked her car on Smith Avenue about a block down the street from where I parked, and I decided to walk her there. Somewhere along the line, we actually held hands.

We were passing my Toyota when they stepped out of the shadows, the African-American blocking the sidewalk in front of me and the Asian behind.

"There you are," the black man said. "I said you'd see me again."

It was just past eleven. The restaurants and clubs up and down West Seventh were still doing good business, and there was enough foot and automobile traffic that any kind of a ruckus would be sure to draw a crowd. That didn't seem to deter either man, though. They closed the distance between us as if they had practiced it. The Asian's long blue shirt with stand collar and Chinese buttons was unbuttoned at the bottom, his hands folded over his stomach as he walked. I would have thought he looked silly, except I knew what was under the shirt. The black guy with the goatee swung his arms like he was a member of the Coldstream Guards in front of Kensington Palace.

My first thought—along with being a pathetic excuse for a human being—I was also extremely stupid. They had tagged my car while I was waiting for them in Dillman's, of course they had. That's why they were waiting for me here instead of at The

Parlour. They knew where my Toyota was, but not where I was.

What really annoyed me, though, was that I had locked my Beretta inside the trunk of my Camry. Why did I need a gun to have a late-night beverage with a university professor?

My next thought—protecting Alex. I turned so that the black man was on my left and the Asian was on my right with a parked car, not mine, at my back. I pulled Alex by her arm in an attempt to move her behind me.

Give her props, she didn't ask questions like "What's going on? Who are these men? What do they want?" She didn't say anything, although in retrospect, a blood-curling scream might have done nicely considering the circumstances.

Instead, Alex shook my hand away and moved the strap of her bag over her head so that it rested on one shoulder and the strap fell diagonally across her body to her opposite hip, keeping the bag secure. Next, she slipped both of her high heels off, holding one in each hand. I figured she was preparing to make a run for it, and I was determined to give her the chance.

As the men approached, I said, "You don't need to do this."

I wasn't hoping for a long discussion, although that would have been nice, only hesitation. There was none.

"You don't need to give me shit in my own place," the black man said.

"Your place?" I asked. "Are you the reincarnation of Michael C. Dillman?"

By then, they were within striking distance.

I decided I should go first, take the black man as quickly as possible and pivot to face the Asian and hope Alex didn't get in the way.

The black man said, "Fuck you."

I hit him before he got the second word out because it's hard for the brain to react to a sudden attack if it needs to switch from one mode—intimidating your victim—to another— keeping your victim from kicking your ass.

First, I raised my right fist.

His eyes followed it, thinking that's where I was coming from.

I moved in with my left leading the way, swiping and scratching his face.

He turned his head down and away, exposing his neck.

That's where I hit him just as hard as I could with a high looping right hand, specifically in the sternocleidomastoid muscle, the one that lets us rotate our heads, like I was taught at Dragons, the dojo in downtown Minneapolis where Freddie and I sometimes train.

The black man started to fall, only I didn't wait to see him hit the ground. Instead, I pivoted toward the Asian, moving into an all-purpose American karate stance, wondering what he had for me which, as it turned out, was nothing.

That's because he was on his knees and rubbing the side of his face where Alex had pounded him with the heel of her shoe.

There was plenty of blood, although I didn't know if that meant she had caused significant damage. The veins were so close to the surface on the face that a simple cut could bleed profusely. In any case, I wasn't interested in finding out.

I grabbed Alex by the hand and ran her down the sidewalk past my car toward her own vehicle. She tried to stop to put on her shoes, only I wouldn't let her.

When we got there, I said "Get in."

Alex unlocked the door.

"Shouldn't we call the police?" she asked.

"No."

"Why not?

"We struck first. Get in."

Alex slid behind the steering wheel. I closed the door. She put her key into the ignition and started the engine. I tapped the top of the roof, telling her to go. She rolled down her window.

"We were acting in self-defense," she said.

"The courts might not agree. They have all kinds of funny

179

little rules about what's justified and what isn't. In any case, I'd have to explain why those guys were after me, and that might prove a little complicated right now."

"You're working a case."

"Yes, now..."

"Can you tell me about it?"

"Alex, go home."

"My heart is pounding a hundred beats a minute. Did you see me hit that man with my shoe?"

"No, I missed it. Alex..."

She grabbed my hand, pulled it through the window, and placed it over her heart.

"Feel that," she said. I felt more than her heart. "Come home with me."

"I need to get rid of the bug first."

"What do you mean?"

"They tagged my car with a GPS transmitter of some sort. Would you please..."

"Why would they do that?"

"Alex, you're killing me."

"I'll leave right now if you promise to come to my house and explain it all."

"I promise, I promise."

Alex put her car in gear.

"Isn't this fun?" she said. "It's just like old times."

Finally, she drove off.

I turned and made my way back down West Seventh, back toward The Parlour. And my Camry. The African-American and his silent Asian sidekick had disappeared from the sidewalk. Which didn't mean they weren't waiting to ambush me again.

I carefully searched the area around my car. When I didn't see them, I searched the car itself. It didn't take long before I discovered a small magnetized black metal box attached to the frame. I didn't open it. I knew what was inside. I tossed it across the street into the gutter before climbing into the Camry and driving off.

I thought about heading home. It had been a helluva day so far. Instead of going right, though, I turned left toward Alex's house. After all, a promise is a promise.

CHAPTER TWENTY-SIX

I was taking a chance with the photos. The kidnap victims' first look at the Asian and the black guy should be in a police lineup. If their defense attorney was to learn that a licensed PI showed pictures of the assailants to witnesses ahead of time, he could argue their identification was tainted and file a motion to have it dismissed. If a judge threw that evidence out, who knows what might follow? On the other hand, I wasn't working for the court. I was working for Charles Boucek.

I contacted Tracy Burrell first. It was early in the afternoon because I didn't get up until early in the afternoon—don't ask, don't tell. She agreed to meet me. I asked where. She told me.

"Are you sure?" I asked.

"I'm sure," she said.

Twenty minutes later, I found Tracy standing on the corner of Western and University Avenues in the heart of Little Mekong in St. Paul. Once again, I thought of a woman with an extreme fear of heights climbing up somewhere high to prove her courage.

"Look at you," I said.

"I will not be afraid."

"Apparently not."

I decided against wasting the woman's time with chit-chat and instead got right to it, showing her the photos that Freddie had taken at Dillman's and forwarded to my cell phone.

"Do you recognize these men?" I asked.

"No."

My enthusiasm for the day quickly drained through my shoes into the concrete sidewalk.

"Are you sure?" I asked.

"The Black man could have been—he has the goatee, but—I'm not sure. I didn't get that good of a look at him. I was concentrating more on the sidewalk behind him, but—it could be him, Holland. I'm just not sure."

"What about the Asian?"

Tracy studied his face for a long time and shrugged.

"Sorry," she said.

I thanked Tracy for her time, trying hard not to let my disappointment reach my voice. I walked her back to her office. She said it wasn't necessary. I told her I knew it wasn't necessary. I just enjoyed her company. She linked her arm through mine.

"Not all men are creeps," Tracy said. "Given what I do for a living and considering what happened to me, it often seems that way. Every now and again though, I meet someone who reminds me that it isn't true."

I told her that was the nicest compliment I've received in a long, long time.

I met Carole Robey in the same place I had seen her last, the parking lot next to the office building where she worked as a business analyst. After exchanging pleasantries, I showed her the photos that Freddie had taken. She stared at the images on my cell phone for about ten seconds.

"Sorry," she said. "I don't really know any African-Americans or Asian people and those I've seen around—there's a man who works in my office—but no, I don't recognize these men. Do you think they're the ones who—who took me?"

"I don't know. They've popped up during the investigation,

and I thought I'd take the chance."

"I wish I could be more helpful."

"You've been great."

"I took your advice and called one of the numbers you gave me. I have an appointment scheduled for tomorrow morning."

"Good."

"You know what? I feel better already. You're a good man Holland Taylor."

Going from not a creep to a good man in the space of an hour, I started to think pretty highly about myself.

Henrietta Weller seemed pleased to see me, which came as a surprise because she didn't seem pleased to hear from me when I called her an hour earlier and asked for a meeting. Apparently, her attitude had changed during the trip to a small club in Uptown not far from her apartment. Or perhaps the Long Island Iced Tea she had nearly finished factored into it.

A Long Island Iced Tea was another one of those ambush drinks. My first experience with it; I was in college. It was hot, not unlike today, so I ordered what the chalk board beneath the Daily Special sign described as a "refreshing" beverage. I liked it so much that fifteen minutes later I ordered another. Fifteen minutes after that I announced I had to leave and stood up. That's when the room started dancing around me. I sat down again and asked "What was in that?" Vodka, rum, gin, tequila and triple sec. Yet all I had tasted was the damn sour mix and a splash of cola.

Henrietta gave me a wave from a small table next to a large window when I stepped past the door, and I made my way through the Happy Hour crowd to her side.

"Hi, Taylor," she said.

"Rhett. How are you? Have you been all right?"

I was looking for some of the PTSD symptoms that Carole and Tracy had displayed and didn't see any. Again, I wondered if the Long Island Iced Tea had something to do with it.

"I'm fine," she said. "Why do you ask?"

"You must know you're not the only one this has happened to."

"You insisted in Boucek's office that the kidnappings would continue, so I kinda guessed when you called. How many?"

"Two that we know of. Women about your age. They're not feeling fine at all."

"Maybe that's because they hadn't fucked up their lives like I had. It's all a new experience for them."

By then, a waitress appeared. Rhett finished her Long Island Iced Tea and ordered another. I asked for Maker's Mark on the rocks.

"Are you driving?" I asked.

"You sound like my mother. No, I'm not driving. Actually, I parked at my place and walked over. I know what you're thinking, Taylor; I thought the same thing myself at first—could it happen again? Will they take me again just walking down the street? I decided I wasn't going to spend the rest of my life worrying about it. Alright, I admit that maybe I'm not feeling fine-fine. I still have moments, only they're not as frequent as they used to be. Yeah, I also know I've been drinking too much lately. I've been cutting back on that, too.

"One good thing—Mom raised my allowance. A nice bump, too. fifty-thousand dollars. Over Bruce Gillard's objections, I might add. He said my mother was throwing good money after bad. Do you believe that? Mom's idea of a compromise, as if she had to compromise a goddamned thing, is that I'm now expected to go back to Carlson in the fall and finish my business degree. How's that for a resounding example of familial affection?"

I wasn't entirely sure how to answer that. When I was a kid, the old man thought nothing of paying my brother and me for good grades—so much for an A, so much for a B, nothing for a C and if we brought home a D or an F, we owed him. I did pretty well; all As and Bs. My brother got mostly Cs. He still resents me for it, especially I think, because I would buy treats from Dairy Queen with my earnings and eat them in front of him.

"Do me a favor and take a look at these," I said.

I called up the pics of the African-American and the Asian and slid my cell phone across the table. Rhett glanced at them.

"The black dude reminds me of a man I used to fuck back when I was drinking and whoring my way through life, but no, that's not him. The Asian, I have no idea who he might be. It's possible I met them during my lost years. I don't remember. Lost years—do you like that? I'm thinking of writing a book. The Lost Years of Henrietta Weller. No, I'm not. Mom would have a heart attack."

I retrieved my phone and slid it back into my pocket.

"She's afraid that you might revert to your rebellious self," I said.

"Have you been talking to my mother?"

"I overheard a conversation she had."

"With whom? The boy-toy? Let me rephrase. At Mom's age, you don't have boy-toys. You have lovers."

"I was in Charles Boucek's office at the time, if that's what you mean."

"That's what I mean. Dad would roll over in his grave if he knew—no, that's not fair. I remember Charles from when I was a kid. He was a friend of my father's; they went to law school together. I always thought he was so humorless, so cold, yet he and my dad and my mom, they all got along fine. Then my father passed, and I didn't see Charles again for God, at least ten years, maybe longer. One day my mother and the rest of my family decided I need to be scared straight and there he was, standing alongside my mom, giving her the courage she needed to intervene in her wayward child's life, his hand resting on her shoulder as she told me I had until Sunday to move out. After which he practically moved in."

"No, that's not fair, either. Mom's been alone for so long. I couldn't prove that she's been with anyone since my father passed. Of course, what do I know what goes on in D.C.? Maybe they conduct orgies on the Capitol Building steps after the tourists move off. That would explain the last spending bill. My mother was so lovely back then with my father; so beautiful. Still is, I guess. I'm talking an awful lot. Dumping a lot of crap on you that you don't deserve. You're a nice guy for listening." She held up her glass. "I blame the iced tea."

"When you went to the hospital after crawling out of that dumpster, did the doctor find anything on your body resembling an insect bite or a bee sting?"

Rhett gave the question serious thought as she sipped her tea.

"Not that he mentioned to me," she said. "Why?"

"The other women, one said she felt as if she had been given a shot, and the other claims she saw a hypodermic syringe."

"I remember falling against my car as if I was tripped without knowing how I tripped," Rhett said. "Beyond that—how long does it take for the body to register pain? Do you know?"

"About half a second."

"Could they have knocked me out in only half a second?"

"I wouldn't think so and yet..."

"Yet they did."

"It would seem so."

Rhett took a long pull of her drink. Something in my expression must have told her something because she laughed at me.

"You look so concerned," she said.

"I am."

"I'm thinking of taking in a few AA meetings, if you must know, kind of like a refresher course. I don't need them. I'm not an alcoholic, but they couldn't hurt, could they?"

"No."

"It'll give me someone to tell my troubles to. What's said in AA stays in AA. In the real world, I can't discuss what happened. Never know who's listening. Who'll start tweeting.

Who'll try to find ten minutes of fame on FOX News or CNN. Lori Hertz keeps asking what happened to me, only I can't tell her because of Mom, and that makes her angry. Did your partner, Mr. Fredericks, talk to her? She mentioned a handsome black man..."

"It couldn't have been him, then," I said.

Rhett chuckled because she knew I was joking.

"Lori said that Mr. Fredericks thought her boyfriend might be a suspect. I told her no. I don't think she believed me. So now Sean Worra is upset with me, too, because Lori is looking at him sideways. Situation Normal All Fucked Up. I heard that in a movie, once. SNAFU. Got that right. I've even considered contacting my ex-boyfriend to have someone to, I don't know, talk to, I guess."

"I thought you said you didn't have a boyfriend."

"Ex, ex—for over a year, like I said. That's how desperate I've become that I'm thinking of calling him even though he was such a...How about you, Taylor? Are you interested in giving a girl a little comfort?"

"Not in the way you're asking."

"I didn't think so. You have scruples. Both you and Fredericks. Dammit. Sometimes I feel so alone."

Rhett started laughing again. She didn't stop until she took another sip of her drink.

"You know, Taylor, I spend a lot of time staring at my ceiling at night trying to remember what happened to me, inventing all kinds of scenarios to explain it. Except that's what they are. Inventions. I would really like to know the truth. Who did this to me? I would like to see them burn in hell for it. I know what I said before about not screwing up my mom's Senate run, and I meant it. I don't want her to be compromised over this. At the same I would really like to get a little justice, which is a lot more than what most people get, I know, but still..."

"That's the plan."

"Except you're doing it for Charles Boucek."

"No, I'm doing it for you and the other women. Boucek is just the guy who's paying for it."

"If he doesn't, I will," Rhett said.

I raised my glass to her.

"We'll call that Plan B," I said.

CHAPTER TWENTY-SEVEN

After I settled in behind my desk, I told Freddie, "I'm a helluva guy."

"Who says?"

"Tracy Burrell, Carole Robey and Rhett Weller."

"They don't know you like I do. What else did they have to say?"

"About that..."

I recapped my meetings with the three women, emphasizing that none of them could identify either the Asian or the African-American as their assailants. After that, I told Freddie about my adventures after leaving The Parlour with Alex the night before.

"If the punks from Dillman's had nothin' to do with the kidnappings..." Freddie said.

"We don't know that for sure. All we know is that neither Tracy, Carole nor Rhett could identify them."

"Then why come after you? By the way, the professor poundin' the Asian in the face with her high heels? I would have paid serious money to see that."

"I missed it, too. My back was turned. The way Alex explained it, the Asian shoved her aside to get at me and wham, wham, wham."

"Nice."

"I thought so."

"What happened after?"

"What happened after is I showed the vics the photos you took and none of them could identify our suspects."

"That's not what I meant."

"I know what you meant, Freddie. Let's stay focused."

"Back to my question then—if the punks had nothin' to do with the kidnappings, why come after you?"

"Because I was going after them. My theory is that the black dude decided to take over Dillman's after the owner—Michael C. Dillman—died ten years ago, only he never made it legal. Instead, he's been pretending that Dillman is still alive, using the bar's bank account to pay the business taxes, insurance, liquor fees, whatever needs to be paid. As long as all of his obligations are met, who's to know if Dillman is alive or dead; who's going to check? Think about it? When was the last time we spoke to our landlord?"

"Now that I think about it—seven years. Everything's been done online since we signed our original lease. But Dillman, what about his family?"

"We don't know if Dillman had any."

"Friends? Acquaintances?"

"They probably know that Dillman died. Let's pretend they were at his funeral."

"If he had a funeral."

"That doesn't mean anyone else knows, though. If there was no doctor present to pronounce his passing, if the county coroner wasn't notified and no death certificate was issued, the feds, the state, the county, they would have his death in the system. If no one contacted his bank or mortgage company, canceled his credit cards or alerted the credit reporting companies, if no one canceled his driver's license, called social security, filed a will in probate court or published an obituary—you prove Dillman's not still running his bar. When you think about it, it wouldn't be all that hard to pull off. Just do next to nothing."

"Why not make it legal?" Freddie asked.

"I can think of a dozen reasons off the top of my head, can't you?"

"Now that you mention it...'Kay, the punks are doin' what they're doin'. Now you come along pretendin' to look for a woman they've never heard of, and instead you find them and start makin' noises about the FBI and shit. They gotta be wonderin' what the fuck, man?"

"That's why they came at me instead of shooting me down in the street—because they don't know what's going on."

"What are we gonna do about it?"

"Why should we do anything? Let 'em marinate. They're still suspects even though they're now way down on the list. Besides, you know what they're doing right this minute while we're talking? They're watching the door and worrying what's going to happen next. It'll drive them nuts."

"It does make for a pretty picture. Don't forget, though—you owe me five hundred dollars."

"What are you talking about?"

"Our bet."

"I bet you a nickel."

"Where I come from, a nickel is five hundred. You started with a dime. That's a thousand dollars."

"Are you crazy? A dime is ten cents. A nickel is five."

"No, no, no, no, no, don't you do that Taylor. A bet is a bet."

"Yes, it is."

I reached into my pocket and pulled out a palm full of change.

"Do you have change for a quarter?" I asked.

"That's low, Taylor. That's low, even by your standards. The professor, man, she hit the wrong guy with her shoe."

"The question is—what do we do next?"

"Besides dissolving our partnership, you welsher?"

"You're being awfully sanctimonious for a guy who bet me ten thousand dollars that the Vikings would win the Super

Bowl. Did they win the Super Bowl, Freddie?"

"I paid you."

"You gave me a ten-thousand-dollar dong bill from the State Bank of Vietnam worth about forty cents American. I still carry it in my wallet."

"So, what are you complain' about? I paid you, didn't I? I can't help it if you didn't specify U.S. dollars, can I?"

"Exactly my point. A nickel is a nickel."

"You're a grifter, Taylor. If you had won, you'd be askin' for your five small."

"No, I'd be asking for my five cents. Next time, you'll have to be more specific."

"Next time we'll put it in writing."

"Okay."

"So, what are we gonna do?"

"Match up the histories of the three vics, and see if we can find a common denominator."

"Besides Boucek?"

"Besides Boucek."

"If we can't?"

"I guess we'll find out if he meant it when he said we could investigate his employees."

"Bet he didn't."

"How much?"

"A fucking nickel."

I spent the next hour transcribing the notes I took when I interviewed Carole and Tracy so Freddie and I would have hard copies when we started comparing the three women's backgrounds. When I finished, we moved to the large combination cork bulletin board and dry erase white board that we had mounted on the wall between our desks. Freddie wrote the names Weller, Burrell and Robey in red marker across the top of the board. Underneath, we started noting in blue ink the things they had in common:

women

"Why kidnap just women?" Freddie asked. "Why not guys, too?"

"They're easier to control."

"Yeah? Tell that to the professor. Or Tracy Burrell. She didn't even have high heels to use as a weapon. Didn't need 'em."

age 25-27
single
gainfully employed
live alone/apartments
no steady boyfriends/recent breakups
rich/prominent families

"That's the key, isn't?" I said. "Rich, prominent families."

"We should be more concerned with what the families have in common instead of the girls."

"Maybe."

"In the meantime…" Freddie wrote:

brown hair
brown eyes

"Do you think that's significant?" I asked.

"You never know why some fuck-up does what he does. Maybe they remind him of his mother?"

"What else?"

"Rhett lives in Uptown; works in the Longfellow neighborhood of Minneapolis. Carole lives near the river in the Merriam Park West neighborhood of St. Paul and works in Mendota Heights. Tracy lives in Prospect Park in Minneapolis and works on the edge of Summit-University in St. Paul. Nothing connects them but maybe Uptown—it's possible that they party in the same clubs."

"Tracy said she hadn't been in a bar or club for over nine months."

"What does she do for fun?" Freddie asked.

"She reads."

"Takes all kinds. Given how far apart they live from each other, it's unlikely they go to the same coffeehouse, eat at the same restaurants, shop the same stores, gas up at the same fillin' stations, have accounts at the same banks, use the same auto mechanic, plumber, travel agent..."

I took my time shuffling through the sheets of biographical information.

"No," I said.

"Healthcare? They use the same clinic?"

More shuffling.

"No," I said.

"Where do they get their hair done?"

I wagged a finger at Freddie, thinking he had a great idea. Turned out he hadn't. Rhett went to a woman in Uptown, Carole used the students who were studying at the Aveda Institute in Minneapolis, and Tracy had a cousin who liked to experiment. "Sometimes I let her, but mostly I don't," she had told me.

"I don't suppose they belong to the same reading group, sipping chardonnay and talkin' Jane Austin," Freddie said.

"Wouldn't that be nice?" I shuffled more paper. "No clubs or social groups for any of them."

"Not even the Brown-Eyed Girl Society?"

"Not unless it's an underground club."

"With a secret handshake." Freddie glanced at his watch. "It's gettin' late. How 'bout we hit it hard first thing tomorrow morning?"

I was hesitant to let it go, but then I didn't have a family waiting for me.

"Alright," I said. "First thing."

"Besides, if they follow their established pattern, the kidnap-pers won't strike again for another two weeks."

CHAPTER TWENTY-EIGHT

I lived exactly nine-point-seven miles from our office in the Butler Square Building in Minneapolis, yet with the rush hour traffic, it took me nearly thirty minutes to get home to St. Paul. I used a security code to gain access to the building and climbed to the second-floor landing. I crossed the landing, rapped three times on 2B, and crossed it again to unlock my door and step inside my apartment. I left the door open, yet Amanda Wedemeyer didn't appear to feed my rabbit. Nor did Claire arrive with leftovers. Nor did Anne Scalasi drop by in search of stress-release. Nor did Alex Campbell call with an invitation to guest star in her latest role-playing scenario.

Ogilvy emerged from wherever he was keeping himself and stared at the open doorway as if hoping for visitors as well. When none arrived, he retreated to his always opened cage and started nibbling alfalfa.

I closed the door and grabbed what remained of a Mexican takeout meal from three days earlier, then finished it in front of the TV. For over two hours, the remote never left my hand. I can't tell you how many channels I flipped through. What was that song Springsteen sang—"57 Channels (And Nothin' On)?" I had two hundred twenty and couldn't find a thing to hold my interest, which probably said more about me than it did about television.

I retrieved a bottle of Makers Mark, filled a glass, and returned to the TV with my remote, telling myself that I might have missed something. That's when my cell phone rang. The caller ID read Elizabeth Jordan. I thought her name was Quinn, I told myself. I answered "This is Taylor."

A woman spoke with a voice I didn't recognize, although I was acquainted with her tone. She was frightened and trying hard not to sound like it.

"Mr. Taylor?" she asked. "Holland Taylor?"

"Yes."

"Quinn gave me your number. My daughter—you know Quinn?"

"Yes, of course."

"I'm Liz Jordan. Quinn said—my daughter told me that if—if something were ever to happen to her, I should call you."

The question I screamed in my head was, "Why me?"

The one I asked over the phone was, "What happened to your daughter?"

"I don't know. She was supposed to come over for dinner and she didn't and when I called, I've called a couple of times now, she doesn't answer. Normally, I wouldn't be overly concerned except..."

I could think of a dozen things off the top of my head that a young woman as smart and lovely as Quinn might be doing instead of spending the evening with her mother, except the first one that came to mind made me shudder. She was, after all, a brown-eyed girl.

"Tell me where you are," I said.

Elizabeth Jordan lived in a small bungalow on a dead-end street in a blue-collar neighborhood nestled between Summit Hill and the western bluffs of the Mississippi River called West End. She was waiting for me at the door; watched as I parked across the street. She opened the door as I approached. I noticed several things at once. Elizabeth was about thirty years older, two inches shorter and twenty pounds heavier than her daughter. Her eyes were the same color yet shaped differently; her hair was cut short and dyed jet black, and she had some sort of motto tattooed to her inner arm I couldn't read. Her chin, mouth and cheekbones were the same, though.

"I apologize for imposing on you," she said. "I wouldn't have, except that Quinn made me promise."

"When did you last speak to her?"

"A quarter to five."

I stepped through the door directly into a small living room furnished with a sofa, two stuffed chairs, coffee table, end table and an HDTV mounted on top of a bookcase. The shelves of the bookcase were full, and Elizabeth had resorted to stacking books on the floor. There were so many titles that I felt a pang of jealousy at the sight of them. There was a time when I used to read like that.

"What did Quinn say when you spoke to her?" I asked.

"She said she had to stop at her apartment before coming over, but that she'd be here no later than six. I timed the meal so that it would be done cooking just after she arrived. Spaghetti in a shrimp sauce."

There was a doorway leading from the living room to the kitchen. I glanced inside and saw two unused place settings arranged on a small table. A clock substituting various species of birds for numbers hung on the wall above the table. I did the math.

"She should have been here at six," I said. "It's now a quarter to nine."

"It's ridiculous, I know. Like I said on the phone, normally I'd be wondering what happened to her, but I wouldn't be—I wouldn't be freaking out."

Elizabeth smiled, yet there was no joy in it. She looked as if she wanted someone to tell her she was being foolish so she could laugh at herself.

"She might still be at work," I said. "Dealing with some

emergency. That's the firm's stock-in-trade, dealing with emergencies."

"I know. It's just that Quinn told me about the kidnappings, and I guess I'm just being paranoid."

"I'm surprised she would tell you about her work. I'd think Boucek and Associates would have rules about that sort of thing."

"Quinn and I never keep secrets from each other. At least not anymore."

"Still, I don't think there's anything to worry about. From what I've seen, Quinn knows how to take care of herself. Besides, she doesn't fit the profile."

"Profile?"

"The kidnap victims have all been from wealthy and prominent families."

Elizabeth stared at me; her mouth hung open slightly as if an unexpected noise had startled her.

"You don't know," she said.

"Know what?"

"Course, the kidnappers wouldn't know, either. How would they know? Quinn has always been so particular about it. At least since she started college."

"Particular about what?"

"Jordan is my name, my maiden name; I went back to it after the divorce. It's not Quinn's though. It's just the name she uses professionally because she wants to make it on her own, she said; because she doesn't want to face charges of nepotism. I think it's also because she doesn't want to be burdened by the sins of her father."

"I don't understand."

"Her real name is Quinn Jordan Boucek. Charles Boucek is Quinn's father."

I didn't have Boucek's private number, even though he had

mine. Nor did Elizabeth. "We don't talk," she said. So, I called Boucek's office number, hoping that he might check his voicemail.

"Ms. Jordan has gone missing," I said. "Call me. Call me now." I also recited my cell number to make it easier for him.

Afterward, I turned toward Elizabeth.

"Who did you call?" I asked.

"I only know a couple of Quinn's friends; that gay guy she likes to spend time with."

"I'm sure she's fine."

"Yes, of course."

Elizabeth Jordan sat in one of her chairs, her legs curled beneath her. I sat in a chair across from her. She had poured us both a cup of coffee, yet neither of us drank it.

"You probably want to know my story," she said.

What I wanted was for Quinn to walk through the door. Listening to Elizabeth was a way to pass the time.

"People make mistakes, don't they?" she said. "My mistake was Jefferson Weller."

"The man who was married to Congresswoman Hudson?" I asked.

"He wasn't married when we met. What happened, I was a waitress down at DeGidio's on West Seventh Street. Do you know it?"

"Family restaurant. Great Italian."

"I was working my way through college. This was over thirty years ago when it was still possible to work your way through college. I was a business major. Both Charles and Jefferson were in law school. They came down to the restaurant, seated themselves in my section, and started flirting with me. One thing led to another, and we began hanging out with each other. Jeff and Charles were good friends. They were also highly competitive. They competed for me. I liked them both immensely, of course. I enjoyed the attention they gave me, too. Yet I always knew it would be Jefferson, right up until he met Abigail. I was prettier than she was. I was also a middle-class girl with a middle-class future. Abby was obscenely rich and had connections up the yin yang. So, Jefferson picked her, and I picked Charles by default.

"And it was fine. I loved him. Charles. I did. The first years of our marriage were wonderful. Unfortunately, Charles soon became obsessed with not only becoming a great lawyer but also being an important lawyer. We had remained close friends with Jefferson and Abigail and seeing how they lived, I think had something to do with his ambition. I was ambitious myself, yet more and more, I found myself sacrificing my dreams to accommodate his.

"Quinn was born, and that helped, especially when she was younger. Only when she was ten, eleven, I began to feel—Charles had neglected me for years; me and Quinn. Meanwhile, Abby was involved in a wide range of charities and foundations and social issues and had been neglecting Jefferson and her daughter; she had a daughter named Henrietta."

I flashed on the first meeting in Boucek's office—*Quinn had come to the reception area to retrieve us; Rhett smiled at her and said, "Good to see you again."*

"Did Quinn and Henrietta know each other?" I asked.

"Charles and I had continued to socialize with Jeff and Abby, so, yes, they knew each other. I don't think they were friends, though. Henrietta was two years older. Why do you ask?"

"What did Quinn tell you about the kidnappings?"

"Only that young women were being kidnapped and sold back to their families. Was Henrietta Weller one of them?"

"Finish your story. You were saying about Jefferson and Abigail…"

Elizabeth stared for a few beats. She knew I was deliberately changing the subject and didn't like it.

"Secrets," she said. "Charles and his secrets."

"Excuse me?"

"Nothing. Umm, Jefferson. He was being neglected by Abby the same way I was being neglected by Charles. An unsatisfied husband is a terrible thing."

"How 'bout an unsatisfied wife?"

"Worse. Much worse. We had an affair. Charles found out. I was shocked by the depth of his anger. A simple divorce wasn't enough to assuage it. He eviscerated me. By the time he was done, I had not only lost custody of my daughter, I was denied all visitation rights. He..." She made a sound I had never heard before; part chuckle and part sob. "...convinced the court to issue a restraining order against me so I would never see Quinn again. He found a way to blackball me in the business community, too. I became unhirable. Jefferson said he'd help, only he didn't. Probably the price he had to pay to keep his name out of the divorce proceedings. He died a year later. I ended up going back to the service industry. I now manage a bar on Selby near Western."

I nearly asked which one yet managed to restrain myself. Instead, I turned my attention to the photographs on Elizabeth's wall across from the bookcase. Most of them were of Quinn when she was a little girl and a few of her as an adult, one of them in cap and gown at a college graduation; another of her in the same cap and gown, only hugging her mother. There was nothing in between.

"How did you and Quinn get back together?" I asked.

"I was working a club on Grand Avenue, and she walked through the door. She was sixteen and the most beautiful thing I had ever seen. I recognized her immediately. She didn't have to say a word. I just knew. My little girl. She had sought me out without telling her father. She wanted to know why I wasn't her mother anymore. Charles had—let's just say he had fudged the facts.

"I didn't say anything to anybody. I left the club and took

her to the Como Conservatory because it had been one of her favorite places when she was a little girl. We sat in the wing with the sunken garden, and I told her the truth. All of the truth, including my adultery. I thought I might never see her again, and I didn't want her last impression of me..."

Elizabeth rested her face in her hand. When her head came up again, there were tears in her eyes. Yet her voice remained strong.

"She kept coming back. Kept calling. We became friends. Her father didn't know. That was my idea. I was afraid of him. I still am. He didn't find out about us until after Quinn graduated from the Carlson School of Management at the U. Quinn insisted that I attend the ceremony. That picture"— she pointed at the photograph of Quinn and her hugging—"she made Charles take it.

"When I said that Charles didn't know about us, that was probably untrue. I think he might have known, but decided it was better not to interfere. I think he was afraid Quinn would blow up at him. She might have, too. I was as surprised as Charles was when she decided to go by the name Quinn Jordan. When was that? Her freshman year? If you know Charles, then you must also know what a courageous act of rebellion that was. Now we have a truce. Charles doesn't talk to me, and I don't talk to him, and neither of us tries to influence Quinn into taking sides.

"Now this. Now I learn that Quinn might have been kidnapped because she's Charles Boucek's daughter. I don't know what to do."

"Tell me something," I said. "Why did Quinn give you my name and number? Why did she tell you to call me if she was in trouble?"

"She said you and your partner were the only two people she knew who were willing to stand up to Charles—besides her."

CHAPTER TWENTY-NINE

Early the next morning, Freddie and I arrived at the offices of Boucek and Associates. This time, we came through the front door. Bruce Gillard was there to greet us.

"Helluva thing," he said.

"What is?" I asked.

"You don't have to play it cagey with me, Taylor. I know everything."

"No one knows everything," Freddie said. "Except maybe my wife."

"You'll see," Gillard said.

He opened the large wooden door and escorted us down the corridor toward the conference room. This time, though, the place seemed strangely quiet, as if no one was doing anything except waiting. Gillard didn't knock on the door as Quinn had done. Instead, he yanked it open like he was in a hurry to show us what was inside.

Boucek sat at the head of the table, as impeccably dressed as ever. His face, though, looked pale and immobile, and I had the fleeting impression that he might be in shock. He hadn't sounded like it when he returned my call the evening before demanding to be told, "What do you mean Ms. Jordan has gone missing?"

I explained.

"How do you know this?" he asked.

"I'm sitting in Elizabeth Jordan's home. I'm looking at her right now."

"Tell her to keep her mouth shut."

"I will not."

My defiance had stunned Boucek into silence, yet it didn't last long.

"*Ask* her to keep quiet about this," he said. "Tell her I will deal with it. Tell her I will bring our daughter home. Will you do that? Please?"

"Yes."

"I need to make some phone calls. Afterward, I will call you back. Holland, I may be asking a lot of you in the coming hours."

"I'll be here."

Boucek did call back about an hour later with a request that Freddie and I meet him in his office the first thing the next morning. There was nothing more that could be accomplished that evening, he said. At the time, he sounded as if he was in complete control, as usual. Watching his blank eyes now, though, I wasn't as sure.

I recognized the woman sitting on Boucek's left immediately, of course. She was dressed in uniform—a crisp white shirt and blue tie, blue skirt and blue jacket, a gold badge glimmering off her left breast and a single gold star pinned to each shoulder as befitting her rank. Normally, Anne Scalasi didn't dress like that. Normally she dressed like she had when we worked homicide together—sports jackets and jeans, sometimes a skirt.

The man to Boucek's right was in his late fifties, early sixties, with short gray hair and a blue suit. He was looking down at photocopies of two extortion letters. I guessed one belonged to Carole Robey, and the other belonged to Quinn.

Gillard did the introductions.

"Holland Taylor, Sidney Fredericks, this is Special Agent Raymond Carr of the Federal Bureau of Investigation."

Carr stood to shake hands. He was taller than he seemed,

sitting down.

"This is Assistant Chief Anne Scalasi of the St. Paul Police Department."

Anne also stood to shake hands with me across the table. From the expressions on both of our faces, you would not have guessed that we had been friends for over twenty years and on-again, off-again lovers for a couple more. In contrast, Freddie's expression was one of happy recognition. He circled the table and hugged Anne as if she had been his first girlfriend.

"Hey, Chief," he said.

"Have you been behaving yourself, Freddie?"

"You know me."

"Yes, I do. That's why I'm asking."

"You've met before," Gillard said.

"We've had dealings in the past," Anne said.

"She arrested me once," Freddie said.

Gillard nodded, as if he had heard everything he needed to know. If Carr was curious, he didn't show it. Boucek continued to stare straight ahead at something the rest of us couldn't see.

I gestured at the photocopies on the conference room table.

"So, it's official, now?" I asked.

Special Agent Carr sat down again and set his cell phone on the table directly in front of him and I wondered—are you recording this, pal?

"Before we proceed, you all must know that I am acting in a strictly advisory capacity," Carr said. "This matter remains under the jurisdiction of the St. Paul Police Department."

"It's our jurisdiction because Ms. Jordan is a resident of St. Paul," Anne said. "We are treating this as a missing persons case at present."

"Are we talking about the same thing?" I asked. "Quinn Jordan has been kidnapped. Hasn't she?"

It occurred to me that no one had actually spoken the words out loud.

"If she were of tender years, we'd initiate an investigation even though there is no known interstate aspect," Carr said. "However, she is not twelve years or younger and there is no evidence of interstate travel. Of course, we will monitor the situation and offer assistance as required."

"Annie," I said.

"Assistant Chief Scalasi," she said.

I spoke the words with a vehemence that made her flinch. "Assistant Chief Scalasi."

"Until events or the level of cooperation evolve, our hands are tied," she said.

"We both know that's not true. Quinn is the victim, not Charles."

"I am merely following my instructions."

I nearly called them out, both Anne and Carr, only I had been a cop for a long time and knew how things worked. So did Boucek. Cops get all large and emphatic when an outsider tries to cover something up, yet they did it all the time to oblige friends and anybody with a little pull. I had done the same thing.

"If there is any confusion, it's my fault." Boucek spoke with a voice as flat as a sheet of paper. "I acted without deliberation; made calls without fully evaluating the situation. I now believe Ms. Boucek will be returned to us unharmed if we agree to the kidnapper's demands, just as in the previous incidents. There is no need for an official presence. I have made my opinion clear to the parties concerned. Afterward, if either the FBI or St. Paul Police Department wishes to initiate an investigation, they will receive my full cooperation."

"Jesus, Charles. Quinn is your daughter."

He had nothing to say to that.

"I don't believe we are accomplishing as much as we could," Special Agent Carr said. He waved at a chair near him. "Mr. Taylor, Mr. Fredericks, please."

Freddie and I sat. I pointed at the photocopies.

"May I?" I asked.

Carr ignored the gesture, which I found infuriating.

"Let's begin with a summary of the current situation," he said. "I believe you are intimately involved in these events," which was Carr's way of telling me to start talking. I glanced at Freddie.

"I told you, man," he said.

You don't lie to the FBI. You don't kid, cajole, tease, holdout on, bargain with, or threaten the FBI. They might have had their ups and downs over the years, but they were still the FBI, so I started talking with as much honesty and attention to detail as I could muster. The fact Carr didn't take notes convinced me he was taping the meeting.

I began with Henrietta Weller and the dumpster, mentioning my confrontations with both the African-American and Asian at Dillman's.

"Do you believe they are suspects?" Carr asked.

"Not at the present time."

I told him why. He didn't reply, although I noticed Anne shaking her head slightly when I mentioned showing their photographs to the kidnap victims. Afterward, I segued into the Carole Robey kidnapping and what we did about it. I started by pointing again at the photocopies in front of Carr and reciting what Paul Dimeski had told me about them and the mail envelope. He nodded when I said that I didn't have the resources to investigate the drop box or the account with the U.S. Postal Service the kidnappers used. He nodded some more when I explained how we had delivered the ransom money.

Carr was looking at Boucek when he said, "It's a pity that no one was there to surveil the drop sight."

"Yeah, about that..."

Carr's eyes shifted from Boucek back to me.

"You were there?" he said.

I explained what happened. Gillard snickered behind his hand. Up until then, I had forgotten that he was there. Now I wanted to smack him in the mouth.

"Hey," Freddie said. I think he was as annoyed with Gillard as I was.

Anne said "You okay, Freddie?"

"I'm good, Chief."

"You've all been very clever keeping these events to yourselves," Special Agent Carr said. "However, in my opinion, all you've accomplished is to encourage the kidnappers. I'm surprised they haven't escalated their ransom demands."

He continued his lecture for a few more minutes. When he finished, I told him about Tracy Burrell. Assistant Chief Scalasi knew all about it, of course, yet she had no idea Tracy and her adventures with the streetcar had anything to do with Quinn's case until that moment. The news caused her to fold her arms over her chest and lean back against the chair. It was difficult to hide my smile. Anne had been trained at the FBI's National Center for the Analysis of Violent Crime to investigate mass murders and serial rape killings, among other things. She had been very good at it. I had always enjoyed watching her work out a problem. You could actually see her think.

After finishing the part of the story involving Tracy, I concluded with the fact that Freddie and I were currently attempting to find a common denominator that linked the first three victims, now four.

"Anything yet?" Carr asked.

"You mean besides Charles?" Freddie asked.

"Yes."

"I learned that at least two of them—Henrietta Weller and Quinn Jordan..."

"Boucek," Charles said. "Her legal name is Quinn Boucek."

"Rhett and Quinn knew each other. Beyond that—we just got started."

"You've done quite well," Carr said.

"Not as well as you could do if you would take charge of the case."

Carr raised and lowered his hand as if that went without

saying.

"Now tell me what you have," I said.

"What I have is a ransom note." Carr slid one of the photocopies across the table toward me. "A copy of the ransom note. The original is in our lab along with the Priority Mail envelope and Ms. Boucek's driver's license. Normally, it would not have arrived until this morning's mail was delivered. However, we were able to expedite matters."

I read it.

> We have your daughter. You will place $50,000 in cash in a small travel bag with the logo of the Minnesota Twins. We require that Holland Taylor deliver the bag to the 29th Avenue North entrance of the Grand Rounds Trail. Taylor will gain the Trail at exactly 6 PM. He will walk north. He will continue walking until we are satisfied that it is safe to approach him. When he is contacted, Taylor will relinquish the bag without discussion. He will resume walking the trail for an additional 30 minutes. If we are content that you have respected our instructions, your daughter will be released unharmed before the midnight hour. If not, she will be executed at 12:01 AM. Do not attempt to contact the authorities. We are watching.

"North Minneapolis again," I said.

"Is that significant?" Anne asked.

"It seems to be."

"The kidnappers asked for you specifically," Carr said.

"I noticed."

"Why?"

I shrugged a reply.

"Who knows that you're involved?"

"Victims," Freddie said. "Their families. All of you."

"I didn't know anything until this morning," Gillard said. "Not until Charles called me."

"The boys and girls at Dillman's," I said.

"Paul Dimeski," Anne said. "Who else?"

"A manageable list in any case," Carr said.

"Whaddaya gonna do about it?" Freddie asked.

"I told you before; I'm here strictly in an advisory capacity."

"'Kay. What do you advise?"

"Pay the ransom and hope for the best."

That caused me to turn my eyes on Boucek.

"I have the money," he said. "I turned it over to the Bureau earlier this morning."

"What are they doing with it?" Gillard asked.

"We're running the cash through a Canon CR-180 scanner featuring optical recognition software," Carr said. "When the process is completed, we'll have a DVD containing the front and back images of the bills, as well as the serial numbers."

"Why?" Gillard asked.

"That's what's meant by marking money," I said.

"Really?"

"What?" Freddie asked. "You think they put a tiny blue dot behind the president's ear? C'mon man."

From the expression on his face, that was exactly what Gillard thought. I nearly told him that marking money wasn't done so that banks could identify the serial numbers of the bills when the kidnappers spent them. That seldom produced results. Mostly it was done so that when the authorities caught the kidnappers and found the ransom money, they could point at the bills and say "Ahh-haa!" Only I was annoyed he was there and said nothing.

"The money will be returned soon," Carr said. "I have sent a special agent to Target Field to secure a Twins travel bag from the pro shop."

"Why a Twins travel bag?" Gillard asked.

212

"They know who I am," I said. "But probably not what I look like. The bag is for identification purposes."

"Will it have a tracking device attached?"

"If the kidnappers are professionals, and they seem to be, a GPS tracker is the first thing they'll look for," Carr said. "If they find it, what happens to Ms. Boucek?"

"Just asking." Gillard was behaving like he was having a wonderful time. "Once the money is ready, then what happens?"

"Taylor will deliver it," Anne said.

She was so matter of fact in her assertion I nearly said no just to prove her wrong, yet of course I was going to deliver the ransom. It would have been nice though, if someone, anyone, had taken a moment to ask me.

"What are the chances that a law enforcement organization with more resources than Freddie and me will conduct surveillance of the drop site?" I asked.

"I would never be allowed to allocate that kind of manpower without assuming jurisdiction," Carr said.

"The drop is in Minneapolis," Anne said, which meant that she wasn't going to do anything, either.

Freddie had been drumming his fingers against the tabletop during all this. He stopped to say, "We want it understood that we're actin' at the behest of Charles Boucek with the approval of both the FBI and the St. Paul Police Department."

"I can attest to that," Gillard said.

"We want it in writing."

No one said a word. It was like they hadn't heard him.

"Yeah, that's what I thought."

Carr stood up. He swept his cell phone off the table, tapped its screen a few times, and slipped it into his pocket.

"That's it then," he said. "I'm sure the Assistant Chief will concur when I say we are deeply concerned for the well-being of Ms. Boucek and pray these events are concluded without further incident. We will reconvene as the situation warrants.

However, unless a federal crime is officially recognized, there is little more that I can do. Mr. Boucek." Charles looked up at him. "I wish that were not true. I wish the system was not being manipulated to prevent me from doing my job."

"Amen," Anne said.

Boucek didn't reply.

Carr started for the door. Gillard hopped up and scrambled to follow him out. Anne circled the table and rested a hand on my shoulder.

"Call me," she said.

I nodded.

She patted Freddie's shoulder and said, "Mr. Fredericks."

"Chief."

A moment later, she was gone, and we were alone with Boucek.

"Well, Charles," I said. "Here we are."

"I will not tolerate a lecture at the present time."

"'Sides," Freddie said. "It's too late now."

"Holland, Sidney." Boucek's voice was quiet. It had a kind of pleading quality that I had never once heard in all the time I've known him. "It's my daughter."

"We'll bring her home," I said.

"Please."

CHAPTER THIRTY

I told Boucek that there was much to prepare. He promised to contact us the moment that the FBI returned the ransom money. We left him sitting alone in his grand conference room and walked the corridor back toward the reception area. There was more noise than before, yet it remained muted. I suspected that Boucek's employees understood something serious was happening, even if they didn't know exactly what, and it made them anxious. Given the nature of Boucek's business, it might have been a feeling that they shared quite often.

We found Gillard in the reception area standing between us and the elevators.

"A moment, please," he said.

He turned and sauntered down still another corridor. I almost didn't follow him, only Freddie gave me a head jerk and a grin as if to say this might be fun.

Gillard led us to a corner office that looked like any other corner office you've ever been in. Apparently, he didn't have Boucek's decorating budget. He motioned toward a couple of chairs strategically placed in front of his desk. Freddie and I sat while he circled the desk and worked his butt into the much larger and more comfortable chair behind it. The moment we did, we noticed that our chairs had been cut down by a couple of inches while Gillard's desk and chair had been elevated by the same amount. The result was that we were looking up at him; a large window showing a clear blue sky at his back.

"Helluva thing," he repeated.

"It is that," I said.

"I didn't even know Ms. Jordan was Charles' daughter. I thought they were—well, never mind what I thought."

I might have expressed my outrage, except there was a time when I thought the same thing.

"I am shocked," Gillard said. "I assure you gentlemen that is the proper word; I am shocked by these—shall we call them Express Kidnappings?"

"Why not?"

"I am equally shocked that Charles would jeopardize the firm by dealing with the kidnappers the way he has, by refusing to cooperate with the authorities."

"It does belong to him," Freddie said. "The firm."

"Of course. However, his blatant disregard for the welfare of his associates and employees is..."

"Shocking?" I asked.

"In a word—yes."

"Guess he was more concerned about the welfare of his clients and their daughters," Freddie said.

"Understandable. However, there are his many other clients and their children to consider as well. Boucek and Associates caters to a specific clientele. The wealthiest families. Families whose portfolios and lifestyles often generate special problems that must be handled with a light and discreet hand. The fear of publicity is often more disturbing to them than the problem they are facing. They will do almost anything to avoid it. I appreciate Charles is striving to keep these matters confidential. However, if it should—what's the term? Blow up? If this should blow up, if Boucek and Associates were to become notorious for its dealings with criminals, I would expect its clients to abandon the firm as quickly as possible. Understand, it would not be the criminal element that would spark the stampede, but rather the firm's apparent inability to keep a secret."

"Where else would they go?" I asked.

"That's the question, isn't it?"

"Course, I'm just a poor black child with no proper education," Freddie said. "I'm guessin' if the first firm should crash and burn, a second might rise from the ashes to take its place in the heavens like a golden Phoenix."

Gillard studied him for a few beats, as if he was trying to figure out if Freddie was putting him on. Finally, he said, "I, as well as my colleagues, remain loyal to Charles and the firm. However, we would be remiss if we didn't also look out for ourselves. There already have been persistent rumors that Charles intends to close Boucek and Associates in order to accept a position in Washington, D.C., or at least greatly reduce his everyday participation in its management, perhaps even attempting to operate the firm from afar like an absentee landlord. This is not to our advantage. I'm speaking for the associates. It would leave us underemployed if not actually unemployed. Now this, the kidnappings. Obviously, they could exacerbate matters. We find ourselves in a precarious position."

"What do you want from us?" I asked.

"The second firm Mr. Fredericks imagined might be in a position to give you so much more business that you would be forced to expand yourselves, become even more successful."

"I appreciate that, Bruce."

He smiled at me.

"Except that doesn't answer my question."

"I want to be made aware of anything and everything that you are doing for Charles, so I will have a better understanding of how his actions might impact the firm we have all worked so diligently to build and maintain."

"You understand we are currently employed by Charles Boucek."

"A situation that is easily rectified."

"We would never betray a client. We take our contacts very seriously."

"Name your price."

Freddie was smiling when he rose from his chair.

"Fuck you, Bruce," he said. "And the horse you rode in on."

We were on the street and walking back toward our office when I asked him, "And the horse you rode in on?"

"It's all I could think of at the time," Freddie said. "You gotta problem with what I said?"

"No, I was merely amused by the way you said it."

"Think we should tell Charles he's got a traitor in his midst?"

"At our first opportunity. In the meantime..."

"You got a plan?"

"I'd like to walk the ground where we're supposed to deliver the ransom, except I'm willing to bet the kidnappers already have it staked out. They'll probably know if we try to set up close surveillance."

Freddie rubbed the back of his head.

"Like last time," he said.

"Our best bet might be for me to just suit up, walk in, make the drop and walk out—if they let me."

"Like sweet cheeks did."

"Yeah."

"What about me?"

"You're in the car."

"You expect me to drive you to the site, sit back while you make the drop, then drive you home after?"

"Let's hope it's that simple."

"If it ain't?"

"I expect you to shoot somebody."

"Be happy to. You know they're leavin' us hangin' out there, right? If somethin' goes wrong Boucek, the FBI, even the Chief are all gonna be indignant as hell, tellin' the world they did the best they could, but those boys just wouldn't listen."

"I know. On the other hand, if we skip out the door, what happens to Quinn?"

"We don't owe her a thing. Or Charles."

"Screw that old man," I said. "If the girl is hurt or worse, though, and we could have prevented it and didn't—that's a pretty heavy debt to carry, don't you think?"

Freddie didn't answer. Instead, we walked in silence until we were halted by the light at the corner near where the Butler Square Building was located.

"If things go sideways," Freddie said. "I think I will shoot somebody."

Anne Scalasi didn't wait for me to call her. Instead, she called me. We were in the elevator going up when my cell rang.

"Assistant Chief Scalasi," I said.

"I can always tell when you're angry."

"How? Is it my tone of voice?"

Freddie started chuckling.

"Hey, Chief." He spoke loud enough to be picked up by the cell's microphone. "Don't let Taylor give you shit."

The elevator stopped, the doors slid open, and we stepped out of the car. Freddie went on ahead to unlock the office while I lingered behind in the corridor.

"Should I tell you what happened?" Anne asked.

"If you like."

"C'mon, Holland. Don't be like that. You know I want this case, especially now that I know it's connected to the Burrell matter. I live for this. Except I received a call at five this morning telling me we are going to cooperate with Mr. Boucek at the present time."

"Who's we?"

"The mayor and me."

"The mayor who may or may not appoint you chief of police when the time comes?"

219

"Yeah, him. Apparently, Boucek had called the St. Paul PD and claimed that his daughter had been kidnapped. An hour later, though, he called the mayor and walked it back. Of course, by then, the mechanism that is a high-priority police investigation was in high gear, so they needed at least a one-star to shut it down. I got the call."

"If it all goes badly, you'll also get the blame. After me and Freddie, of course."

"So don't let it go badly."

"Sounds like a plan."

"In the meantime…"

Anne told me that while her hands were tied concerning Quinn Jordan's disappearance, there was nothing keeping her from expanding the Tracy Burrell investigation.

"There must be a hundred traffic and store security cameras in Little Mekong that we can access," she said.

"Anne…"

"What?"

"I love you."

From the way she laughed, I got the impression Anne thought that I was being funny.

"Besides this insanity, how have you been?" she asked. "I haven't spoken to you for a while."

"I've been better."

"In case you're wondering, Ashley Leighton Redman, the famed architect who was born in Des Moines yet behaves like he's the Prince of Wales, is in Bangkok supervising the construction of a hotel, so when this is all over, if you want to drop by and talk…"

"Seems to me we had a discussion before about you, me, and your husband."

"I remember."

"Annie, when this is over, I would very much like to come over and talk."

"You know where I live."

As I ended the call, it occurred to me that a statistically im-
probable number of attractive women—Claire, Alex, and
Annie—all wanted to sleep with me.

"Apparently, I'm a catch," I said out loud.

Freddie was sitting behind his desk when I entered the office.
He heard what I said and seemed to know exactly what I was
talking about.

"Catch and release," he said. "Women think you're a poor
little broken boy and they want to fix you. Afterward,
though..."

He threw a thumb at the door.

"Mr. Fredericks, you are a cynical man."

The Grand Rounds Trail was a paved pedestrian walkway that
looped in an irregular circle for fifty miles through the City of
Minneapolis. Bikers and hikers and people just out for a stroll
used it not only for exercise but also to access the city's spider
web of lakes, parks, and trails. Some even used it for daily
travel, taking the scenic route from their homes to their jobs.
That's why it was cleared of snow and ice at six every single
morning in the winter.

Freddie and I hovered over a 3D map of the trail on his
computer.

"God knows how far they're gonna ask you to walk," Freddie said. "Walk 'til you drop."

"Then they wouldn't care where or when I started. Instead,
they want me to go off at exactly six PM from 29th Avenue.
They'll probably be watching to make sure I'm not being
followed. I'm guessing they'll approach me before the sun sets
at eight-fifty-seven, according to the weather people."

"Three hours. The average person walks three-point-one
miles an hour."

"I can do better than that."

"How much better? Remember you'll be carrying a four-pound bag, wearing a six-pound vest and it's hot outside."

"I can do twelve miles in three hours."

"Which would put you way over here by sundown." Freddie tapped the computer screen at a spot where the trail crossed a bridge spanning the Mississippi River and looped south. "That would take you out of North Minneapolis by several miles."

"Assuming North Minneapolis is important. I'm betting..." I did some tapping of my own. "Here."

"How much?"

"A nickel."

"The Victory Flagpole is the cornerstone of Victory Memorial Parkway," Freddie said. "It was built a hundred years ago to commemorate those guys from Hennepin County that were killed in World War One. Don't know if people know that so much, but it's a park, man. This whole area, one really long park; I mean miles long, narrow park. There'll be a lot of civilians hangin' around."

"I believe that's why the kidnappers want us on the trail at six PM in the first place. They know by the time I follow the trail into the park, the place will be crawling with bikers and hikers and joggers, people walking their dogs. We'll never see them coming."

"On the other hand, they would never see the FBI coming, either."

"They're not afraid of the FBI," I said.

"Sure don't seem to be. Alright, what we'll do, we'll take both of our cars and park here on Bottineau Boulevard. Then we'll take your car and sweep around the neighborhood before I drop you here, where 29th Avenue North and the Grand Rounds Trail intersect. At exactly six, you'll start walking up the trail.

"You'll enter Victory Memorial Parkway here." Freddie tapped the computer screen again. "The trail runs straight like a ruler for several miles through the park until it reaches the flagpole. On your right will be Victory Memorial Drive, a two-lane street, twenty-five-mile-an-hour speed limit, no parking.

There'll be plenty of open space between you and the drive, fifty yards or more. On the other hand, we have York Avenue on your left, two lanes of traffic and plenty of places to park. It runs parallel to the trail all the way up to the flagpole, plus the grassy median between the avenue and the trail is only ten yards wide. If they come at you with a car, they'll be doing it from York."

"I agree."

"They want you to deliver the ransom because they know who you are," Freddie said. "We don't know how they know this; only that they do. Unfortunately, we don't know them. Every single person you encounter on the trail, man or woman, could be one of the kidnappers. It would be easy for them to approach you, say gimme the bag, run to York or even Memorial Drive for that matter, hop in a car and boom, they're gone."

"That's one way of doing it."

"Meantime, I'll be two blocks over from York on Zenith Avenue. After I drop you off, I'll drive a couple of miles out of the way to make sure I'm not being followed, head back to Bottineau and switch cars. They might know your vehicle from before, but they won't know mine. Then I'll get on Zenith and skip along the avenue a half mile at a time, trying to keep pace with you. You'll have a radio like before. Talk to me. Call out the side streets as you pass them. Let me know exactly where you are and what's going on around you."

"Freddie, if it does go down the way you expect, you can't give chase," I said. "We can't put Quinn in danger."

"I know. I'll just be there to drive you home. Or identify your body. Whichever."

After that, we hung around the office. Freddie ran a couple of skip traces while I managed a few employee background checks, working on automatic pilot, killing time. Freddie asked me if I was thirsty. I said I was, and we each had a Grain Belt beer, but only one. Finally, our landline rang. Gillard said the FBI had returned the money. I was surprised it had taken so long.

"It's a bureaucracy," he said. "What did you expect? Mr. Taylor, I must apologize for what I said to you and your partner this morning. I spoke out of turn. My concern for the well-being of Charles and, of course, for the safety of Ms. Boucek, got the better of me. I hope we can forget the matter and move on."

I told Gillard I'd be right over and hung up. Freddie asked if I wanted him to tag along. I said he should otherwise, all that cash, I might be tempted to jump a plane and fly to Costa Rica. He said change the destination to Jamaica, and he'd go with me.

Ten minutes later, we were standing in Charles Boucek's outer office. Quinn would have been gratified by our promptness.

A dark blue travel bag with the red and white logo of the Minnesota Twins sat open on a table. Gillard hovered over it like a kid waiting for someone to announce it's time to eat cake. Charles Boucek was sitting straight up in one of his comfy chairs. As always, he was impeccably attired, as always, the lines of his suit jacket straight. He was staring at the bag as if it were a bomb.

"There it is," Gillard said.

I looked inside. The eyes in many portraits of Andrew Jackson arranged in neat packets looked back. I zipped the bag shut and lifted it by its two handles. Gillard exhaled as if he had been holding his breath.

"Nervous, Bruce?" Freddie asked.

"Not at all. I know you both will do the right thing."

"Charles," I said. "Charles?"

His eyes darted from the bag to my face. This is a man, I told myself, who prided himself on being at all times in complete control of any situation, yet now he appeared as if he were incapable of buttering a slice of toast.

"It'll be alright," I said.

He didn't answer.

"What are you going to do now?" Gillard asked.

Freddie glanced at his watch.

"I'm hungry," he said. "You wanna get some Chinese?"

I glanced at my own watch.

"Sure," I said. "We have time."

Freddie and I headed for the door. Gillard followed us.

"I know a place," he said.

Freddie put a hand on his chest to stop him.

"You're not invited," he said.

Fifteen minutes later, we were back in our office. A half hour after that, we were on the road. We never did stop to eat.

CHAPTER THIRTY-ONE

I had underestimated the heat. Under normal conditions, eighty degrees and sunny would have been very pleasant, a perfect summer day in Minnesota. Only I was carrying an extra twelve pounds, including the nine-millimeter Beretta holstered behind my right hip. Plus, I was wearing a windbreaker zipped to my throat. I have no idea what people might have thought as they passed me on the Grand Rounds Trail.

"I'm sweating like a pig," I said.

The two-way radio was hidden beneath the windbreaker, the speaker clipped under my chin and the earpiece in my left ear.

"Pigs don't actually sweat," Freddie said.

"What are you talking about?"

"They have sweat glands, but they don't sweat. At least not a lot. The saying—it comes from smeltin' pig iron. They call it pig iron, by the way, cuz the iron is shaped in molds that branch off like piglets sucking on a—what do they call a mamma pig? A sow, yeah, yeah, yeah."

"A helluva thing to tell a guy while he's marching to his certain doom."

"Bitchy, bitch, bitch. Every time we do something like this, you get so whiney. Can't you just appreciate what a beautiful day it is? Women walkin' 'round in short shorts and short skirts...This is why I live in Minnesota, man."

I had been on the trail for well over thirty minutes, having worked through the concrete spaghetti that had been the convergence of Theodore Wirth Parkway, West Broadway Avenue, Lowry Avenue, Oakdale Avenue, and Bottineau Boulevard. I had just passed 34th Avenue North and no one had yet tried to kill me.

"So you got that goin' for you," Freddie said.

I kept moving north, the travel bag bouncing against my thigh as I walked. Various vehicles drove past me on both York Avenue and Victory Memorial Drive, yet none of them slowed down. I couldn't tell if any of the drivers had paid much attention to me, and I looked hard. I noticed the middle-class houses that lined both sides of the park were well maintained. They had a welcome-home vibe that reminded me of the house where Laura, Jenny and I had once lived and were happy.

I passed 35th Avenue, 36th, and 37th, calling out the names for Freddie. I encountered several joggers and more than a few hikers. Half gave me a smile and a nod; half ignored me completely, which was about average in Minnesota. A couple with a small dog who wanted to be my friend slowed me down. I gave the dog a pet and kept moving.

Thirty-eighth, 39th, 40th...

"There are all these plaques with crosses and stars imbedded in the ground," I said.

"Near the trees."

"Yeah."

"Those are the monuments, man. I told you before, this whole park area was designed to commemorate the 568 soldiers and nurses who got killed in the First World War. They planted the monuments with the name and rank of the fallen and they planted the trees, 568 trees exactly, back in 1921. How come you don't know these things?"

"I grew up in St. Paul."

Forty-first, 42nd, 43rd and I was beginning to wonder if this was the best plan I've ever had.

"You could've been a business guy like your old man

wanted," Freddie said.

"You could have become an actor like your mom wanted."

"We are great disappointments to them both."

"I'm nearly there."

I was talking about the Flagpole, where I was convinced the kidnappers would contact me. That's where both the trail and the memorial drive took a hard right and went due east for about three miles. It was nearly a half mile away. I didn't even get close.

Instead, I was intercepted by a black man. He was tall and thin and wore a goatee. I knew him without ever having seen him before. He was dragging a dog along on a leash. I say dragging because the dog seemed determined to run off in a different direction.

I described it all to Freddie.

"Call me if you need me," he said.

The black man tried hard not to look me in the eye. Mostly he was watching the Twins travel bag in my left hand. He didn't speak until we were nearly side by side.

"Taylor?"

The question told me I had been correct before. He hadn't known what I looked like.

I stopped.

He stopped.

"Take this."

The black man gave me the leash. The dog it was attached to tried to pull me off the trail, yet I held firm.

"I'll take that."

The black man made a gimme gesture toward the travel bag with his now empty hand.

I gave him the bag.

"Keep walking," he said.

I did—one step, two, three, four...

"What the fuck?" the black man said.

I spun toward him.

"What the fuck is this?" he asked.

He was holding what should have been a fistful of twenty-dollar bills in his hand. Except they were sheets of newspaper cut to the size of dollar bills.

"I don't get it," I said.

"You sonuvabitch."

The black man threw the bag to the ground and pulled a Sig Sauer 9mm. At the same time, a silver Kia Rio pulled to a stop along York Avenue. The driver leaned on his horn.

"No, wait," I said.

He knew how to shoot.

He fired three rounds.

They all hit me center mass.

The bullets lifted me off my feet and threw me down on the pavement.

I lost my breath when I hit the ground.

I tried to gain some more, but my lungs didn't seem to be working properly.

I don't know how I got the word out. "Freddie."

CHAPTER THIRTY-TWO

Freddie half walked me, half carried me into the same emergency room at North Memorial Hospital in Robbinsdale where they had treated his head injury. Along the way, I tried to explain what had happened. I must have done a nice job of it because he didn't ask many questions beyond "You're not going to die on me, are you Taylor?"

"If I do, I expect you to sue DuPont."

DuPont is the company that manufactured the Kevlar vest I had been wearing beneath my windbreaker.

"You need to call Boucek," I said. "Tell him about the ransom money. The ransom money was switched. I shoulda counted it. Or at least looked at it. Why didn't I look at it? He's gotta know that. The girl. They shot me, Freddie. They shot me three times. What'll they do to Quinn? This is so messed up. What happened to the dog?"

"What dog?"

"The shooter—he gave me a leash and the dog. You don't think they stole a dog, do you?"

"I didn't see any dog. Just a bunch of people standing around and asking themselves what they should do about you."

"What did they decide?"

The same emergency medical specialist who had treated Freddie also treated me.

"How do you feel?" he asked.

I wanted to say I felt like I had been smacked full force three times with a baseball bat or that I felt as if someone had hit me with a sledgehammer, except I've never been hit by a baseball bat or a sledgehammer. And I couldn't imagine that either would hurt as much as this did.

"I feel like I've been shot," I said.

I was lying on an examining room table and clothed in nothing but my briefs, socks, and a hospital gown. I was cold and in pain, but my head had cleared. I was suddenly able to speak in coherent sentences and hold an adult conversation.

There was a light box next to the examination table, and the doctor slid an x-ray over it.

"You have two cracked ribs," he said.

I didn't see the cracks in the ribs pictured in the x-ray, yet I took his word for it. Certainly, the pain on my left side seemed to support his conclusion.

"Nothing we can do for that except to let them heal," the doctor said. "A month, maybe longer."

"I've fractured ribs before." I spoke like I was proud of myself. Go figure.

The doctor removed the x-ray and put up a different picture of my chest.

"The CT scan we took reveals that you're also suffering from a pulmonary contusion," he said.

The words "pulmonary contusion" were new to me and they made me flinch.

"Sounds serious," I said.

"You have a bruised lung. That could have been very serious except in this case there's some swelling but no bleeding. I don't think the injury is severe enough to require oxygen therapy. So, we'll let it heal itself like your ribs. It'll hurt. Breathing, especially taking deep breaths, will be painful and somewhat difficult for a few days. We can give you something for the pain."

"Okay."

"Your other bruises…"

There were three of them hidden beneath the hospital gown, two on my chest and one on my abdomen. Despite the comparatively small size of the bullets, the bruises they left were as large as softballs. There was a dime-size burn mark in the center of each of the two on my chest where the heat from the 9mm rounds seared my flesh. People who watch a lot of detective shows might be surprised by this. On TV, the bullets just bounce off the vest, and the hero goes out for pizza. What viewers don't understand is that in real life bullet-proof vests, including the Kevlar vest I had been wearing, aren't actually bullet proof. They're "bullet-resistant." They might stop the rounds, but their energy has to go somewhere. It's basic physics.

"You were lucky," the doctor said.

"I know."

"The hospital is required by law to report any and all gunshot wounds to the police department. Even superficial wounds like these." He held up a finger as if that would reverse time. "Forgive me. I'm sure they don't feel superficial."

"I was a cop for a long time, Doctor. I'll take superficial any day."

"Tell me the name of your favorite pharmacy. We'll call in a prescription, and you can go pick it up. In the meantime, there's a police officer waiting outside who wants to interview you."

"Can I get dressed first?"

"Get dressed and go out for coffee for all I care."

"I can leave?"

"There's nothing more that I can do for you. I'd tell you to take it easy for a month or so, but I think your body will speak more forcefully than I can."

"Thank you, Doctor."

"You're welcome. By the way, I hope you and your friend Frederickson…"

"Fredericks."

"I hope you and he don't make a habit of this."

"We'll try not to. About the pain—I don't suppose I could lobby you for a little medicinal marijuana?"

"For a lung injury? Nice try."

Freddie wasn't always the most diplomatic when it came to dealing with what he insisted on calling "the white man's police department" yet he and the MPD officer were chatting in the waiting room like they were brothers from a different mother. Clearly, Freddie was trying to use charm to limit official involvement. When I arrived, he introduced the officer by his first name and not his last.

"I'm required to ask a few questions, Mr. Taylor, if you're up to it," the officer said.

"Call me Holland, please…"

I told the officer just enough to keep him from pursuing an investigation beyond the hospital door. All the while I watched Freddie pace the waiting room. He was as anxious to get out of there as I was.

Once I finished with the officer, Freddie practically sprinted to his car in the parking lot. I was forced to move at a much more deliberate pace. I told him why. He was less sympathetic than I thought he might be.

"Did I tell you about the time my head got caved in by a tree branch?" he asked.

"By all means, explain how that's so much worse than getting shot three times."

"I wasn't wearing Kevlar."

He had me there.

"Let's get your car and then we should go see Boucek," Freddie said. "He's waitin' on us."

"Did you tell him what happened?"

"I called right after I brought you to the hospital."

"He must be going crazy with worry over Quinn."

"You'd think so, but he seems to be holdin' up pretty well. Better than this mornin', anyway."

"How is that possible?"

Bruce Gillard was waiting for us at the security desk in the lobby. It was nearly ten o'clock, and unaccompanied guests weren't allowed to wander the building where Boucek and Associates was located. We called ahead, and Boucek sent Gillard down to escort us up.

"What happened?" he wanted to know. "I've been waiting with Charles for news about Quinn."

"Was that your idea or his?"

"Mine until, well, until you called, and then he told me to stay close."

Gillard spent a lot of time staring at the Twins travel bag Freddie was carrying. Freddie had recovered it from where the kidnapper had dropped it at the crime scene. I think he might have grabbed the bag before he grabbed me. I'd have to ask him about that later, I decided.

"What's going on?" Gillard asked.

By then we had crossed the lobby to the bank of elevators. Once again, I was moving gingerly.

"Are you alright?" Gillard asked.

"Damn, you ask a lot of questions," Freddie said.

We took the elevator; a weak cover of *The Girl From Ipanema* was spilling from the hidden speakers.

"How many crooners does it take to sing *The Girl From Ipanema*?" Freddie asked. "All of them."

I thought that was funny, but laughing was like being punched in my left side. I lost my breath, and it took several floors for me to recover it. Gillard looked on with an expression of alarm.

Freddie said, "This is going to be fun."

"Fun?" I asked.

"I have a bunch of Chris Rock jokes memorized. *If you haven't contemplated murder, you ain't been in love...*"

The elevator stopped just in time. We left the car and marched down the corridor to Boucek's outer office, or at least as close to marching as I could manage. Gillard hopped in front of me and opened the door. I passed through it without breaking stride. Boucek was sitting in one of his comfy chairs. He stood as I walked up to him. Behind me, Freddie closed the door and leaned against it. Gillard halted midway between Freddie and where Boucek and I were standing.

"If you had asked me when she was alive, I would have told you I loved my daughter so much I would have given my life to keep her safe," I said. "After she died, I realized I loved her even more than that. What's your opinion on the subject?"

Boucek didn't hesitate. It was like he had been anticipating the question.

"I'd not only give my life for Quinn," he said. "I'd also give yours and Freddie's and my ex-wife's and Abby Hudson's and every other human being I know."

"I believe you. Bruce?"

I looked over my shoulder at him. He glanced at Freddie and moved cautiously forward until he was within striking distance.

"Yes?" he said.

I spun and hit him with my right hand as hard as I could—and promptly felt as if I had been shot again. The pain in my ribs caused me to slump against Boucek's chair. Breathing became nearly impossible. It was like sucking oxygen through a straw.

Gillard recoiled from my blow. Unfortunately, I hadn't been strong enough to knock him down. He covered his face with one hand, spun around, and headed for the office door. Freddie blocked his path.

"Goin' somewhere?" he asked.

"Let me pass."

Freddie pushed him backward. Gillard didn't want to go. Freddie pushed him again, putting more weight into it. Gillard nearly fell, yet managed to retain his balance.

"Charles, what is this?" he asked.

"I'm not sure."

"Yes, you are," Freddie said.

He gave him another shove, and Gillard fell against one of the Chesterfields.

"Why are you doing this?" he asked.

By then, I had regained my composure.

"Where's the money, Bruce?" I asked.

"Money? I don't know what you're talking about."

Freddie opened the travel bag and dumped its contents on top of Gillard. Mostly it contained packets held together with rubber bands, each with a twenty-dollar bill on top, a twenty on the bottom and cut up newspaper in between. At least one of the packets had been undone, however, and the loose paper fell on Gillard like snow.

Freddie leaned in close and screamed—"Where's the money, Bruce?"

I thought Gillard was going to break into tears. "Please, please," he chanted.

Freddie looked at me and smiled.

"Sometimes how you speak matters as much as what you say," he said.

"Meh," I said.

Gillard witnessed the exchange and knew we were laughing at him. He decided to man up, yet his voice was shaky.

"Charles," he said. "Call off your dogs."

"Dogs?" I asked.

I drew the Beretta that had done me no good whatsoever when I was on the Grand Rounds Trail. I didn't even need to point it before Gillard covered up and started chanting "Oh please, oh, please, oh please…"

"Bruce, what did you do?" Boucek asked.

"Oh please, oh please…"

"Holland," Freddie said.

"What?"

He gestured at the Berreta in my hand and said, "The guards down at the security desk saw us come up with him."

"You're right." I holstered the Beretta, making sure Gillard saw me do it. "If you don't tell us what we want to know, we'll shoot you when no one's looking."

"Tell me about the money," Boucek said.

He was talking to his business associate. However, since Gillard demonstrated no inclination to answer, I did.

"The ransom money was switched. If you didn't do it, then Gillard must have." I pointed a finger at his face like it was a gun. "Don't even think of blaming the FBI. I gave the bag containing the ransom to the kidnapper. He looked inside and found newspaper disguised as twenty-dollar bills. He was understandably upset. So much so that he shot me, Bruce. He shot me three times. If I wasn't wearing Kevlar, I would be dead right now, so imagine how upset I must be."

"That wasn't supposed to happen," Gillard said.

"What did you think was going to happen?"

Gillard didn't answer.

"What? Did you think the police would become involved and that would be it? What the fuck, Bruce?"

Gillard still refused to answer. He closed his eyes and became still, like a child who thought that's all it took to become invisible.

"What about my daughter?" Boucek asked.

"I don't know," I said.

"Shootin' Taylor was a spontaneous act," Freddie said. "The kidnappers will take their time, think it through before they decide t' hurt Quinn. I believe they'll contact us in a day or two and offer a second chance to pay the ransom, although the amount will probably go up."

"On what do you base this hypothesis besides wishful thinking?" Boucek asked.

"You said it yourself; the kidnappers are businessmen. They want t' keep doin' business. Besides, right now they know they're dealin' with just you and me and Taylor. They hurt Quinn, they gotta know all the cops in the world will come after 'em."

Freddie had been right about Boucek. That morning, he seemed incapable of rational thought, yet now he appeared as sharp as ever. I didn't know why. Perhaps the shock of Quinn's kidnapping had affected him the same way getting shot had affected me. It took awhile before the surprise wore off.

Boucek moved to where Gillard lay sprawled on the Chesterfield and hovered above him.

"Tell me about this," he said.

Gillard shook his head. I didn't know if that meant he wouldn't answer or didn't know how.

"He was trembling at the rumors that you might move to Washington with Abigail Hudson if she's elected to the Senate," I said. "He was looking for a way to wreck your business, pick up the pieces, and start his own. In a small way, Freddie and I might be responsible for what happened next. Bruce all but admitted his plans to us and asked for our assistance. We not only told him to stick it in his ear, we might have left him with the impression that we were going to give him up. He panicked."

"Or not," Freddie said. "Could be he thought that a couple of dead bodies was a small price t' pay."

"In any case, Bruce was sure if Quinn were hurt, you'd bring in the FBI and the media would probably learn about the other kidnappings you negotiated. All hell would break loose. Your business would suffer, and he'd take advantage. Course, I'm just speculating."

"Is this true, Bruce?" Boucek asked.

Gillard tried to meet his gaze, yet failed.

"Answer me."

"It's fake news," Gillard said. "Taylor and Fredericks are making it up. They're inventing stories to hide their own ineptitude. They probably kept the money for themselves."

"A viable response," Boucek said. "Faced with comparable circumstances, I might have said something similar. I might even have attempted a coup just as you have. However, to deliberately endanger the life of a young woman…" He tapped his chest. "My daughter. Anyone's daughter. I like to believe that there are lengths to which even I won't go."

Boucek turned away from Gillard and moved back to his comfy chair. I noticed he didn't mention the danger to my life or Freddie's yet. I decided not to make a thing of it. Boucek sat, pulling the hem of his jacket beneath him to maintain his straight lines.

"You may go," he said.

Gillard scrambled to his feet.

"We'll speak again tomorrow," Boucek said.

Gillard seemed confused. He hadn't even been fired, much less threatened. I thought I had it figured out, though. It went back to Chinese General Sun Tzu and his book *The Art of War—keep your friends close and enemies closer.*

Boucek seemed to confirm my theory when Gillard reached the office door.

"Bruce," he said. "I expect you to return the fifty thousand dollars before you leave. In addition, you must realize from personal experience working for me that there is nowhere you can hide that I can't find you. My recommendation is to stay close and pray for the safe return of my daughter."

CHAPTER THIRTY-THREE

After Gillard departed, I again lobbied Boucek to involve the FBI. Again, he refused. I told him events were spiraling out of control. He didn't agree. Apparently, Freddie's theory concerning the kidnappers' next move seemed reasonable to him. I told him that Freddie and I would remain all-in until Quinn was safely returned. He thanked us. I also told him that afterward all bets were off. He said he understood.

Ten minutes later, Freddie and I were back on the street.

"I've never been this tired before in my life," I said. "I keep yawning."

"I realize I'm just a poor black child with no proper education…"

"Here we go again."

"I think the yawnin' is cuz the paraventricular nucleus of the hypothalamus of the brain ain't gittin' enough oxygen. You need to take a couple of deep breaths."

"First—each deep breath is like being stabbed with a knife, okay? Second—poor, uneducated black child? You went to the University of Iowa."

"On a football scholarship."

"Are you telling me you didn't learn anything?"

"I learned that low oxygen levels in the paraventricular nucleus of the hypothalamus of the brain can cause yawning. Other than that…Saturday. If the 'nappers keep usin' the Postal

Service, we won't hear from 'em until Saturday. They wouldn't have had time to get an envelope in the mail t'night. That means we have all tomorrow to figure it out."

"Assuming they haven't already dropped Quinn's dead body in the Mississippi River."

"Would you do that?"

"No, but I wouldn't have kidnapped her in the first place."

"The fact they snatched sweet cheeks so quick after botchin' the Burrell kidnappin' tells us something, though."

"What does it tell us?"

"They've got a list."

"I wonder what it takes to get on it."

"Not much more we can screw up tonight," Freddie said. "See ya in the office first thing, a'ite?"

"Sounds like a plan."

"I'd give you a ride home, but it'll take longer to heal if people start babyin' you."

"I appreciate that you're looking out for me."

"What partners do."

Every bone in my body ached, not just my ribs. I parked my Camry in the asphalt lot behind my apartment building and cautiously unfolded myself as I slid out of the car, wondering if this is what it felt like to be 100 years old. If it was—kill me at 95, I decided. I shuffled to the concrete steps leading to the back door. There were only four, yet climbing them made me feel like George Mallory attempting to summit Mount Everest. Wait, I told myself. He's the one who didn't make it.

I was standing on the concrete landing and imputing the security code when I heard him.

"Taylor, right?"

I pivoted toward the voice. It took me a few seconds to find it. Douglas Wedemeyer was standing between two parked cars. I didn't realize that my hand had moved to the butt of my

Beretta until I released it or that I had been holding my breath until I exhaled.

"Oh, did I startle you?" Wedemeyer asked. He quoted the air around the word "startle." "Were you"—more quotes—"frightened?"

"What are you doing here?" I asked.

"What are you doing here?"

"I live here."

"Do you?"

Wedemeyer left his position between the cars and moved toward me like we were friends and he wanted to say hello. Except we weren't friends. It was past eleven PM, and he had been hiding in my parking lot. Was he waiting for me? A dozen scenarios played out in my head as he approached, none of them pleasant. I felt his fingers on my fight or flight switch.

"What do you want?" I asked.

"What do you want?"

He reminded me of a child purposely repeating every word a sibling might say in order to accomplish what? Anger me enough to call my parents to make him stop?

"I want to be left alone," I said.

"I'll leave you alone if you leave me alone."

Most of the bullying I've endured in my life was mental, sometimes emotional. It came from teachers, coaches, instructors at the police academy, my superiors in the SPPD, other cops, prosecutors and defense attorneys, a few criminals, the occasional client now that I work private, and a lady lawyer who stomped on my heart. That didn't mean I couldn't recognize a physical bully when I saw one.

"Are you trying to be funny?" I said.

"Are you trying to be funny?"

Wedemeyer climbed the stairs until he was standing on the narrow concrete landing. I moved away from him, pressing my backside against the iron railing, putting as much distance between us as possible. He clearly enjoyed my discomfort.

Why would he do this? I wondered. Did Wedemeyer really think he could bully me? Why would he want to? Yeah, I was in piss-poor condition if it came to a fight. I couldn't even knock down Bruce Gillard. Wedemeyer didn't know that, though. Did he?

I felt the pain as I inhaled.

"You shouldn't be here," I said.

"You shouldn't be here."

"Why are you being such a jerk?"

"You're the jerk—jerk."

It didn't make sense. Until I saw a slight movement out of the corner of my eye and the far-away glint of light off something metal, and then it did. I was willing to bet a nickel that there was someone hidden in the parking lot with a camera. I folded my arms across my chest and waited.

Wedwemeyer did the same. It was almost laughable. He wanted me to start babbling, maybe bring up his wife and daughter. Tell him he doesn't deserve Claire or Amanda, tell him I'm twice the man he is. Shove him or perhaps take a full swing. He'd get it on film and edit the footage to prove to a jury that I was a deranged hothead who posed a clear and present danger to Amanda. He'd blame Claire for allowing me to get close to her, accuse Claire of putting her sexual needs before her child. It was the kind of thing I might have done for a client. Actually, no. I wouldn't do that.

I took slow, shallow breaths because I didn't want Wedemeyer and his partner to know I was in pain. I remained still for the same reason. In this one regard, it was good that I had been hurt. Given my nature, I probably would have popped Wedemeyer ten minutes ago.

You'd have thought that a long jolt in prison would instill Wedemeyer with a modicum of patience. It didn't. After a few moments of my staring at him and saying nothing, he said, "Well?"

"Well, what?"

"Have you got something to say?"

"Have you got something to say? You're the one who's trespassing on private property." I decided Wedemeyer was probably wired for sound; I spoke quickly so my words couldn't be easily edited. "Say? Aren't you supposed to be locked up in a halfway house somewhere so the authorities can monitor your criminal behavior? What is an ex-convict doing hiding in a parking lot at midnight, anyway?"

Of course, it was closer to eleven, but midnight sounded more ominous.

Give him points for gall. Wedemeyer wasn't about to give up his game just yet. He started to mimic me again, repeating "What are you doing hiding in parking lot..."

I cut him off.

"You're a thief," I said. "You came here to rob people."

That caught him off guard. He tried to recover by saying, "Stay away from my family."

"Okay, I get it now. You're stalking your ex-wife. You want to hurt my neighbor, Ms. Wedemeyer."

"You want to hurt Ms. Wedemeyer."

I put my hand in my pocket. Wedemeyer flinched. Perhaps he thought I was reaching for a weapon. Instead, I retrieved my cell phone and tapped the "Emergency Call" icon on the screen.

The operator said, "Nine-one-one, where is your emergency?" She asked where because I was calling from a cell phone.

I gave her my name and location and said, "There's a man hiding in the parking lot behind the building. He's an ex-convict named Douglas Wedemeyer. I think he came here to assault his ex-wife and daughter."

Wedemeyer exploded with a half dozen obscenities and threats. I held the phone up. When he realized what I was doing, he stopped talking. I asked the operator, "Did you get all that?"

"I'll get you for this, Taylor," Wedemeyer said. "I'll get you."

The operator said that a St. Paul police officer was on his way.

I said I'd wait.

Wedemeyer leapt off the steps and dashed across the parking lot. He gestured at a figure I couldn't recognize as being a man or woman and the two of them took off down the alley.

The patrol car arrived seven minutes and thirty-two seconds later, which was actually a pretty good response time. All the while, the 911 operator remained on the line.

"I don't want to tell you your business," I said. "Only you might want to hang on to the tape of the 911 call."

The operator said that they always did.

Of course, I knew that.

The officer was young and eager. He arrived anticipating an "unstable scene" with an imminent threat to life and property yet instead found a "priority two." Still, he was good at making a detailed report, especially after I informed him with no prodding whatsoever that I had been on the job myself. I was tempted to drop Anne Scalasi's name as well to see if that might snap him to attention, only I knew she wouldn't approve.

After he finished with me, we went up to 2B and knocked on the door. Claire was wearing a pink robe she cinched tightly around her waist when she answered. I looked her up and down like I was seeing her for the first time and then cursed myself out for it. *What is wrong with you?* I asked myself. She's a friend. Like Annie's a friend.

The officer was as apologetic as hell for disturbing her and said he needed to ask a few questions.

Claire answered them.

Yes, she was Wedemeyer's ex-wife; they had divorced while he was in prison.

No, she didn't know he was stalking her although he contacted her several times since he was released from prison.

245

No, she didn't know how he got her address and phone number.

She disappeared inside the apartment and then reappeared with the address of Wedemeyer's halfway house on the eastside of St. Paul as well as the name of his parole office. Wedemeyer had supplied both, she said, because he claimed he had nothing to hide.

Afterward, Claire apologized to me, in front of the officer, for everything that happened since we were merely neighbors and barely knew each other, which I thought was a nice touch.

The officer apologized again for disturbing her and told Claire if she saw her ex-husband in the area again to immediately contact the police. Claire asked if that was necessary. The officer said "We don't know for sure if he's stalking you. The fact he was seen near your apartment this late at night raises questions, however. In any case, residential rehabilitation centers have curfew requirements, and obviously he is in violation. So we'll see."

Claire thanked the officer for his service.

I thanked him, too, and drifted to my apartment.

After he departed, I went back to see Claire.

"You said Douglas might do something like this," she said.

"Yes."

"Will this hurt his chances of gaining custody of Amanda, do you think? The police report and everything?"

"I don't know. He could easily say I made it all up."

"We have the 911 tape. The police will have it."

"He could also argue that he was here because he feared for the safety of his daughter because of your poor parenting and immoral conduct."

"Would anyone believe that?"

"I'm just saying—this is the beginning, not the end."

"What should I do?"

"Nothing. You and Mandy are innocent bystanders in all of this."

"What are you going to do?"

"Nothing as far as you know. If anyone should ask, I'm just your neighbor with a rabbit that your daughter likes to play with from time to time."

Claire decided I was more than that. To prove it, she wrapped her arms around my waist and pulled me close. I winced at the pain it caused. She quickly released me.

"Are you all right?" she asked.

What was I going to tell her? That I had been shot five hours ago?

"A pulled muscle," I said. "Hug me again in the morning. I'll be feeling much better."

CHAPTER THIRTY-FOUR

I didn't see Claire Wedemeyer Friday morning, which was just as well. For one thing, I felt much worse than I had the evening before. It was more difficult and painful to draw a full breath, and because of my tender ribs, I had slept for about six minutes. I considered taking the pain pills that were waiting for me at the pharmacy, only I was afraid they would cloud my judgment which, let's face it, hadn't been operating at peak efficiency recently.

I was also feeling conflicted. I received a phone call first thing from Assistant Chief Anne Scalasi, who wanted to know what had happened to me. So I explained in glorious detail. Unlike Freddie, she seemed genuinely concerned for my health and well-being.

"How's the investigation going?" I asked.

"Burrell? About what you'd expect. We're gathering plenty of film, but we don't know exactly what we're looking at."

"I can't speak to the Asian, but the African-America is tall, thin, and is sporting a goatee."

"That'll narrow it down. I don't suppose you could be prevailed upon to examine some footage."

The remark dinged my conscience.

"I'm sorry I didn't call you last might as promised, Annie," I said. "The way I was feeling, I didn't think I'd be of much use to you. Or anyone else for at least a couple of weeks."

"Did it ever occur to you when I asked you to drop by and talk that I actually meant talk? You and I were very close for a long time, Holland. I miss you. I miss hearing about your adventures with Freddie and your girlfriend troubles. I miss having someone to tell all my troubles to."

I silently called myself a few names before saying "I'm sorry" again.

"You're my friend, and I don't have that many," Anne said.

"I don't have many friends, either."

"Sex would have been nice, Holland. Don't get me wrong about that. Have you noticed though—it's much more fun when it doesn't mean anything?"

I flashed on Alex Campbell and her endless imagination.

"Yes," I said.

"I'll call you if I learn anything new about the Burrell incident I can share. Holland? Please be careful."

I beat Freddie into the office by fifteen minutes. I was sipping a mug of chocolate caramel brownie coffee, a flavor provided by Cameron's Coffee, a local company based in Shakopee. He took one look at me and said "You look like shit."

"Good morning to you, too."

"Git any sleep?'

"Do I look like I got any sleep?"

I explained briefly about my neighbor and her trials and tribulations involving her ex-husband; Freddie had met Claire and Amanda and liked them both.

"Married guys know more about women than single guys." I knew from the way he was speaking that Freddie was channeling Chris Rock again. *"Single guys have girlfriends. Girlfriends are always auditioning, always on their best behavior. Wives are like Supreme Court justices. They do whatever the fuck they want."*

I refused to laugh. The effort hurt more than if I had just let it out.

"Have we heard from Boucek?" Freddie asked.

I shook my head, adding "No news is good news."

"Don't know 'bout that. You read about that body they found in a drainage ditch in St. Paul? Couldn't even decide if it was male or female it's been there so long."

"On that cheerful note…"

"We made the papers." Freddie waved a folded copy of the Minnesota *Star Tribune* at me. "Second page of the local section."

"What's it say?"

Freddie read it to me:

> Police are investigating a shooting that took place inside the Victoria Memorial Parkway near 44th Avenue No. in North Minneapolis early Thursday evening. According to a statement, officers responded to a call at 7 PM of a shooting and found a number of witnesses yet no shooter and no victim. Witnesses claim two unidentified men were involved in a loud confrontation over a blue gym bag when one of the men pulled out a semi-automatic handgun and shot the other. The shooter then fled the scene in a car that had been waiting for him on nearby York Avenue. A third man was spotted at the scene immediately after. Witnesses claim he recovered the gym bag, helped the shooting victim to his feet and escaped with him across the parkway to a second waiting car. The extent of the victim's injuries remains unknown. A police spokesperson said the investigation is on-going but that they had no suspects at this time.

"A lot of nothin'" Freddie said.

"Let's hope it stays that way. Now, you want to get to work or what?

I used to work at McDonald's making minimum wage. You know what that means when someone pays you minimum wage? You know what your boss was trying to say? Hey, if I could pay you less, I would, but it's against the law."

Okay. That time I did laugh, and except for the pain, I felt better.

We had index cards with the names of all four victims pinned with thumbtacks to the cork side of the large combination bulletin board and dry erase white board mounted on the wall between our desks. We used a length of red yarn to connect Henrietta Weller with Quinn Jordan Boucek because they had known each other when they were young. After reexamining my notes again, I remembered Tracy Burrell also knew Quinn—*Her friends call her Q*, she had told me when I interviewed her at her apartment in Prospect Park—so we connected her index card to Quinn with more red yarn.

"How does she know sweet cheeks?" Freddie asked.

"I didn't ask."

"Now seems like a good time."

I called Tracy. Unfortunately, there was no answer.

On the white board side of the bulletin board we had tried to add to our list of traits that the four women shared with a blue marker yet didn't get much further than "brown-eyed girls."

After a couple of hours, Freddie slouched in one of our stuffed chairs and propped his feet on the round table. I was sitting behind my desk looking just as defeated.

"You know, it's probably something very simple," I said. "So simple that we've been staring at it for days and still can't see it."

"Maybe we're going about this the wrong way," Freddie said.

"I'm open to suggestions."

Freddie didn't have any. After a few minutes, he asked "Lunch?"

"What do you have in mind?"

He went to our small refrigerator, produced two Grain Belts, opened both, gave me one, and returned to his chair.

Half a beer later, Freddie said "What would the Chief do?"

"Hmm."

"What does 'Hmm' mean?"

"About twelve years ago there was a serial killer terrorizing northern Minnesota near the Canadian border—Roseau, Warroad, International Falls, Baudette, up in that area. You must remember. It was big deal in the papers."

"I was stationed at Clark Air Base in the Philippines twelve years ago," Freddie said.

"Thank you for your service. Anyway, the guy was killing young boys, thirteen, fourteen years old, and the Bureau of Criminal Apprehension had nothing, so it asked Anne to help out. Anne had been trained for this sort of thing at Quantico. The BCA filled our conference room in the Griffin Building with cartons containing evidence or at least what they thought was evidence for her to examine, only Anne pushed it all away and said, 'No, no, no, just give me everything from the first crime scene, the first killing.' She argued the first crime, that was when the killer was most likely to screw up, to make mistakes, that this was when he was still figuring out his MO."

"Did she catch him?"

"Of course she caught him. She's Anne Scalasi for God's sake. Anyway, you ask what she would do. She would go back to the first kidnapping."

We left the index cards up yet erased the white board. At the top, we wrote the name Henrietta Weller and underlined it twice. Beneath it we started noting facts that applied to her case and hers alone. One stood out. I wrote it down.

"Timeline," I said. "Rhett leaves her apartment at exactly five-thirty-five PM. The kidnapper is waiting for her."

"No." Freddie took the marker and started writing above the line I had written. "First Rhett and her girl, Lori Hertz, exchanged text messages between four-thirty and five arranging to meet at a club called Nightingale on Lyndale Avenue."

"Only Rhett never showed up."

"She went home to change clothes first."

Freddie put a check mark next to Girlfriend/Hertz.

"It wasn't unusual for the two of them to meet," he said. "They did it a couple times a week, except..." He wrote the word Boyfriend next to Girlfriend/Hertz. "Usually, Lori's boyfriend was there. This time he wasn't."

"Where was he?"

"Girl didn't know. That's why we were going to check him out, remember? Before Boucek and the congresswoman derailed us."

"Do you still think that's a good idea?"

"Seems to me the point of the exercise is to ignore the other kidnappings and concentrate on this case, so, yeah, I think we should check him out."

"Do we have a name?"

Freddie went back to his original notes.

"Sean Worra," he said.

"That's right. Rhett mentioned him. Apparently, he's annoyed because you all but accused him of committing a heinous crime against her without specifying what crime and Rhett can't tell him about it because she's sworn to secrecy by momma."

Freddie barked out the words, "*J'accuse...!*"

"What?"

"*J'accuse...!* It's the title of the letter Émile Zola published in the newspaper in 1890-something that accused the French Army of a massive cover-up. He wrote they had falsely convicted a Jewish captain named Alfred Dreyfus of treason and sentenced him to Devil's Island, even though they not only knew he was innocent. They also knew who the real traitor was."

I stood there blinking.

"Dreyfus," Freddie said. "You don't know who Dreyfus was? Damn, Taylor, read a book."

"Tell me again how you're just a poor black child with no proper education."

"Better than yours, that's all I can say."

"I'm missing something."

"Alfred Dreyfus was…"

"Not about that, Jesus. I know who Dreyfus was. I saw the movie."

I kept staring at the board. A stray thought was nagging at me, only I couldn't grab hold of it. Or maybe the paraventricular nucleus of the hypothalamus of the brain wasn't getting enough oxygen.

"Something, something…"

"What?" Freddie asked.

"Something you told me about Rhett and Lori Hertz. What was it? Where are your notes?"

He gave me half a dozen loose sheets of paper. The words looked as if they had been scribbled there while he was on horseback.

"You expect someone to be able to read this?" I asked.

Freddie pulled the sheets away.

"I can read it. That's the important thing."

"What did you say about how Rhett and Lori knew each other?"

"Ahhh…" he perused his notes. "Here. They went to school together. They were roommates in college before Rhett was kicked out."

"Where?"

"Carlson School of Management at the University of Minnesota."

I pointed at Freddie.

"What?" he said.

I grabbed a pen and wrote Lori Hertz's name on a three-by-five inch index card. I pinned it to the bulletin board and ran a length of red yarn from it to Rhett's card.

"They both went to Carlson," I said.

"'Kay."

I ran more red yarn from Lori to Quinn Jordan.

"So did Quinn," I said. "She graduated summa cum laude with Bachelor of Science Degree in Business Management. I saw the photograph they took of her on graduation day at her mom's house Wednesday night."

Freddie grabbed a stack of paper off my desk and started shuffling through it.

"You interviewed the Robey girl, remember?" he said. "She said that nearly everyone in her family worked for her dirt-bag uncle in one capacity or another except for her because…Here it is." My handwriting was much easier to read than his. He recited, "*Carole worked for Brian Haskins until she earned BSB from Carlson…*" BSB stands for Bachelor of Science in Business.

"That's right," I said.

Freddie connected Lori to Carole with yarn.

"What about Tracy?" he asked.

"I don't know." I gestured at the red yarn connecting her card with Quinn's. "They're pals, though. We know that much."

"Try reaching her again."

I didn't need to. As if on cue, my cell rang. The caller ID read Tracy Burrell.

I said "Ms. Burrell, hello. Thanks for calling back."

She said, "No problem, Taylor. You left a message asking how Q and I knew each other, how we became friends? We went to school together. First at Breck and later at the Carlson School of Management. We weren't friends in high school. I knew who she was, only we didn't socialize. She always seemed to have something important on her mind, you know? Carlson, though, was very hard and very scary, at least at first, and since we knew each other from Breck we kind of bonded over that; became close friends. She insisted I call her Quinn Jordan. I was probably the only one at the U who knew that her real name was Boucek. Why do you ask?"

We now had Lori Hertz's index card connected to all the others with red yarn.

Freddie said, "That ain't right, man."

"What do you mean?"

"Tracy just now told us she knew Quinn, but she didn't know Rhett or Carole and, although Lori's name sounded familiar to her, she couldn't place it."

"She wouldn't have met Rhett at Carlson," I said. "Tracy and Quinn were two years behind Rhett. Rhett would already have been kicked out of school by the time they started as freshmen. As for Carole, she was one year older, a sophomore. Sophomores and freshmen don't mix. At least they didn't when I was in school."

"Juniors and freshmen don't mix, either, and Lori would have been a junior when Tracy and Quinn started."

"How many students are enrolled at Carlson, anyway?" I asked.

Freddie looked it up on his computer.

"Five thousand, including grad students," he said. "See, that's my point."

He labeled another index card with the name Carlson and pinned it to the bulletin board. Next, he rearranged the yarn so that it ran from the victim's cards to that one instead of Lori's.

"It's possible none of the women knew each other while in school," I said. "But anyone who gets the Carlson School Alumni Magazine has access to names."

"Question is," Freddie said. "Goin' t' Carlson—does that make Lori a suspect or a potential victim?"

"We know she's not a brown-eyed girl. You told me she was a blue-eyed blonde."

"Ain't got a rich family, either."

"How do you know that?"

"She said she went to Patrick Henry Public High School and that she had a lot of college debt."

"What?"

"What?" Freddie repeated.

"Patrick Henry High School. Damn. I drove right past it the night we were setting up surveillance of Camden Central Pond. Patrick Henry is in North Minneapolis."

The first words out of Freddie's mouth: "Let's not get crazy."

"You're right," I said. "You're right. Lori went to Carlson like all the vics, okay. She knew one of the victims personally; Rhett was on her way to meet her when she was kidnapped. She's from the north side, too, where most of the action seems to be taking place. There are enough coincidences for us to take a look at her, but they don't prove anything. Carlson is a good school, a prestigious school. I bet a million students have passed through it, and I bet more than a few came from North Minneapolis."

"So we're calm?"

"We're calm."

"'Kay. Cuz there's somethin' I forgot to tell you—Lori said her boyfriend is also from North Minneapolis. He also went to Patrick Henry."

"I keep telling myself this is too good to be true, but it keeps getting harder and harder," I said.

"Could be 'nother coincidence."

"You said his name is Worra?"

Freddie grabbed his beer bottle by the neck and carried it to his desk. He sat, fired up his computer, and started surfing.

"Nothin'," he said. "Almost nothin'. Google Sean Worra

and you get half a dozen guys with similar names, but that's it. No Facebook account, no Twitter, no LinkedIn; no images. The only thing with his name is a white pages address—Sean Thao Worra. Oh, this is interestin'. The name Worra? It's rare in the U.S.; only about a hundred people have it. Know where it's not rare? Laos."

"Laos, which is in Southeast Asia?"

"Last time I looked."

"If Lori Hertz has a Facebook page, her boyfriend's photograph will be on it."

Ten seconds later Freddie said, "Here ya go."

I peered over his shoulder. Lori Hertz had 751 friends. Sean Worra was one of them. His photograph in the nine-pic grid located under Friends was conveniently tagged for us. It also appeared three times under Photos, once with Lori draped over his shoulders, once with him in a kitchen cooking and once with him standing next to a desk while wearing a blue suit. He was a good-looking young man, and yeah, his features appeared Asian.

"See if you can find a black guy with a goatee," I said.

Freddie surfed both the Friends and the Photos sections. Apparently, Lori didn't know any African-Americans.

"I saw a dozen or more pics of Rhett Weller," I said. "I didn't see any of the other vics, though."

"All that means is that they're not her friends."

"Apparently, neither is the black guy who shot me. Dammit, Freddie, I'd really like to interview this woman or have you do it again, since she seems to like you. Rhett said she called you a handsome black man."

"'Cept we need t' step lightly. If Lori and her crew are holdin' sweet cheeks, rappin' on her door and sayin' 'Hey' might not produce a positive outcome."

"Just being seen by them might be enough to make them freak."

"If they haven't freaked already after yesterday. They've

tried t' kill us both, so I'm not thinkin' they'll show any restraint when it comes t' Quinn."

"How do we get close to them without making them suspicious—that's the question?"

While I was thinking about it, Freddie kept working his computer. It didn't take long before he came up with an address for both Lori Hertz and Sean Worra.

"The Hertz girl is in an apartment building on Johnson and 22nd in Windom Park. Look."

I did. Freddie had pulled up a street view of the place, a simple square brick building three floors high that I guessed housed two dozen units. There were two entrances, one facing the street and one facing the parking lot in the back.

"Not likely they'd stash our girl there," he said. "But here…" Freddie manipulated his mouse, pressed a few keys, and the apartment building was replaced by a small yellow split-level house with a porch, crumbling sidewalk, and an attached garage. "This is where Worra lives. Logan Avenue, two short blocks away from Patrick Henry, two long blocks from Camden Central Pond and within easy walking distance to Victory Memorial Parkway. Drive into the garage, close the door, who's to know what you have tied up in your trunk."

"What are your feelings concerning first degree burglary?"

"Crash the joint with guns blazing? Yeah, only good things can come from that."

"If we were convinced that Quinn was inside…"

"We'd call the FBI, wouldn't we? Give Special Agent Carr a shout?"

"We should put eyes on this place," I said. "If we can ID the shooter coming or going…"

"Tall, thin brother with a mustache and goatee—I'm on him."

"What do you mean, you're on him?"

"He sees you, he's gonna know he's been made. We don't want that."

"No, we don't."

"So, I'll be the one sittin' on the house. I see a brother like you described, I'll take a pic and send it your way. If it's the same guy…"

"We'll call the cavalry," I said.

"In the meantime, we wait t' see what the Saturday mornin' mail brings."

"We could do that. Or we could give 'em a nudge and see which way they jump."

"If they jump at all. We still don't know if they're involved."

I went to the bulletin board and stood staring at it for a moment.

Freddie asked, "You got a plan?"

I tapped the index card with the name Rhett Weller.

"As a matter of fact, I do," I said.

CHAPTER THIRTY-FIVE

Rhett didn't answer her cellphone, so I called the number of the Mother of Mercy Community Church. A woman with a chirpy voice asked how she could help me. I told her.

"Sister Henrietta is on another line," she said. "Would you care to hold?"

"Sure."

It took Rhett only a couple of minutes to get to me although the recorded music they played while I was holding made it seem longer.

"This is Henrietta Weller," she said.

I identified myself.

Rhett said "Good afternoon, Taylor. How are you this bright and sunny day?" which I thought was nice of her. Most people, the first thing they ask is what do you want?

"The woman who answered the phone called you Sister Henrietta," I said.

"That's the way they talk around here. I kind of like it, to be honest. Taylor, you're not a guy who calls just to chit-chat. There's been another kidnapping, hasn't there?"

"Yes."

"And Charles still won't call the police."

"Freddie and I are re-interviewing everyone connected to the case. We're hoping to find something that we missed before."

"I don't know if I can tell you anything more than I already have. If you want to talk though…I had planned to meet Lori Hertz in Uptown, but I can cancel."

"Don't do that."

"She pretty much knows everything, anyway. At least she knows what I know. I told Lori what happened because I just had to tell someone, and I wanted her to stop worrying about the deep, dark secret I was keeping from her. I didn't want her to think it was her fault. If you don't mind that she's there…"

"No," I said. "I don't mind."

"Her boyfriend Sean might come by, too."

"The more the merrier."

Rhett gave me a time and place. I arrived an hour early. Traffic and parking in Uptown are brutal, yet within that hour I managed to move my car close enough to the club that I had a perfect view of the entrance and the parking lot next to it.

Lori Hertz was the first to arrive; I recognized her from the pics on her Facebook page. She went inside the club without hesitation. A few minutes later, Sean Worra parked a decade-old red two-door Honda Accord in the last open space in the lot and slipped out. He was wearing a dark blue blazer and a matching tie. He removed both and set them on his car seat. I realized in that instant it wasn't just a jacket and tie. It was his uniform. Worra worked security for someone.

He didn't enter the club, though. He lingered between his car and the one next to him while he played with his phone. A few moments later, I spied Rhett Weller approaching the stop light a block up from where I was parked; I guessed she had walked there from her apartment. She was also working her cell phone. The light changed, and Rhett crossed the street, sliding the cell into her bag. She was wearing a short skirt that kind of swished as she moved. I approved, although I doubted that her mother would have.

Rhett surprised me by strolling purposefully past the entrance of the club and into the parking lot. She stopped and looked for Worra. He waved; I guessed that was what Worra and she were doing with their phones, texting each other. She looked around again as if she half expected someone to be watching and quickly made her way to where Worra was standing. Worra immediately kissed her. Rhett didn't kiss him back, but she didn't resist, either. He pressed his body against hers until Rhett was pinned against the car. His mouth found her neck and his hand slipped between her legs and under her skirt. Rhett's hands gripped his shoulders tightly. A few moments later, though, she used them to push Worra off her. She waved a finger as if she was scolding him and moved away. He attempted to follow. Rhett pressed a hand against his chest. Words were exchanged, and she started walking toward the entrance to the club. Worra glanced at his watch.

"Hey, Freddie," I said.

I heard his voice through my earpiece. It was too loud, and I adjusted the volume on my radio.

"I'm here," he said.

"Rhett Weller is fucking Lori Hertz' boyfriend."

Freddie paused long enough that I wondered if he had heard me.

"Let's hope that's all she's doing with Lori's boyfriend," he said.

"Are you in position?"

"I am. Good sight lines. I can see Worra's front door and the entrance to his garage. All the drapes and shades have been pulled shut, so there's nothing to see."

"Okay." By then, Worra had started moving toward the entrance of the club, too. "I'll be signing off for a while."

"Get back to me whenever. I'll be here."

Never mind the happy-hour horde, men and woman standing together wherever they could find an empty space because there were no vacant tables or stools at the bar. Never mind the noise, either; the loud, laughing voices or the fact that the sound system was playing music I had never heard before. What made me aware that I was in the wrong place at the wrong time was the realization that I was probably the oldest person in the club. Everyone, including the bartenders and wait staff, was at least fifteen to twenty years younger than I was. I was convinced that they were all watching me, too, as I weaved through the crowd until I found the table where Rhett and the others were already enjoying their drinks. Rhett had been kind enough to save a chair.

She saw my approach and rose to greet me.

"Hi," I said.

She wrapped her arms around me and squeezed.

"Oh, I get a hug." I tried to sound upbeat despite the pain that surged through my body. "Thank you."

"I want to introduce my friends," Rhett said. "This is Lori Hertz."

"Ms. Hertz," I said.

"Please, call me Lori. Ms. Hertz sounds like I'm about to be given another lecture on resource allocation, task duration, and deliverables."

"Lori." I shook her hand. "I have no idea what you just said."

Lori laughed.

Rhett said, "Lori works for a biotech."

"I have a friend who's also working for a biotech," I said. "They're trying to come up with—I think she called it an index that'll measure the freshness of fruit and vegetables."

"Sounds like more fun than what I'm doing," Lori said. "Right now, my group is attempting to develop an anesthetic for the U.S. Army…"

"Lori," Worra said.

Lori both chuckled at Worra and shook her head dismissively. She leaned toward the center of the table, pressed an index finger against her lips and said, "Shhhh. It's a secret. Only eight thousand people know about it. I need another drink. Where's the waitress?"

"Allow me," I said.

Lori told me what she wanted, and I went to the bar to fetch it, plus bourbon for myself. When I returned, Worra was speaking earnestly to her even while Lori waved her hand as if she wasn't interested in a word he had to say.

"I should report you," Worra said.

"I know I did wrong, Mr. Man," Lori said. "What can I do to pay my debt to society?"

From the expression on her face, I decided that she and Alex Campbell would get along just fine.

"Stop it," Rhett said. "You're embarrassing me."

I set Lori's drink in front of her.

"Bless you," she said.

I sat next to Rhett. She was drinking another Long Island Tea, only this time it seemed as if she was trying to make it last.

"You haven't met Sean," she said. "Sean Worra, this is Holland Taylor. He's the private investigator I told you about."

I reached across the table despite the discomfort it caused me and shook his hand. He didn't seem pleased to meet me. He did notice that I was in pain.

"What happened to you?" he asked.

"I zigged when I should have zagged," I said. "Did Rhett tell you what happened to her?"

"Everything," Rhett said. "I told them everything."

"Everything?"

"It was too hard to keep it a secret. They're my friends. I trust them."

"Then I'll trust them."

"I'm just..." Lori shook her head and took a sip of her drink. "It seems so unbelievable. A kidnapping ring?"

"Who else was taken?" Rhett asked. "Who were the other girls?"

"I can't divulge that," I said.

"I thought you said you trusted us," Worra said.

"What do you do?"

"I work security for SLP Biotech."

"That's where I work," Lori said. "My very first day on the job, I walked through the front door into the lobby and there he was sitting behind the desk. He looked so cute in his blue suit and tie; I almost didn't recognize him."

"Lori and Sean went to high school together," Rhett said. "They didn't see each other for what was it? Six years? Seven? Then they end up working for the same company. It's like one of those Hallmark movies."

"It's a small world," Lori said.

"It really is."

"You haven't told us about the other kidnap victims," Worra said.

"Privileged information," I said. "You work security; you should know what I'm talking about."

"But another girl was taken," Rhett said.

"Yes."

"Like I was taken."

Rhett looked down at the Long Island Tea as if she wanted to drain the glass, yet didn't. Good for her, I told myself.

"Is her family going to pay the money like mine did?" Rhett asked. "Will the kidnappers send her home?"

"We're deeply concerned about that," I said. "Someone screwed up on our side yesterday, thought he was being clever. We're hoping that the kidnappers will see past it and give us another chance to pay the ransom." I was deliberately looking at Rhett when I spoke, yet I wanted Lori and Worra to hear what I had to say, in case they really were involved. "If not—right now it's just between us and them. If the girl is hurt, though, every cop in the country will come after them and they won't stop; it'll never become a cold case. The family of the victim is like your mother. They have enough clout to make that happen. We're hoping that cooler heads will prevail."

"At least I'm not a suspect anymore," Worra said.

"Who told you that?"

Worra looked shocked.

"I'm just messing with you," I said. "You were never a suspect."

"Mr. Fredericks thought so," Lori said.

I couldn't read the expression that flared on Worra's face. Was it anger or jealousy?

"I was hoping to see him again," Lori added.

"Why?" Worra said.

"I like him."

Okay, jealousy.

"My partner and I were grasping at straws," I said. "We still are."

"Rhett said you had photographs," Lori said.

"Of the wrong guys."

"Are you sure?"

"Yes."

"Can I see them?"

I fetched my smartphone from my pocket and called up the pics. I handed the phone to Lori.

"These two don't look anything like you, Sean," she said.

Worra reached for the phone to take a close look, but I snatched it from Lori's hand before he could. I didn't want Worra to see the black man with the goatee for fear that it would remind him of someone he knew.

"Anyway," I said. "My partner and I are backtracking, hoping the people we interviewed the first time might remember something we missed."

Rhett shook her head.

"I'm sorry," she said.

"No," I said. "I'm the one who's sorry I keep making you relive this."

"Do you think the kidnappers will stop?"

"I don't know why they would. They seem to be winning."

I thanked Rhett and her friends for their time and stood. Lori said she had to depart soon as well. Something about her parents' anniversary dinner. I was the first to leave and retreated to my car. I was safely inside when Lori, Rhett, and Worra left the club. There were hugs and kisses outside the front entrance, and the three of them went off in different directions. Worra reached his vehicle first, yet sat unmoving behind the steering wheel. Lori reached her car and drove off. She waved at Rhett who was standing in front of the stoplight at the intersection. Rhett waved back. After Lori was gone, she spun around and half walked, half jogged in her heels to the parking lot where Worra was waiting for her. Rhett climbed into his car. Worra started it and put it in gear. He pulled out of the lot onto Lake Street. I followed. A couple of quick turns later, they parked on the side street next to Rhett's place near Lake Bde Maka Ska. They entered the building through the door facing the parking lot. Rhett threw a wave to a woman who was watching them through a basement window.

I activated my radio and called Freddie.

"Anything?" I said.

"Nothing. You?"

"Rhett and Worra are in Rhett's apartment."

"Doing what?"

"Your guess is as good as mine."

"Where's Lori Hertz?"

"Helping to celebrate her parents' wedding anniversary."

"I'm not sure I like Henrietta as much as I did an hour ago."

I flashed on Dr. Alexandra Campbell.

"I don't know," I said. "She's not the first person to look for love in all the wrong places."

"You speaking from experience, partner?"

"I'm going to hang here," I said. "Catch Worra when he

leaves. I'll let you know."
"Could be a long night."
"For us both."

CHAPTER THIRTY-SIX

It wasn't a long night for Sean Worra, however. He skipped out of the rear entrance to Rhett's apartment building a short thirty minutes later by my watch with his shirttails hanging out and most of his buttons undone. So much for the stamina of youth, I decided.

He crossed the lot to the street. I started my own car and waited while Worra climbed into his. He was in no hurry to leave, though. Instead, he pulled out his cell phone, tapped his screen a couple of times, and started talking.

While he was talking, yet another vehicle passed us both on the side street and turned into the parking lot. The way the driver drove and stopped abruptly made me think that he was in a big hurry. He exited his vehicle, slammed the door, and approached the rear entrance. The sun was still high in the sky, and I got a good look at him. Bruce Gillard.

What the hell is going on? I thought. Or maybe I said the words out loud. At the same time, a short, thin woman brandishing a sixteen-inch Louisville Slugger flew out the door and charged across the parking lot toward him.

Gillard raised his hands as if he was surrendering.

The woman looked to be in her early seventies, yet she waved the bat as if she was trying out for the Twins Triple-A farm team.

At the same time, Worra started his car and slowly worked

his way out of his parking space into the street.

I needed to make a quick decision.

While my curiosity was aroused, I decided Worra was the most important character in this drama. Where he drove, I drove, following as he made a casual loop back toward Hennepin Avenue and headed north. Because of the heavy Friday evening traffic, it was slow going. Yet I managed to keep with him through the numerous traffic lights while remaining two car-lengths behind and one lane over until he approached the complicated Hennepin-Lyndale-I-94 interchange. It had been easy to follow him on Hennepin without looking like it. Now not so much. I called Freddie on the radio.

"If Worra turns I'll turn," I told him. "Otherwise…Okay, he's going straight. I'm guessing he'll get on 94 and head for home. If I maintain surveillance, he's probably going to make me. Unless he's a moron."

"Pull off," Freddie said.

"I am. Besides, there's interesting things going on over at Rhett's apartment that I want to check on."

"Like what?"

I explained.

"Fuckin' Gillard," Freddie said. "What's he up to now?"

"With a little luck, I'll find out."

It was only a four-mile round trip, yet the traffic pushed my driving time to nearly fifteen minutes total. By the time I returned to Rhett's apartment building, Gillard's car was missing from the parking lot. I cursed my luck until I saw it parked in the same spot that Worra had vacated, then I praised my luck, or rather the feisty old parking lot sentinel who had made him move.

I managed to find an empty spot myself with a good view. Part of me wanted to call Rhett and invite myself up to her place, only I couldn't conceive of a gag that would explain my presence. I suppose I could have made it sound as if I had reconsidered the suggestion that she had made two days earlier, the one where I provided her with comfort. Only she had been right about that. I did have scruples. Such as they were.

I wondered—was Gillard offering her comfort? If he had been there before, he would have known not to use the parking lot.

I waited, wondering what I would do when Gillard showed up again. Then he did show up, coming out of the front entrance and circling the building toward his car. Rhett Weller flew out the front door and trailed after him. She shouted something I couldn't make out. Gillard stopped. Rhett threw something at him, but missed her mark. Gillard bent to pick it up, a paperback novel. He brushed it as if it didn't deserve the treatment it was receiving.

More words were exchanged that I didn't hear.

Rhett moved toward Gillard.

He moved toward her.

The distance between them lessened along with the volume of their conversation.

When they became close, Rhett used two hands to push against Gillard's chest.

He used one to slap her face with enough force to send Rhett spinning to the sidewalk.

He shouted and shook the paperback at her.

By then I was out of the Camry and closing on them.

"It doesn't need to happen this way," Gillard said.

"I won't hurt my mother," Rhett said.

"How's she going to feel when she finds out her daughter's a whore?"

"Don't do this, please. I'll pay you."

"Pay me what? Thousands? I'm talking about millions."

"Not just money."

"You really are a whore."

"Hey," I said.

Gillard spun toward me.

I hit him as hard as I could and remembered instantly that I had two cracked ribs and a bruised lung—dammit!

Gillard went to the ground next to Rhett.

The woman scrambled to her feet as if she was afraid he was contaminated.

Clearly, Gillard wasn't used to being hit because, instead of trying to make a fight of it, he rolled into a ball and covered up. I was grateful. It meant I didn't need to hit him again, which I wasn't sure I'd be able to do. Also, it allowed me to hover above him while pretending I wasn't in acute pain, although the way I was attempting to suck oxygen back into my lungs might have told him something if he had been paying attention.

"Hurts, doesn't it?" I said.

"Taylor, what are you doing here?" Rhett asked.

I pointed down at Gillard.

"I was following him."

"Why?" Rhett asked.

"I mentioned before that yesterday someone screwed up the ransom drop for our latest kidnap victim." I pointed at Gillard. "It was him. We wanted to keep an eye on him to make sure he didn't do it again."

You must admit, few people lie as well as I do. Truly, it's a gift.

Gillard attempted to stand up.

"Stay down," I said. "Swear to God, Gillard, I'll beat your brains in."

Apparently, he believed my bluff and remained suiting on the sidewalk. He had set the paperback next to him—*50 Shades of Grey* by E. L. James.

"What the hell is going on?" I asked.

"He's trying to blackmail me."

"How so?"

"He has evidence, pictures..."

"Of what?"

"Of me. And him."

I gave it about three beats before deciding to skip to the chase.

"What does he want you to do?" I asked.

"Go public about the kidnapping; tell the media that Charles refused to contact the police and because of it, other kidnappings have taken place. He wants to ruin Charles. I don't care about that. But I won't hurt my mother."

"You don't know when to quit, do you, Gillard?"

He didn't answer.

"Should I tell you about the pictures?" Rhett asked.

"If you like."

"I told you about me and my family, about how they disowned me, except they didn't, really. They kept an eye on me from a distance. They hired Charles, who assigned Gillard to keep an eye on me and report to them. When they decided I had reformed enough to resume my place in the Hudson hierarchy, they started paying me a stipend through the family foundation; just a few dollars at first but the amount increased, with Gillard acting as my banker. I was impatient though and traded with him—sexual favors for an increase in my allowance. Gillard kept evidence of my debauchery. But that was years ago, Taylor. A lifetime."

I gestured at the book.

"What that's about?" I asked.

"Gillard gave it to me to read," Rhett said. "He said it would teach me how I should behave toward him."

I don't know why I thought that was so funny, yet it made me laugh, which hurt both my ribs and lung, but what the hell. I pushed a toe against Gillard's leg.

"You are so screwed," I said. "First, we're going to have you disbarred and then we're going to take away everything you have, including your reputation. You'll be lucky to get a job at Walmart. Blackmailing a client—the Lawyers Professional Responsibility Board is going to eat you alive and spit you out."

Gillard's fight-or-flight instinct kicked in, as I knew it would, and he quickly regained his feet.

"What proof do you have?" he asked. "Only the word of a whore."

"The pics, you dipshit. What are you going to do? Erase them? Freddie and I make a pretty good living finding shit that people erase from their computers and their phones; that they try to take off the Internet. You're done, man. You are so totally fucked."

I took Rhett's arm and led her down the sidewalk back toward the entrance to her building. I called to Gillard over my shoulder.

"Oh, and try hiding your assets in offshore accounts," I said. "That always works."

When we reached the door, I looked back. Gillard was still standing there, so I gave him a parting shot.

"If you're not afraid of us, think about Charles Boucek," I said. "Think about what he did to his wife. And he loved his wife."

There was no elevator. Rhett and I had to walk up three flights of stairs, which didn't do my ribs or lung any good. Inside her apartment, she turned on me.

"Are you really going to do those things you said?" Rhett asked. "If you do—I don't give a damn about Gillard, but I don't want my mother to know what I did. I don't want to disappoint her any more than I already have."

"It'll be okay, Rhett. Do you know what Gillard is doing right this minute? He's covering his tracks. He's working very hard to eliminate any possible evidence that connects him to you, including obliterating any pics he might have taken. If that means tossing his cell phone, camera, and computer into the Mississippi River, that's what he's going to do. He's going to move heaven and earth to protect himself, and by doing so, he'll also protect you."

"Are you going to tell Charles?"

"He's already drawn a bullseye on Gillard's forehead, so no, probably not. Besides, there's no reason for Boucek to know your business, is there?"

"You were bluffing then."

"No," I said. "If Bruce comes after you, Freddie and I will destroy his life because that's the way we're wired. We'll let him make the first move, though. Think of it like an old western movie. The good guys never draw first."

"Guys in white hats protecting the virtuous schoolmarm— except now you know I'm not virtuous. I'm a whore like Bruce Gillard said."

"Don't talk like that."

"I've done so many incredibly stupid things that seemed like a good idea at the time. This was only one of them. I just can't stop myself."

"You were ready to sacrifice yourself to protect your mother, Rhett. There's plenty of virtue in that. Besides, what is it they say in AA? One day at a time?"

Rhett used that as an excuse to hug me tightly. I was actually glad for the pain it caused. It kept my mind from wandering. Sure, I had scruples. But I didn't necessarily trust them.

"If I knew more men like you, I'd know fewer men like Guillard," Rhett said.

And Worra, I almost said, yet didn't.

I took a deep breath because I knew it would hurt.

Rhett asked if I would share a drink with her. I told her there was much to do. She said she didn't blame me for wanting to get away from her.

"Is that what I'm doing?" I asked.

"I'm sorry, Taylor. That was uncalled for. I hate being alone. Anyway, I have things to do, too." There was a Carlson School Alumni Magazine on her coffee table and she picked it up. "I've enrolled. My grades are subpar, but apparently the school is happy to welcome back the daughter of Congresswoman Abigail Hudson. Funny how that works. The people in the admissions office were happier to see me than my mom. Are you sure I can't convince you to stay?"

I said, "Rain check?" but I was only being polite.

A few minutes later I was inside my Camry and working my radio.

"Where the hell have you been?" Freddie wanted to know.

"The stories I could tell."

"Yeah, I got one for you. Sean Worra showed up twenty minutes ago. He used a remote to open his garage door and parked inside."

"Okay."

"It's been quiet ever since," Freddie said. "Nothin' movin' at all."

"Not much of a story."

"You expectin' *War and Peace*?"

"Should I tell you what's wrong with *War and Peace*?"

"Oh, please, I really want to know."

"Too much peace and not enough war."

"You're a fuckin' philistine, Taylor."

"Do you want me to take over surveillance?"

"No, I'm good."

"I could bring you some food; a couple beverages."

"I'm afraid any movement on the street might alert them. I'm good, like I said. I got a couple of energy drinks and an empty plastic milk jug."

"You're going to toss it when you're done, right? You're not going to take it home and use it on your cereal?"

"I thought I'd bring it to the office. You can pour it int' your coffee instead of cream."

"I like my coffee the way I like my women."

"Whitish?"

"With a little extra flavor."

"There ya go."

"How 'bout I find a parking place in North Minneapolis, not too close, not too far, just in case? Besides, you never did finish telling me about your trip to that plantation in Charleston, South Carolina. What was it called? Middleton Place?"

"I'd appreciate that, Taylor."

CHAPTER THIRTY-SEVEN

We waited until two-forty-five AM before we took a chance that we wouldn't be seen, Freddie pulling out of his parking space and me pulling in without using our headlights. A quick meal and three hours of sleep later, Freddie returned, and I drove to a spot where I could get a few hours of shut-eye myself without having a Minneapolis cop tapping on my window and demanding I take a PBT.

At about nine-thirty Charles Boucek sent us a text DEMANDING—the word was in all caps—that we come to his office IMMEDIATELY. I arrived at ten. Boucek greeted me outside the elevators near the reception area. He didn't look like he had enjoyed any more sleep than Freddie or me but his suit was nice. Boucek led me down the corridor. There was no one else working at Boucek and Associates that I could see or hear. We entered his outer office and crossed it to his inner office. He stood behind his desk yet made no effort to sit down. I made no attempt to sit, either. Boucek wanted to know where my partner was. I told him. Afterward, I pulled Freddie up on speakerphone.

"Do you believe that Ms. Jordan is being held in the house?" Boucek asked.

I was surprised to hear him refer to his daughter that way yet didn't mention it.

"We don't know," I said. "We're not even sure if Worra is

involved in any of this. We're just nit-picking leads as best we can."

"We were hoping we might spot someone who looked like the brother who capped Taylor, who tried to take Tracy Burrell in Little Mekong," Freddie said over the speaker. "If we did, we could take it to the feds or Chief Scalasi, only no such luck."

"How many times do I have to tell you—we will not involve the authorities at this juncture," Boucek said.

"Your priorities are all fucked up, you know that, man?"

Boucek stared at my cell phone as if he wanted to smash it with a hammer.

"Charles." That brought his gaze from the phone to my face. "Why am I here?"

He handed me a Priority Mail Express envelope from the U.S. Post Office. There was a single sheet of white typing paper inside. I pulled it out and read what was written there.

"What?" Freddie asked.

I read the letter to him.

> This is the final time you will be contacted. For Ms. Boucek's sake, you will place $100,000 in twenties and fifties—the price of your previous offense—in a small travel bag emblazoned with the logo of the Minnesota Twins, just as before. We insist that Holland Taylor deliver the bag to Folwell Park. He will enter the park from the corner of Knox Avenue and 36th Avenue North at exactly 12 PM. He will follow the sidewalk to the wading pool located in the center of the park. He will sit on the park bench on the west side of the pool. He will remain there until he is contacted. He will be prepared to follow any and all instructions that he is given without hesitation. He will not be wearing a bullet-proof vest or any kind of garment that might conceal it. He

will not be armed. If these simple demands are met, Ms. Boucek will be released immediately. If not, she will be executed immediately. If you contact the authorities, she will be executed. Do not try our patience a second time. We are watching.

Freddie paused for a few beats before speaking.

"They know you're not dead," he said. "They know you're not seriously injured."

"They might have guessed based on the newspaper article."

"Or they might have a more direct source of information."

"They might."

"Why you again?"

"They know me by sight now."

"Or maybe they just want to blow your head off; get it right this time."

"There's that possibility, too. Of course, Folwell Park on a sunny Saturday afternoon is bound to be crawling with witnesses."

"That didn't seem to bother them the last time."

"No, it didn't."

"You want my advice. Holland?"

"No."

"I probably wouldn't take it, either. I like her, too."

I turned toward Boucek.

"Do you have the money?" I asked.

He opened a drawer, pulled out the Twins travel bag we had used before and set it on the desk. I glanced inside. It was filled with cash. I rummaged briefly through the bag just in case, zipped it shut, and removed it from the desk.

Boucek hadn't spoken a word since he gave me the ransom note and didn't look like he was going to anytime soon. I stood for a moment, staring at him. He didn't ask me to risk my life to save his daughter the first time, and he didn't seem inclined to do so now. Somehow, he couldn't manage it. The way he lived his life, it was either a favor too big to ask or he simply didn't know how. It didn't make me angry, though. Just a little sad.

"Freddie?" I asked.

"I'm here."

"I'm signing off for now. I'll call you back on the radio in about twenty minutes. Call me though if something happens I should know about."

"Okay."

I ended the phone call and slipped the cell into my pocket. "Charles," I said.

Blank eyes stared back at me.

"I have a neighbor, a friend named Claire Wedemeyer. There's something I want you to do for me if I can't."

Folwell Park was vibrating with activity—happy children playing in the wading pool under the watchful eyes of their parents, singles, doubles and mixed-doubles on the tennis courts, teenagers shooting hoops, a women's softball team practicing on one of the diamonds, couples spreading blankets beneath trees, families gathering at picnic tables—yet I felt as safe as a canary in a mine shaft.

I remained inside my Camry parked on Knox Avenue, the windows open, while my digital clock marked the passing of each agonizing minute as I waited for high noon. The bag filled with cash was on the seat next to me. Every couple of minutes, I would pull it closer until it was resting on my lap. It wasn't that I was anxious. I just wanted to get on with it even as my brain kept telling me to relax, be calm, chill...

Freddie barked into my ear.

"The garage door is opening...I'm watching them through the telephoto lens of my camera...There's two of them, Taylor. Worra behind the wheel and a brother in the passenger seat...It's him. He's wearing a goatee. It's gotta be him...They're outta the driveway, headin' down Logan. I'm going to follow."

"No, no, no, Freddie. We talked about this. Take the house, not the car. If Quinn's in the house, we need to get her out. If she isn't, we know where the car is headed..."

"What about you?"

"Dammit Freddie, we already decided this. If we can free her from the bad people, I won't need to go into the park. Now get going."

I tapped my watch. Eleven-forty-nine.

I told myself that Sean Worra lived five minutes away from Folwell Park if he took his own sweet time getting there. Still, that was cutting it close if he wanted to set up surveillance, make sure I was alone when I began my long walk. Or maybe he was so sure of me he wasn't worried about it. Or maybe he didn't give a damn. I watched the street waiting for his red two-door Honda Accord to appear. It didn't.

Eleven-fifty.

Freddie said, "I'm parking in his driveway, going to walk up to his front door casual like and knock. Don't want the neighbors to get suspicious..."

Eleven-fifty-one.

Freddie said, "I'm knocking and using the doorbell...No answer. The shades and drapes are all pulled shut. Can't see inside. I'll knock again..."

I watched Knox and that part of 36th Avenue that I could see through my front windshield. Two cars and a pickup, no Hondas of any kind.

Eleven-fifty-two.

"I'm circling the house," Freddie said. "If I can't get in through the backdoor, I'll use a window. How you doin' Taylor?"

"I haven't seen Worra's red Honda yet. I'm wondering if he's setting up on the opposite side of the park."

"I'm beginnin' t' think these assholes aren't as professional as we thought they were."

"Just now you're thinking that?"

"Notice how the ransom note referred to sweet cheeks as Ms. Boucek?"

"I did," I said.

"Makes a brother go Hmm."

"It does."

"Back door has a knob lock and a deadbolt. It also has a window."

"Do you have your burglary tools?" I was referring to the assorted picks and wires that were illegal for him to carry.

"Fuck it," Freddie said.

The next thing I heard over my ear bud was the sound of breaking glass. I wasn't happy about it. If there was someone in the house, they'd come running. Or call 911.

Eleven-fifty-four.

"I'm in." Freddie was speaking softly now. "The place feels empty."

"Go slow."

"We ain't got time for slow."

"Quinn comes first."

"Alright, alright, fuck…"

The sounds I heard after that were muffled. It could have been heavy breathing. It could have been footsteps. I imagined Freddie moving from one room to another, his Colt Command-er gripped with both hands, leading the way.

Eleven-fifty-six.

"Downstairs is clear," Freddie said. "I'm going upstairs."

I took hold of the handles of the Twins travel bag, wishing there was a gun inside, wishing I was wearing my Kevlar vest, wishing I was role-playing in Alexandra Campbell's bedroom. "What do you mean, you can't pay the rent?" Wishing I was anywhere but where I was.

Eleven-fifty-seven.

"There's no sign of her," Freddie said.

"Try the basement."

"I should be lookin' for the car."

"Freddie..."

The volume of his breathing increased along with sound of his footsteps. A door was opened. A click of a light switch. The pad of shoes on wood.

"I'm goin' downstairs."

Eleven-fifty-eight.

"There's a door on the right," Freddie said. "Some kind of storage room. Padlock, but it's open; just hangin' on the loop. Give me a second."

Eleven-fifty-nine.

"She was here," Freddie said. "Taylor, she was here. There's a mattress on the floor. A pot for her waste. A chain attached to the wall. They must have taken her out in the car. Taylor..."

Twelve PM.

"Times up," I said.

CHAPTER THIRTY-EIGHT

I left my Camry, crossed the street, and gained the sidewalk that led from 36ᵗʰ Avenue into the center of Folwell Park. I was wearing a blue polo shirt, khakis, and deck shoes without socks. My shirt was hanging loose, better to hide the radio transmitter attached to my belt at the center of my back. The microphone was clipped to the inside of my collar, just below my chin, the ear bud in my right ear. The travel bag was in my left hand and bouncing against my thigh as I walked.

"I'm on my way," Freddie said.

"Don't mind me, find the car."

"What was it again? A blue Chevy?"

"You're killing me, Freddie."

Folwell was as nice a park as any you've ever strolled through. There was plenty of well-kept grass and trees and amenities and a large number of people enjoying it all. It made me think North Minneapolis would have been a great place to live if not for the crime and violence. I strolled as I had at Memorial Park—was it just two days ago that I was shot?—nodding at those people I met, giving them the Minnesota wave, and getting more waves back than I expected. The tennis courts were on my left, and I watched a young woman snapping passing shots past her male opponent, who became increasingly frustrated. I hoped she wouldn't let up and that he'd take it like a man and wondered if that meant I was becoming more "woke" as I grew older.

In the center of the park was the wading pool, a large circle of water with a fountain made to resemble a seal. At least I think it was a seal. What did I know about modern art? The pool was surrounded by benches, which were surrounded by a cyclone fence. There were at least twenty children and nearly twice as many adults inside the fence. A dozen more children and adults were enjoying the playground that had been built outside the fence north of the pool. I found a bench on the west side facing the pool with my back to the tennis courts and made myself comfortable.

"Take your time," I said.

"I'm comin' as fast as I can," Freddie said.

"Not you, the bad people."

"Yeah, let's hope they spend a couple of hours checkin' you out."

Only they didn't. It was only a matter of minutes before I saw Mr. Goatee on the far side of the wading pool. He was leaning against the cyclone fence and watching me. I pretended not to see him.

I told Freddie about it.

"Where's Worra?" he asked.

"I don't know. If Quinn's in the Honda, he's probably with her."

"I'm on Humboldt Avenue. That's the street bordering the east side of the park. There's parking on only one side of the street. Nothin' yet. I'll keep drivin' around the park until I find the Honda."

Mr. Goatee pushed himself away from the fence and started circling it counterclockwise.

"He'll be coming up on my left, so he won't see the ear bud in my right ear," I said.

"So, we got that goin' for us."

Mr. Goatee kept circling, and I kept pretending not to see him.

"There's no parking on 36th so I'm speeding up to—okay, I'm hangin' a right on Knox Avenue," Freddie said. "That's the street on the west side of Folwell."

Mr. Goatee kept circling until he was on my side of the pool. There was no pretending now. He stood several feet in front of me. And smiled. And I thought how much I'd like to kick that smile off his face with my shoe.

"Nothin'," Freddie said. "Taylor? I can't find the Honda."

"Try the side streets directly behind me. Mr. Goatee wanted me on the west side of the park so he could make a quick getaway."

"You talkin' to me?" Mr. Goatee said. "I didn't hear ya. Whadyou say?"

"I said you're blocking my view of the pool. Mind moving?"

"Stall," Freddie said. "Stall as long as you can and then do whatcha gotta do."

"You better have the fuckin' money this time," Mr. Goatee said.

"I have it," I said.

"Let me see."

I deliberately moved the travel bag from my left side to the right so that it was behind me.

"You tryin' to be funny?" Mr. Goatee said.

He moved in close and lifted his shirt with both hands so I could see that gun he had stuck between his pants and his belly. I thought—what a punk. All I had to do was jump up. He'd drop the tails of his shirt and reach for the gun. He might even be able to grab hold of it before I put hands on him, yet not with enough time to pull it from his jeans. He'd probably end up shooting his balls off, which would have suited me fine if I had known that Quinn was safe.

"Amateur," I said.

"Whadyou call me?"

I patted the bench next to me.

"Sit," I said. "Let's talk."

"Show me the money."

"I need to see proof of life first."

"Fuck is that?"

"You tried to kill me. You tried to kill my partner. How do I know you didn't already kill the girl?"

"We didn't."

"Prove it."

"What?"

"Call your partner. Put her on the phone. Have her tell me her complete name. Just three words. Then I'll give you the money."

Mr. Goatee reached under his shirt. He spoke nice and slow.

"Give—me—the—fucking—money," he said.

"Look around you. How many people do you see? Fifty? How many cell phones do they have? All it takes is for one of them to snap your picture and then you're done. What you did last time was stupid. Yeah, you got away with it, but it was stupid to throw down on me in front of so many witnesses when you didn't need to. I get you were pissed off. But it was stupid, okay?"

"Don't fuckin' call me that."

"I see it," Freddie said. "Red Honda Accord parked on a side street just off 37th Avenue. I'm drivin' past…"

"I'm just saying there's a better way to do this," I said.

"You're the one who's fuckin' stupid," Mr. Goatee said.

"It's him," Freddie said. "It's Worra sittin' behind the steering wheel like he's waitin' for a light t' change."

"The money is right here." I patted the travel bag next to me. "It's all yours. Just let me hear the girl's voice."

Mr. Goatee sat next to me. At first, I thought he was giving into my demands. When he pulled his gun and jammed it into my cracked ribs, I thought differently.

"Fuck you," he said.

"I'm pulling a U-turn," Freddie said. "I'm going to ram him."

"What about the girl?" I said.

"Fuck the girl," Mr. Goatee said.

"Alright, alright, alright," Freddie chanted.

"Give me the fuckin' money," Mr. Goatee said. "Do it now."

I slowly reached for the travel bag.

Mr. Goatee poked me some more with his gun.

I heard the screech of tires as Freddie stopped his car next to the Honda.

I picked up the bag and set it on Mr. Goatee's lap.

Freddie jumped out of his car without even putting it into park; he told me later that it rolled twenty feet before it came to rest against the curb.

Mr. Goatee set his free hand on top of the bag, only now he was confused. He couldn't open the bag with one hand and he liked that his other hand was pushing the business end of his gun against my side.

Freddie said that Worra hadn't been paying attention, that he caught him by surprise when he snatched open the Honda's door and grabbed Worra by the throat and hair. He dragged him from the vehicle and threw him onto the street.

"Open it," Mr. Goatee said.

I moved the bag from his lap to mine and found the zipper.

Worra was unarmed, but Freddie did not suffer from the same handicap. He told me later that he pressed the barrel of his Colt Commander against Worra's temple while he shouted the words that I heard clearly through the ear bud. "Tell me where the girl is or I'll kill you."

I unzipped the bag and held the sides open for Mr. Goatee to see. His eyes lit up like a child on Christmas morning.

"One hundred stacks," he said.

"In the trunk," Worra said. "In the trunk, in the trunk."

"Close the bag," Mr. Goatee said.

Freddie found the trunk latch next to the driver's seat and opened it.

I slowly zipped the bag shut.

"Give it to me," Mr. Goatee said.

I slid the bag back onto his lap.

"She's in the trunk," Freddie said. "She's alive, Taylor. She's good."

"Stand up," Mr. Goatee said.

I moved slowly to my feet, then pivoted quickly toward Mr. Goatee. He didn't seem alarmed until I pushed his hand so that the gun was now pointed at the back slats of the wooden bench.

I attempted to punch him as hard as I could in the throat.

He angled his head at the last moment, though, and I hit the side of his neck instead.

Pain from my injuries rippled through my body. If that wasn't enough, Mr. Goatee managed to get his leg up and kick me in the chest.

I fell backward onto the ground.

Despite the pain, I quickly rolled to my knees. It was a case of too little too late, though.

Mr. Goatee had scrambled to his feet and was holding his gun with both hands.

The gun was pointed at my face.

In that instant when I was sure I was about to die, when my only thought was how could I have been so damned careless, a half dozen special agents appeared all around us as if by magic and shouted "FBI drop the gun."

Mr. Goatee looked at the agents as if it was the most amazing sight he had ever seen. Certainly, it was the most amazing sight I had ever seen.

The agents kept shouting and moving. Mr. Goatee didn't drop his gun, so the agents snatched it from his hands and drove him to his knees. Handcuffs appeared and pinned his arms behind his back.

I remained on my knees, watching.

And laughing.

I don't know why I was laughing; the situation didn't seem

all that funny, and yet I was.

Special Agent Raymond Carr appeared at my side and looked down at me.

"Having fun, Mr. Taylor?" he asked.

"Let's just say it's an unexpected pleasure to see you."

"You, too."

"What are you doing here? Did Boucek send you?"

"The FBI doesn't work for Mr. Boucek."

I thought that was funny, too.

"Quinn Boucek is safe, by the way," I said.

"We know. That's why we intervened. We would have done the same at Victory Memorial Parkway the other day when you were shot, but we didn't have eyes on her then."

"It sounds like you're saying I was expendable, but she wasn't."

Carr patted my shoulder.

"Is that how it sounds?" he asked. "We couldn't ID your assailant or his partner at Victory. Nor were we able to put a tail on the Kia Rio they drove, although we did find it abandoned later. We were forced to wait until the kidnappers contacted you again."

"All this without telling Boucek?"

"Should I recite the oath we take when we're sworn in as special agents of the Bureau?"

It took me a half beat before I had the presence of mind to ask, "Freddie, are you there?"

"I'm here," he said. "I am surrounded by several gentlemen and one lady, all with guns and federal badges."

"Quinn?"

"Sweet cheeks seems to be okay. Owww..."

"What?"

"She slapped me."

"So, all is right with the world?"

"I don't know, Taylor," Freddie said. "I think we're in trouble."

CHAPTER THIRTY-NINE

As it turned out, we weren't in trouble. In fact, Special Agent Carr shook both of our hands and thanked Freddie and I for our cooperation in this matter.

"We'll take it from here," he said.

I asked to see Quinn and was informed that Ms. Boucek had been taken to the North Memorial Hospital in Robbinsdale for examination and would subsequently be debriefed at FBI headquarters in Brooklyn Center.

I suggested that there were aspects to the crimes committed by Sean Worra and his partner that Quinn didn't know about; that the FBI didn't know.

Carr patted my shoulder—he seemed to like doing that—and said "I'm sure the Assistant United States Attorney will contact you if she has any questions."

It turned out that she hadn't.

The next day, the Minnesota *Star Tribune* announced on its front page that

> The FBI has arrested two North Minneapolis men for the alleged kidnapping of the daughter of a well-known local attorney...

Ten days later, a second story reported that

The suspects in the kidnapping of the daughter of a prominent Minneapolis attorney had unexpectedly plead guilty in Federal Court to their crimes...

"You need to give the man credit," I said. "Charles Boucek is very good at what he does."

"I wonder what he offered Sean Worra and his partner to convince them to cop a plea and keep their mouths shut while doing it."

"My guess? A shorter sentence than they'd serve if they spoke up, plus an offshore bank account."

"Do you think he knows exactly what happened?"

"Maybe not exactly, but, yeah, he knows."

That's how Freddie and I figured the story would end, too, not with a bang but a whimper. Until the phone rang a week later. Freddie answered it.

"Fredericks and Taylor Private Investigations," he said.

"Whom am I addressing?" a woman's voice asked.

"Sid Fredericks. And you are?"

"Quinn Jordan."

"Sweet cheeks."

"Mr. Fredericks, the next time I see you, I'm going to slap your face."

"When have I heard that before?"

"Mr. Boucek requests to speak with you and Mr. Taylor in his office."

"When?"

"Immediately. I will greet you in the lobby. Please be prompt."

"We're on our way."

Freddie hung up the phone, placed two fingers against his cheek and said "Hmm."

***

We met Quinn in the lobby of the glass and granite building that housed Boucek and Associates. She tried mightily to maintain her usual nothing-but-business demeanor, but the effort lasted only about twenty seconds.

I said, "Are we late again?"

She said, "Hell no," and immediately closed the distance between us. First, she hugged Freddie—lucky him—and then she hugged me. She stopped for a moment, a look of concern on her face, and asked if I was alright.

"Healing nicely," I said.

Quinn hugged me some more and then hugged both of us together.

"I'm so sorry," she said. It was difficult to understand her words because she was both laughing and crying at the same time. "I wanted to thank you in person for what you did for me or at least call, only I was ordered not to. My father..."

Our mutual embrace was loosened so we could look at each other. People entering and exiting the building glared at us for breaking one of Minnesota's unwritten commandments—no overt public displays of affection.

"How is the old man?" Freddie asked.

"He cried," Quinn said. "When I finally came home, he broke down and wept. At first, I was gratified, but then I was like 'What have you done with my old man?' He's been so kind to me since all this happened. He's even been nice to my mother. You two—I don't know how to thank you."

"Not slapping me again was a good start," Freddie said.

Quinn smiled at him and patted his cheek.

"Next time," she said.

"Why are we here, Ms. Jordan?" I asked. "I noticed you kept your mother's name, by the way."

"It seemed easier. Come on."

We followed her across the lobby. As we approached the door marked Authorized Personal Only Freddie said, "Sneaking us up the back way, again?"

Quinn stopped abruptly; I nearly walked into her.

"Fuck that," she said and changed direction for the main elevators.

"Sweet cheeks, look at you being all rebellious," Freddie said.

Quinn stopped again and glared at him.

Freddie raised his hands in surrender.

"Never again," he said. "I promise."

If Boucek was surprised that we walked through the front door into his outer office, he didn't show it. He graciously shook both of our hands and gestured to his guest seated on one of his Chesterfields.

"I believe you've met," he said.

"Good morning, Congresswoman Hudson," I said.

"Good morning."

Freddie nodded and received a nod in return.

Quinn moved to the far wall where she could silently view the proceedings.

Boucek gestured toward his bar.

"Would you care for a drink?" he asked.

"It's a little early for me," I said.

"Mr. Fredericks?"

"I'm good," Freddie said.

"Please, have a seat."

We sat.

Boucek stared at us as if he didn't know where to begin. Representative Hudson just stared. Finally, Boucek said "We received your invoice." As if to prove it, he held up a sheet of paper printed with our letterhead for all of us to see.

"Did you bring us here to quibble?" I asked.

"Not at all," Boucek said. "Not at all. It's a very fair price. If anything, I thought that you had grossly undercharged for your services."

"No one has ever told us that before," Freddie said.

"I hope this meets with your approval."

Boucek attached a check to the invoice with a paperclip and passed it to Freddie. Freddie read the number written on the check. He tried hard to appear indifferent only I've known him long enough to know when he's faking. Freddie passed the invoice to me. The number was big enough to be a bribe yet small enough that you could argue it was merely a generous bonus.

"I don't know what we did to deserve this," I said.

"It's not what you did but what you're going to do," Representative Hudson said.

"What's that?" Freddie asked.

Representative Hudson shifted in her seat as if she was about to engage in a long and involved explanation only Boucek stifled her with a hissed "Abigail."

I found myself shaking my head. You'd think that after a couple decades in public service the congresswoman would know how these things work.

"You guaranteed our silence when you signed the contract," I said. "You remember the contract we made you sign, don't you Charles?"

Boucek gave me a slight shoulder shrug, and I understood that if it wasn't for Representative Hudson, we probably wouldn't be having this conversation. She's the one who needed assurances. She proved it when she said, "Silence about what?" in a hushed voice.

"That your daughter was behind the kidnappings," I said.

"You can't prove that."

"I never said I could. I never said I'd try. Sean Worra and his partner might have been able to, but I read in the newspaper the other day that you've already managed to resolve that issue. How is Rhett, anyway? Is she still working for the church?"

"Unfortunately, Henrietta has been confined to a private psychiatric facility in Virginia for a period of observation,"

Boucek said. "Nervous breakdown."

"Oh?"

"We're all sure that it's a temporary condition."

"At least until—when are the primaries?" Freddie asked. "August fourteenth?"

"Did she go willingly?" I asked.

"Quite willingly," Boucek said. "Once the situation was explained to her."

"Poor Rhett."

"What do you know about it?" Representative Hudson asked.

"The first kidnapping, her kidnapping, was a cry for attention; the money meant nothing to her. At least no more than it meant to you. Only it didn't get your attention, did it? At least not the way Rhett had envisioned. She realized when you didn't attempt to contact her after paying the ransom that you concluded she had staged the kidnapping. Which, of course, she had. She hired Freddie and me after the fact to convince you she really had been victimized. It worked, too. Suddenly, you were a loving mother—for a time, anyway."

"You know all this because…"

"Rhett has a nosy neighbor. If she had been taken from the parking lot of her apartment building, the neighbor would have known it. Also, the other victims had been attacked with a syringe. Rhett was not, at least according to the rape kit examination she had submitted to at the Hennepin County Medical Center."

"The other victims?"

"The fake kidnapping went so well that Rhett's accomplices decided to try it for real. They had the means, too—a drug being developed by SLP Biotech for the Army, an instantaneous anesthetic. Apparently, it works; the Army should be pleased. Anyway, Lori Hertz, Rhett's former college roommate, was involved in its development. Lori no doubt told Rhett and her boyfriend Sean Worra about it; she was not a discreet woman.

I'm guessing that Worra stole some of the drug, using his position as a security guard for SLP to gain access; Lori had nothing to do with it. I'm guessing because I don't think Lori would have given up Worra as readily as she had when we first questioned her about Rhett's kidnapping if she was involved. Also, it was obvious she didn't know that Worra and Rhett were sleeping together, so...

"For what it's worth, I don't think Rhett wanted the kidnappings to continue. That's why she started drinking again. She fingered victims for Worra and his partner using the Carlson School Alumni Magazine and Charles' client list because she was afraid of being outed by them and because she was sleeping with Worra behind Lori's back, and she—well, I think Rhett was desperate for attention. Again, I'm just guessing.

"What I know for sure is that the first ransom note Charles received after Quinn was kidnapped referred to her as his daughter. The second note called her Ms. Boucek. Hardly anyone knew Quinn was Charles's daughter, including the people who worked with her. Nor did she go by the name Boucek. Most people knew her as Quinn Jordan, even her classmates at the Carlson School of Management. Rhett knew who she was, though, because they had met when they were children."

"Anything else?" Representative Hudson asked.

"No, that pretty much covers it."

"Mindless supposition that would never stand up in a court of law," Representative Hudson said.

"As you say."

"If you were to repeat a word of this in public, I would sue you for slander."

"My partner and I would deserve it, too," I said. "Anything else?"

Representative Hudson shook her head. I think she was surprised when I refused to argue with her.

I stood.

Freddie stood. He took the invoice and check from my hand because he was afraid I would rip it up. Yet I had no intention of doing such a silly thing.

"Normally, I'd tell you what you could do with your check," I said. "But if it makes you happy, I'll take your money."

We turned for the door. Quinn left her place against the wall and moved to join us. Only Boucek raised a hand to hold her back. Instead, he led us out into the corridor alone.

"I apologize for that display of—let's call it misplaced suspicion," he said. "Representative Hudson did not trust your discretion and would not take my word for it. She needed to see it for herself. The House had recessed for the Fourth of July week and…"

Boucek flicked his hand as if the subject no longer interested him.

"All I can say is she lost my vote," Freddie said.

"I apologize for allowing so much time to pass without thanking you personally for what you did for me and my daughter. I know we didn't always agree on how to handle these past events, yet you must know now and forever, you will always have a friend in me."

"Stop it," Freddie said. "I'll get all misty-eyed."

"By the way," I said. "Whatever happened to Bruce Gillard?"

"Who?" Boucek asked. "I'm not sure I know a person by that name. I doubt anyone else doing business in Minnesota has, either."

"That's what I thought."

"One thing's for sure, Charles," Freddie said. "It's better to be your friend than your enemy."

CHAPTER FORTY

I decided to go home early. Freddie didn't seem to mind. He said he might call it a day, too, right after he deposited Charles Boucek's check. I was surprised, though, when I arrived at my apartment to discover that Claire Wedemeyer was also playing hooky from work. She was wearing a modest two-piece swimming suit, lying in a reclining lawn chair, and catching rays in the large square of grass located between the building and the rear parking lot. I paused for a minute or two to watch her. At no time did she resemble a woman with a daughter pushing thirteen. Claire spoke without moving her head, without opening her eyes to look at me.

"See anything you like?" she said.

"Nothing at all."

"A funny thing happened today, Holland. I received a phone call at work from Douglas' parole officer. It upset me. That's why I came home early. Not upset exactly, but it did throw me a little bit."

"What happened?"

"The St. Paul police raided a high-stakes poker game three days ago, which, the parole officer said, very rarely happens. Douglas was in the apartment at the time, although he claims he wasn't gambling. He said he met a woman who invited him to her apartment. He claims he didn't know anything about the poker game until he arrived and said he was going to leave, but the cops knocked on the door before he could. Douglas was taken into custody along with the other gamblers, and his probation officer was notified. Douglas isn't supposed to gamble as a condition of his parole, which meant he was in big trouble.

"The next day, yesterday, he went to work," Claire said. "Douglas works for his uncle who owns a construction firm; I think I told you that. The firm just won a big contract to work on a project for a large real estate development firm called Burrell, Inc."

"David Burrell?" I asked.

"Do you know it?"

"The name sounds familiar."

"Douglas' uncle claimed that there was money missing from the till; that someone had been embezzling funds from the company. Suspicion fell on Douglas, of course. The uncle contacted the parole officer and said he didn't want to pursue the matter any further because Douglas was family, but he couldn't allow him to work there. The parole officer began taking steps to help Douglas find another job. Before he could, though, a judge issued a warrant for Douglas' arrest, and he was taken into custody.

"The next day, this morning, a parole hearing was convened, which, the parole officer said, also rarely ever happens. At least not that quickly. Sometimes it takes as long as six months to get a hearing. The woman who invited Douglas to the apartment testified. She claimed it was the other way around; that Douglas had invited her to the apartment, that he was carrying a lot of money with him. Douglas called her a liar but couldn't provide any evidence to prove it or explain what her motive was. It was decided Douglas had violated the conditions of his parole and that his original sentence should be reinstated. He was sent back to Stillwater. He won't get out of prison now until—well, not until after Amanda's sixteenth birthday, anyway."

"I'm sorry to hear that," I said.

"Are you? I'm not sure that I am although...It does seem unfair. That's what the parole officer said, anyway. He said Douglas was railroaded, that the fix was in. He all but blamed me. I told him I didn't know what he was talking about, which was true. After talking to him, though, I came home to think about it. Holland, was the fix in?"

"It sounds like it."

"Did you do it?"

"No," I said. "I don't have those kinds of resources."

"Who does?"

"I couldn't say."

Claire turned her head and opened her eyes. She stared at me for a long time. I have no idea what she saw. Eventually, she closed her eyes again.

"Amanda should be home in less than half an hour," Claire said. "Otherwise..."

She didn't finish her sentence. I gave it a few beats and continued toward the entrance to the apartment building. Once inside and climbing the stairs, I flashed on Charles Boucek and what I told him before I took Quinn's ransom money to Folwell Park, the favor I asked him to do if something unpleasant happened to me.

I thought about giving him a call and thanking him for the extra bonus, but, of course, that's not something you do.

ACKNOWLEDGMENTS

Special thanks to Eric Campbell and Lance Wright at Down & Out Books, Tammi Fredrickson, and Renee Valois for all their help in writing and publishing this book.

A past president of the Private Eye Writers of America, **DAVID HOUSEWRIGHT** is best known for his Rushmore McKenzie and Holland Taylor detective novels, as well as other tales of murder and mayhem in the Midwest. He earned the Edgar Award from the Mystery Writers of America, a Shamus nomination from the PWA, and three Minnesota Books Awards. A reformed newspaper reporter and ad man, he also taught at the University of Minnesota and Loft Literary Center in Minneapolis. He was recently added to "Minnesota Writers on the Map" by the Minnesota Historical Society and Friends of the St. Paul Public Library.

Find him online at DavidHousewright.com.